# Family and Succession Law in Cyprus

# Family and Succession Law in Cyprus

**Second Edition**

**Achilles C. Emilianides**

This book was originally published as a monograph in the International Encyclopaedia of Laws/Family and Succession Law.

Founding Editor: Roger Blanpain
General Editor: Frank Hendrickx
Volume Editor: Walter Pintens

Wolters Kluwer

*Published by:*
Kluwer Law International B.V.
PO Box 316
2400 AH Alphen aan den Rijn
The Netherlands
E-mail: international-sales@wolterskluwer.com
Website: lrus.wolterskluwer.com

*Sold and distributed in North, Central and South America by:*
Wolters Kluwer Legal & Regulatory U.S.
7201 McKinney Circle
Frederick, MD 21704
United States of America
Email: customer.service@wolterskluwer.com

*Sold and distributed in all other countries by:*
Air Business Subscriptions
Rockwood House
Haywards Heath
West Sussex
RH16 3DH
United Kingdom
Email: international-customerservice@wolterskluwer.com



*Printed on acid-free paper*

ISBN 978-94-035-0924-2

e-Book: ISBN 978-94-035-0925-9
web-PDF: ISBN 978-94-035-0930-3



Printed in the United Kingdom.

# The Author

Dr Achilles C. Emilianides is Professor and Dean of the School of Law of the University of Nicosia and a practicing advocate, senior partner of the firms Achilles & Emile, Constantinos Emilianides LLC, and A&E C. Emilianides, C. Katsaros and Associates LLP. He holds PhD in Law and LLM from the Aristotle University of Thessaloniki and LLM from Leicester University. He is the Editor of the Cyprus and European Law Review and the Chair of the Royal Commonwealth Society Cyprus Branch. He has handled several high-profile cases and has been involved in legal consultancy and funded research. During the Cypriot Presidency of the Council of the European Union in 2012 he acted as the Chairman of two working groups of the European Council. Major publications include: *Labour Law in Cyprus* (Kluwer, 2016), *Private International Law in Cyprus* (Kluwer, 2015), *Media Law in Cyprus* (Kluwer, 2015), *Cypriot Succession Law* (3rd ed., Hippasus, 2015), *Religion and Law in Cyprus* (Kluwer, 2014), *Constitutional Law in Cyprus* (Kluwer, 2013), *Religious Freedom in the EU* (2010), *The New European Private International Law of Contracts* (2009 in Greek), *Cypriot Law of Public Procurement* (2007 in Greek), *Professional Law of Advocates* (2007 in Greek), *Parliamentary History of Cyprus 1964–1976* (2007 in Greek), *Beyond the Cyprus Constitution* (2006 in Greek), *The Cypriot Law of Marriage and Divorce* (2006 in Greek), *Bibliography of Cyprus Law* (2005), *The Parliamentary Co-Existence of Greeks and Turks in Cyprus* (2003 in Greek). He has written and practised extensively on family law and law of succession.

**The Author**

# Preface

This study consists of an extensive analysis of Cypriot family and succession law. This is the second edition of this work, the first edition having been published in 2012. It is the first time that a detailed monograph concerning Cypriot family and succession law has been published in the English language. There are unique characteristics in Cypriot family and succession law. Cypriot family law has been the outcome of a lengthy process of secularization and modernization during which the family institutions have been detached from the Orthodox Church and its ecclesiastical courts. Cypriot succession law is an interesting mixture of common law and civil law provisions. The defining characteristics of the system are therefore better understood through knowledge of the country's history.

A significant number of people have influenced my views on Cypriot family and succession law, and it would be impossible to mention all of them here. I would like to thank my colleagues at both the University of Nicosia and my law firm for their perspectives and comments. The work of and discussion with Judge Georgios Serhides and the guidance of my later Professor Charalambos Papastathis have been instrumental in shaping my views on Cypriot family law The International Encyclopaedia of Laws and Kluwer Law International have been kind enough to include this monograph in their publications. I would like to thank my family and friends for their support during all these years, without which nothing else would be of significance.

My father Constantinos Emilianides has been, however, the most instrumental in the development of my reasoning about both family and succession law. His comments to my work have always been of extreme importance. Unfortunately, this second edition is published following his death, and therefore, I did not have this time the opportunity to benefit from his comments and his overall presence in my life. This work is dedicated to his memory.

*Achilles C. Emilianides*

# Table of Contents

# List of Abbreviations

| | |
|---|---|
| CJEU | Court of Justice of European Union |
| CLR | Cyprus Law Reports |
| ECHR | European Convention on Human Rights |
| ECtHR | European Court of Human Rights |
| ECR | European Court Reports |
| EHRR | European Human Rights Reports |
| EU | European Union |
| JSC | Judgments of the Supreme Court of Cyprus |
| RSCC | Reports of the Supreme Constitutional Court of Cyprus |

## List of Abbreviations

# General Introduction

## §1. General Background of the Country

*1.* The Republic of Cyprus was established as an independent and sovereign republic on 16 August 1960, when its Constitution came into force and the British sovereignty over Cyprus, as a crown colony, ceased. On 20 July 1974 the Republic of Turkey, one of the guarantor powers of the independence, sovereignty and territorial integrity of Cyprus, invaded the country with its armed forces and occupied the northern part of the country. As a result of the occupation, the Greeks and the other Christians of the northern region became displaced persons, having fled to the southern part of the island. In addition to that, the Muslim Turks of the southern part of the island were induced to relocate to the north. The area occupied by Turkey amounts to 36.4% of the territory of the Republic of Cyprus. The Turkish occupation in Cyprus continues to the present day, and therefore, the Republic of Cyprus is prevented from exercising its powers over the occupied territory.

*2.* Since the Turkish invasion providing precise figures with respect to the population of Cyprus has presented certain difficulties, due to the abnormal situation prevailing in the island. The Statistical Service of the Republic of Cyprus has estimated, however, that by the end of 2006 the population of Cyprus was 867,600, out of which 660,600 (76.1%) belonged to the Greek community, while 88,900 (10.2%) belonged to the Turkish Community. The remaining 118,100 (13.7%) were foreign residents, including mainly Greek and British citizens, as well as citizens of Russia, Philippines, Sri Lanka, Romania, Bulgaria, and other countries. According to the 2011 official census the population of Cyprus was 840,407, out of whom 667,398 (79.41%) were Cypriots, 106,270 (12.64%) were European citizens and 64,113 (7.62%) were third country nationals (the majority being Asian or Russian nationals).[1] Out of the members of the Greek community, 2,700 (0.4%) were Armenians and 4,800 (0.6%) were Maronites, while 900 (0.1%) were Roman Catholics. With the exception of few agnostics, atheists, or naturalized foreign citizens, members of Greek origin normally adhere to the Greek Orthodox religion. In view of the fact that many non-Cypriots, such as mainland Greeks, Russians, Romanians and Bulgarians, also adhere to the Orthodox Christian religion, it is estimated that approximately 82% of the total current population of Cyprus are Orthodox Christians. It is further estimated that the number of Roman Catholics residing in Cyprus, if foreigners are also included, is approximately 2%.

1. The remaining 0.33% were unidentified. Source: Statistical Service of the Republic of Cyprus.

*3.* The actual number of Turkish Cypriots residing in Cyprus is difficult to estimate with precision. After the Turkish invasion in 1974, there has been an effort by Turkey to change the demographic character of occupied Northern Cyprus through the implantation of settlers. The indigenous population of the island (Greek and Turkish Cypriots) has always insisted that the possible legalization of the Turkish settlers would not only illegally modify the demographic structure of the island and constitute a constant source of tension but also would further threaten the stability and security of the Republic.[2] This view was also adopted by the Council of Europe.[3] It is estimated that 57,000 Turkish Cypriots have emigrated from Cyprus following the invasion of 1974. The number of settlers currently residing in Cyprus is not known. It is estimated, however, that more than 100,000 settlers from mainland Turkey are currently residing in the occupied areas. Illegal settlers are not included in any estimation of the current population of Cyprus. While the Statistical Service of the Republic of Cyprus estimates that the number of Turkish Cypriots currently residing in the occupied areas reaches approximately 88,900, it is suggested that the actual number might be closer to 120,000 as estimated by Turkish Cypriot sources. Therefore, it is estimated that approximately 12% of the current total population of the Republic, excluding the Turkish settlers, are Turkish Cypriots.

## §2. Historical Background of Family and Succession Law

### I. Roman and Byzantine Era

*4.* An understanding of the peculiarities of Cypriot family law presupposes an understanding of the turbulent Cypriot history.[4] During the early period of the Roman rule, Christianity was introduced in Cyprus. On his first missionary journey in 45 AD, Paul, accompanied by Barnabas, a Cypriot, and Mark, landed in Cyprus and preached there the new religion.[5] The conversion of Cypriots to Christianity had been completed by the beginning of the fifth century. With the exception of sporadic Arab invasions, Cyprus remained for more than eight-and-a-half centuries, between 325 and 1191, a province of the Byzantine Empire. Thus, Christianity was the State religion of the island, similarly to other parts of the Byzantine Empire. The

2. L. Loucaides (ed.), 'Expulsion of Settlers from Occupied Territories: The Case of Turkish Settlers', in *Essays on the Developing Law of Human Rights* (Dordrecht: Martinus Nijhoff, 1995), 108–138; A. De Zayas, 'The Annan Plan and the Implantation of Turkish Settlers in Northern Cyprus', *Cyprus Yearbook of International Relations* (2006): 163 ff, M. Stavrinos, *Settlements as a Crime in International Law* (Nicosia: Parga 2013, in Greek).
3. Council of Europe, 2 May 2003, Doc. 9799, *Colonisation by Turkish Settlers of the Occupied Part of Cyprus* (Rapporteur Mr Laakso).
4. For an extensive history of Cyprus *see*, *inter alia*, C. Kyrris, *History of Cyprus* (Nicosia, 1985); G. Hill, *A History of Cyprus*, vols 1–4 (Cambridge: Cambridge University Press, 1940–1952).
5. For a history of the Orthodox Church of Cyprus *see* J. Hackett, *A History of the Orthodox Church of Cyprus* (London: Methuen & Co, 1901), V. Egglezakis, *Twenty Studies on the Church of Cyprus* (Athens: Leventis Association, 1996, in Greek).

ecclesiastical courts of the Orthodox Church applied Byzantine law and had competences over religious matters and matters of personal status, including family and succession law matters.[6]

*5.* The period of the Byzantine rule in Cyprus ended in 1191, when Cyprus came briefly under the rule of the crusader then King of England, Richard the Lionheart, or Coeur de Lion, who immediately sold Cyprus to the Order of the Knight Templars for 40,000 gold besants; the transaction was, however, short-lived, and it was cancelled. The island was once again sold, for the second time in the same year, to the King of Jerusalem, Guy de Lusignan, who was a French knight; this time Richard received 100,000 gold besants as consideration. The island remained under the rule of the Lusignans for nearly 300 years, from 1191 until 1489, which is considered to be the period of the Frankish rule of Cyprus.

## II. Frankish and Ottoman Rule

*6.* During the period of Frankish rule, Roman Catholic (Latin) Christianity became the official religion of the island. However, the great majority of the population still adhered to the Orthodox Christian religion and were Greeks. Pope Alexander IV issued the Bulla or Constitutio Cypria on 3 July 1260, according to which the then existing fourteen Orthodox Metropolises were reduced to four, so that their number and geographical limits would coincide with the respective Metropolises of the Roman Catholic Church. The legislation during the Lusignan period was the one contained in the Assizes of Cyprus, which were modelled after the Assizes of Jerusalem.[7] However, the ecclesiastical courts of the Greek Orthodox Church applied, with respect to the family and succession law affairs of members of the Orthodox Church, the so-called *Hellenic law* of Cyprus, which essentially consisted of a codification of Byzantine law.[8] During the Venetian rule from 1489 to 1571, the Roman Catholic Church remained the dominant Church of the island and Assizes (as well as the Hellenic Laws) continued to be the governing legislation.[9]

---

6. *See* C. Tornaritis, *The Ecclesiastical Courts especially in Cyprus* (Nicosia, 1976): 15, D. Seremetis, 'The Administration of Justice in Cyprus during the Byzantine and Post-Byzantine Era', in *Proceedings of the First International Cyprological Conference*, v. III (Nicosia: Society for Cypriot Studies, 1973 in Greek), 309ff (in Greek).
7. *See* N. Coureas, *The Assizes of the Lusignan Kingdom of Cyprus* (Nicosia: Cyprus Research Centre, 2002), P. Zepos, 'The Law of Cyprus during Frankish Rule', *Yearbook of the Centre of Research of the History of Greek Law* 23 (1976): 123–141 (in Greek), A. Emilianides, 'Polyarchy in the Frankish Rule of Cyprus', in *Mélanges à la Memoire de Michel Dendias* (Athénes–Paris, 1978), 7–13, T. Papadopoulos, 'Cypriot Legal', in *Studies*, vol. I (Nicosia: Foundation of Archbishop Makarios III, 1984), 1–142 (in Greek).
8. A. Emilianides, 'The Hellenic Laws of Cyprus during Frankish Rule', *Yearbook of the Cyprus Research Centre* 25 (2004), 51–74 (in Greek), A. Emilianides, 'The Hellenic Laws of Cyprus and the Hexabiblos of Armenopoulos', *Yearbook of the Faculty of Law of the Aristotle University of Thessaloniki* (1951): 33–38, D. Simon, *Zyprische Prozessprogramme* (München: Beck, 1973).
9. A. Aristidou, 'Assizes in Cyprus during the Venetian Rule', *Yearbook of the Cyprus Research Centre* 22 (2001): 95–101 (in Greek).

*7.* The period of Ottoman rule lasted for more than 300 years, from 1571 until 1878, and marked the first appearance of adherents of the Islamic faith in Cyprus. The Sheri law, namely the interpretation of the Qurani law, was not only the personal law of the Muslims of Cyprus, but also the State law, thus replacing the law of the Assizes which had been the State law during the period of Frankish and Venetian rule. The Sheri law was applied by the Sheri courts, which were the competent courts for the legal affairs of all people living in the island, irrespective of their religion.[10] The only exception to such exclusive competence of the Sheri courts was the law of personal status and family relations of members of the Orthodox Church. The ecclesiastical courts of the Orthodox Church continued to be the only competent courts with regard to the family relations of their members and continued to apply the Byzantine law.[11]

*8.* The right of all Christian communities to administer their religious and family law affairs was eventually recognized, following the Tanzimat reform of the Ottoman Imperial rescript, Hatt-i-Humayun of 18 February 1856.[12] It is indisputable that the Hatt-i-Humayun also applied in Cyprus.[13] The Hatt-i-Humayun granted spiritual advantages and exemptions, as well as a form of religious autonomy to the various Christian and non-Muslim religious communities living within the boundaries of the Ottoman Empire. As a result the Maronites and the Roman Catholics gradually referred their family law disputes to their ecclesiastical courts in Lebanon and Jerusalem respectively, while the National Constitution of the Armenians was confirmed by a firman of the Sultan of the Ottoman Empire.[14] Succession law disputes were governed by Sheri law; however, the succession law disputes of Christians or non-Muslims could, following a petition of the parties, be adjudicated by the respective leader of the religious community or the respective ecclesiastical courts (Article 18 of Hatt-i-Humayun).

---

10. M. Zekia, 'A Short Historical Survey of the Laws Administered by the Ottoman Civil and Criminal Courts and of the Constitution of such Courts during the Ottoman Era in Cyprus During 1571–1878', in *Proceedings of the First International Cyprological Conference*, v. III, (Nicosia: Society for Cypriot Studies, 1973), 457–464, V. Bedevi, 'A Survey of the Cyprus Sheri Courts Registers', in *Proceedings of the First International Cyprological Conference*, v. III, (Nicosia: Society for Cypriot Studies, 1973), 29–36.
11. A. Emilianides, 'The Evolution of the Law of the Mixed Marriages in Cyprus since the Frankish Rule', *Cyprus Studies* 2 (1938): 197–236 (in Greek).
12. G. Dionyssiou, 'The Ottoman Administration of Cyprus and the Tanzimat Reforms', *Yearbook of the Cyprus Research Centre* 20 (1994): 361–366 (in Greek), G. Young, *Corps de Droit Ottoman* v. II (Oxford, 1905), 22ff, D. Nicolaides, *Ottoman Codes*, 3rd edn, v. III (Constantinople, 1890): 2858–2866 (in Greek).
13. *Parapano and Others v. Happaz* (1893) 3 CLR 69, *Tano v. Tano* (1910) 9 CLR 94. *See also* the observations of G. Serghides, *Internal and External Conflict of Laws in Regard to Family Relations in Cyprus* (Nicosia, 1988), 32ff.
14. C. Tornaritis, 'The Legal Position of the Armenian Religious Group', in *Idem.*, *Constitutional and Legal Problems of the Republic of Cyprus*, 2nd edn, (Nicosia, 1972), Case 172/32 *Takvorian v. Nassibian and Others*, (District Court of Nicosia).

## III. British Rule

*9.* With the signing of the Convention of Defence Alliance on 4 June 1878 in Constantinople,[15] the period of British rule in Cyprus officially began. Great Britain was granted the power to enact laws and conventions for the island of Cyprus and to regulate its commercial and consular relations and affairs. Immediately after the outbreak of the First World War in 1914, Great Britain annexed Cyprus by Order in Council of 5 November 1914.[16] While it could be argued that such unilateral annexation was invalid, it was eventually recognized by Turkey in 1923 by Article 20 of the Treaty of Lausanne. By Article 16 of the Treaty of Lausanne, Turkey renounced all rights and titles whatsoever over Cyprus. The island was proclaimed as a Crown Colony on 10 March 1925.[17] With respect to religions, Great Britain maintained the existing state of affairs,[18] with the sole exception that the Islamic faith was no longer the prevailing religion. Essentially, the system could be characterized as post-Millet, in the sense that the right of all religious communities, either Muslim, or non-Muslim, to administer their religious and family affairs without any State intervention, was recognized.

*10.* The application of the canon law of the Orthodox Church, with respect to the adjudication of the family law disputes of its members, was also recognized. During the early years of the British Rule, the Privy Council held that the canon law of the various Christian communities continued to apply in family law cases, as it did according to the Ottoman law formerly prevailing in Cyprus.[19] The status of the Orthodox Church, with respect to the adjudication of family law disputes, was also confirmed by the Administration of Justice Law 38/1935; Article 34(c) of Law 38/1935 expressly provided that family law matters would continue to be governed by the law of the religious community of the parties. Furthermore, Article 50 of Law 38/1935 explicitly excluded from the jurisdiction of State courts any marital disputes between members of the Greek Orthodox Church, whenever the marriage was celebrated in accordance with ceremony. Thus, the ecclesiastical courts of the

15. *See* G. Georgallides, *A Political and Administrative History of Cyprus 1918–1926 with a Survey of the Foundations of the British Rule* (Nicosia: Cyprus Research Centre, 1979), 3ff, L. Dwight, *Great Britain and the Cyprus Convention Policy of 1878* (Cambridge: Harvard Historical Studies, 1934).
16. Cyprus Annexation Order in Council of 5 Nov. 1914 in J. Howarth, C. Gerahty, *Statute Laws of Cyprus*, v. II: (London, 1923): 184, C. Orr, *Cyprus under British Rule* (London: Robert Scott, 1918): 175.
17. Cyprus Gazette 1 May 1925, Notification No. 266.
18. A. Emilianides, 'Private International Law', in *Symposium on Cypriot Juridical Issues* (Thessaloniki, 1974): 90 (in Greek).
19. *Parapano and Others v. Happaz and Others* (1893) 3 CLR 69. *See* further A. Emilianides, 'The Parapano Judgment: Conflict of Laws with respect to Legitimization of Children and Succession in Cyprus during British Rule', in *Idem.*, *Five Studies in the History of Private Law* (Nicosia: Dikaionomia, 2007 in Greek): 67–78.

Orthodox Church continued to enjoy exclusive jurisdiction regarding family law disputes of their members, while the canon law of such Church continued to be applicable in those disputes.[20]

*11.* Smaller Christian religious communities of the island also continued to enjoy spiritual autonomy with respect to their internal affairs. Consequently, the family law disputes of members of the smaller Christian Churches continued to be governed according to the law of the religious community of the parties. In addition the ecclesiastical courts of the smaller Christian communities maintained their exclusive jurisdiction with respect to family law disputes of their members until 1935. Article 50 of Law 38/1935 excluded from the jurisdiction of State courts, not only any marital disputes of members of the Greek Orthodox Church but also any other matter, which according to the principles of the Ottoman Law that was formerly in force in Cyprus, was subject to the jurisdiction of an ecclesiastical court of the religious community of the litigants. The Supreme Court held that the above reference to 'any other matter' intended to cover matters such as election of bishops, and not family law matters.[21] Marital disputes of members of the Greek Orthodox Church were expressly excluded; should the legislator have intended to further exclude marital disputes between members of the smaller Christian communities, this would have also been explicitly mentioned. Thus, since 1935 the State courts had acquired jurisdiction to adjudicate the family disputes of members of the smaller religious communities of the island; State courts should, however, apply the canon law of the religious community of the parties. The restriction of the rights of the smaller Christian religious communities referred only to jurisdiction, and not to applicable law.

*12.* With respect to succession law of Christians and non-Muslims, the Wills and Succession Law 20/1895 was enacted; such law remained in force until 1946 when the current Wills and Succession Law was enacted, and governed the succession of non-Muslims. Law 20/1895 constituted a curious mixture of elements, not only from English and Ottoman law but also from the Italian Civil Code and consequently the Roman law. Sections 720–1049 of the Italian Civil Code were first translated into Greek and subsequently into English and formed the basis of an original Cypriot legislation. As noted:

> *It is in part English, in part Italian, in part Turkish and in part wholly Cypriot. Yet the English parts are not wholly English, the Italian parts have been so altered that in some instances they are quite unrecognisable and the Turkish parts are subject to modifications unknown to Turkey.*[22]

20. *See* further A. Emilianides, *The Cypriot Law of Marriage and Divorce* (Thessaloniki: Sakkoulas, 2006, in Greek): 48ff, G. Serghides, *Internal and External Conflict of Laws in Regard to Family Relations in Cyprus,* (Nicosia, 1988): 54ff.
21. *See* G. Serghides, *Internal and External Conflict of Laws in Regard to Family Relations in Cyprus* (Nicosia, 1988), 61–62, A. Emilianides, *The Cypriot Law of Marriage and Divorce* (Thessaloniki: Sakkoulas, 2006, in Greek): 91ff.
22. A. Bertram, 'The Law of Wills and Succession in Cyprus: A Study in Comparative Legislation', *Journal of Comparative Legislation and International Law* 12 (1911): 324–339, at 326.

*13.* The Treaty of 1878 expressly provided that Great Britain would respect Sheri courts and Sheri law, with respect to the religious affairs of Muslims. In 1902 the Supreme Court of Cyprus held that the phrase 'religious matter' is vague, while ecclesiastical courts in different ages and countries have at times assumed and exercised jurisdiction in almost every kind of matter, on the ground that such matter was religious or affected religion. It was thus held that matters relating to religion are in particular questions which affect or arise out of marriage, divorce, maintenance, infancy, wills, and inheritance.[23] Article 17 of the Cyprus Courts of Justice Order of 1927 further interpreted the term 'religious matters', as covering all cases concerning marriage, divorce, maintenance, hereditary succession, wills and registration of wakfs. The competence of the Sheri Courts with regard to the religious matters of Turkish Muslims was confirmed by Article 50 of the Courts of Justice Law 38/1935.[24]

*14.* However, the Interim Committee of Turkish Affairs observed in its Report in 1949 that, while the matrimonial relations of the Turkish Muslim sought to retain their religious character and derive their origin and basic principles from Quran, they should also be modified on the basis of Kemalic reforms and of the principles of Articles 82–145 of the Civil Code of Turkey of 1926.[25] On the basis of the observations of the Interim Committee, two laws were enacted: (1) the Turkish Family (Marriage and Divorce) Law 4/1951, Cap. 339 in the 1959 Edition of the Laws of Cyprus and (2) the Turkish Family Courts Law 3/1951, which was eventually replaced by the Turkish Family Courts Law 42/1954, Cap. 338 in the 1959 Edition. According to Article 2 of Cap. 338, the term 'religious matters' for which the Turkish Family Courts have exclusive competence was defined as covering any matters concerning marriage, divorce, maintenance and registration of wakfs, but not matters concerning hereditary succession or wills.

## IV. Independence

*15.* The 1960 Constitution of the Republic of Cyprus provides that Cyprus is a unitary State, comprised of two communities;[26] (1) the Greek community and (2) the Turkish community. According to Article 2 of the Constitution, the Greek Community comprises all citizens of the Republic who are of Greek origin and whose

23. *Sabri v. Ibrahim* (1902) 6 CLR 1, *Effendi v. Irikzade* (1906) 7 CLR 37, *Abdullah v. Hassan and Others* (1909) 8 CLR 123.
24. *See* further A. Emilianides, 'Islamic Faith as One of the Main Religions: The Case of Cyprus', in *Islam in Europe* (Bratislava: Institute for State-Church Relations, 2005), 220–228.
25. Cyprus Government Printing Office, *Interim Report of the Committee on Turkish Affairs: An Investigation into Matters Concerning and Affecting the Turkish Community in Cyprus*, (Nicosia, 1949).
26. A. Emilianides, *Constitutional Law in Cyprus* (The Hague: Kluwer, 2013), *Beyond the Constitution of Cyprus* (Thessaloniki: Sakkoulas, 2006, in Greek), A. Markides, 'The Republic of Cyprus', in *Constitutional Law of 10 EU Member States: The 2004 Enlargement*, ed. Kortmann et al., (The Hague: Kluwer, 2006), I-3–I-77, G. Pikis, *Constitutionalism, Human Rights, Separation of Powers, The Cyprus Precedent* (Leiden: Martinus Nijhoff, 2006).

mother tongue is Greek, or who share the Greek cultural tradition, or who are members of the Greek Orthodox Church. However, the Turkish Community comprises all citizens of the Republic who are of Turkish Origin and whose mother tongue is Turkish, or who share the Turkish cultural traditions, or who are Muslims. Citizens of the Republic who did not fulfil any of the above criteria opted to belong either to the Greek or the Turkish Community, within three months of the date of the coming into operation of the Constitution.

*16.* The Constitution provided, in addition to the organs of the central government which exercise the executive power and the House of Representatives which exercises the legislative power, for two communal chambers: (1) a Greek Communal Chamber and (2) a Turkish Communal Chamber. Such communal chambers were to exercise executive, legislative, as well as judicial power in educational, cultural, religious and other matters of purely communal nature and personal status; family law affairs fell predominantly within the jurisdiction of the Communal Chambers. However, following the constitutional crisis of 1963 the Greek Communal Chamber was self-dissolved. On the basis of Law 12/1965 the legislative competences of the Greek communal chamber were transferred to the House of Representatives, while its administrative competences with respect to educational matters were transferred to the Ministry of Education and Culture; the remaining competences of the Greek Communal Chamber were transferred to the Council of Ministers.

*17.* According to Article 110 §1 of the Constitution, the Autocephalous Greek Orthodox Church of Cyprus shall continue to have the exclusive right of regulating and administering its own internal affairs and property in accordance with the Holy Canons and its Charter in force for the time being. The same right is accorded to the Islamic religion through Muslim religious institutions, and to the three constitutionally recognized religious groups.[27] A 'religious group' in the constitutional sense is, according to Article 2 §3 of the Constitution, a group of persons, ordinarily resident in Cyprus, professing the same religion and either belonging to the same rite or being subject to the same jurisdiction thereof. All three religious groups (Maronites, Armenians, and Roman Catholics) opted to belong to the Greek Community.[28]

*18.* According to Article 111 of the Constitution, prior to the 1989 Amendment, any family matters of the members of the Greek Orthodox Church were governed by the law of the Greek Orthodox Church and were cognizable by a tribunal of such

---

27. *See* in general A. Emilianides, *The Status of the Armenian Church of Cyprus* (Nicosia: Cyprus Institute of Church and State Relations, 2006, in Greek), *Idem*, 'The Legal Status of the Latin Community of Cyprus', in *Minorities of Cyprus*, ed. A. Varnava, N. Coureas, M. Elia, (Cambridge: Cambridge Scholars Publishing, 2009), 229–240, C. Tornaritis, 'The Legal Position of the Armenian Religious Group', in *Id.*, *Constitutional and Legal Problems of the Republic of Cyprus*, 2nd edn (Nicosia, 1972), 85–90.
28. For Art. 110 of the Constitution *see* A. Emilianides, *Law and Religion in Cyprus* (2nd edn The Hague: Kluwer, 2014).

a Church.[29] All the aforementioned rights of the Orthodox Church were also granted to the ecclesiastical groups of the three religious groups of the Republic. The Constitution does not contain a similar provision stipulating for competence of Muslim religious institutions concerning their family relations, because of the radical amendments of the Turkish Cypriot institutions, following the acceptance of the Kemalic reforms mentioned above;[30] the Turkish Communal Chamber exercised exclusive jurisdiction with respect to the family law of the Turkish Cypriot Community.

*19.* Thus, Article 111 provided for the competence of the ecclesiastical courts of the Greek Orthodox Church or the ecclesiastical courts of the three religious groups, as well as for the application of ecclesiastical law, to any matter relating to betrothal, marriage, divorce, nullity of marriage, judicial separation, or restitution of conjugal rights or to family relations other than legitimization by order of the court or abortion. In the case of *Tylliros*, however, it was held that Article 111 was intended to preserve and not to extend the competences of the ecclesiastical tribunals of the Greek Orthodox Church (as well as of the three religious groups), as exercised at the time of the coming into operation of the Constitution. It was thus held that the term 'matter relating to marriage or to family relations' did not include applications for maintenance, since the ecclesiastical courts did not exercise competence with respect to maintenance applications prior to Independence.[31]

*20.* In view of the above, marital disputes between members of the Orthodox Church, who had celebrated a religious marriage according to the rites of such a Church, used to fall under the jurisdiction of the ecclesiastical courts of the Orthodox Church. When both of the prospective spouses were Orthodox and citizens of Cyprus, it was not possible for them to perform a civil marriage in Cyprus.[32] In 1977 the Supreme Court of Cyprus held that a civil marriage between members of the Orthodox Church is null to begin with, wherever it has been celebrated;[33] consequently, the only appropriate form of marriage for the Orthodox, the Armenians, the Maronites, and the Roman Catholics was the religious form according to the rites of their respective Churches. The 1980 Charter of the Orthodox Church included detailed provisions with regard to the institutions of family law that come under the jurisdiction of ecclesiastical courts, namely betrothal, marriage, divorce, and adoption (Articles 217–235), as well as for the organization and operation of the ecclesiastical courts (Articles 236–335).

---

29. *See* G. Serghides, *Internal and External Conflict of Laws in Regard to Family Relations in Cyprus* (Nicosia, 1988).
30. A. Emilianides, 'Private International Law', in *Symposium on Cypriot Juridical Issues* (Thessaloniki, 1974): 91 (in Greek).
31. *Tylliros v. Tylliros* [1962] 3 RSCC 21.
32. *HjiHanna v. HjiHanna* [1973] 1 CLR 186, *De Stefano v. De Stefano* [1982] 1 CLR 367.
33. *Metaxa v. Mita* [1977] 1 CLR 1, adopted in *Neophytou v. Neophytou* [1979] 1 CLR 685, *Platritis v. Platritis* [1980] 1 CLR 324, *Panayiotou v. Constantinou* [1980] 1 CLR 533, *Koutsokoumnis v. Christodoulou* [1981] 1 CLR 58, *Farmakallidou v. Theocharides* [1981] 1 CLR 724, *Venglis v. Venglis* [1982] 1 CLR 223, *Papasavvas v. Johnstone* [1984] 1 CLR 38, *Televantos v. Kyza* [1985] 1 CLR 412.

*21.* The family law disputes of members of the Greek Community, who were not under the jurisdiction of the ecclesiastical courts in accordance with Article 111 of the Constitution, fell under the jurisdiction of the Greek Communal Courts, while the family law disputes of members of the Turkish Community fell under the jurisdiction of the Turkish Communal Courts in accordance with the provisions of Article 160 §1 of the Constitution.[34] Family law disputes of persons who were not citizens of the Republic fell under the jurisdiction of the Supreme Court of Cyprus in accordance with section 19(b) of the Courts of Justice Law 14/1960 or the District Courts in accordance with section 21 of Law 14/60.[35] Following the self-dissolution of the Greek Communal Chamber in 1963, the competences of the Greek Communal Chambers were transferred to the District Court in accordance with section 11 § of Law 12/1965. With Laws 29/83 and 51/84 the competences of the Supreme Court with respect to family law disputes was also transferred to the District Courts.

## V. The 1989 Constitutional Amendment

*22.* The compulsory character of religious marriage and the jurisdiction of ecclesiastical law were criticized as being inconsistent with contemporary legal principles and social perceptions.[36] The need to adjust all matters relating to personal institutions to the commitments of the Republic of Cyprus towards international conventions led to the First Amendment of the Constitution (Law 95/1989), which amended Article 111.[37] The First Amendment was held to be constitutional on the basis of the Cypriot doctrine of necessity.[38] According to the provisions of Law 95/1989:

(a) All matters relating to divorce, judicial separation or restitution of conjugal rights or to family relations of the members of the Orthodox Church came under the jurisdiction of a Family Court. In divorce cases the court is composed of three members. It is presided over by a clergyman, while two laypersons act as its other two judges. If the Church does not appoint a presiding judge, which has been the established practice since 1989, a judge is appointed by the Supreme Court of the Republic. The Family Courts came into force with Law 23/1990.

---

34. G. Serghides, *Internal and External Conflict of Laws in Regard to Family Relations in Cyprus* (Nicosia, 1988), 247–282.
35. *Ibid.*, 287–342.
36. *See* L. Savvides, 'Sex Discrimination in Family Law in Cyprus', *Cyprus Law Review* 4 (1983): 708–714, C. Tornaritis, *Is Reform Needed in Family Law and on which Areas?* (Nicosia, 1979, in Greek).
37. *See* A. Emilianides, *The Cypriot Law of Marriage and Divorce* (Thessaloniki: Sakkoulas, 2006, in Greek): 145ff.
38. *Nicolaou v. Nicolaou* [1992] 1 CLR 1338 (in Greek). For the Cypriot doctrine of necessity *see* A. Emilianides, C. Papastylianos and C. Stratilatis, *The Republic of Cyprus and the Doctrine of Necessity* (Athens-Thessaloniki: Sakkoulas, 2016, in Greek), P. Polyviou, *The Case of Ibrahim, the Doctrine of Necessity and the Republic of Cyprus* (Nicosia: Chryssafinis & Polyviou, 2015), C. Kombos, *The Doctrine of Necessity in Constitutional Law* (Athens-Thessaloniki: Sakkoulas, 2015).

(b) All matters relating to divorce, judicial separation or restitution of conjugal rights or to family relations of the members of the three religious groups, came under the jurisdiction of the Family Courts of the religious groups, which eventually came into force with Law 87/1994.
(c) The Constitution specifically provides for grounds for divorce. The ground of irretrievable breakdown rendering the marital relationship intolerable for the claimant is introduced, while the grounds of divorce, mentioned in the Charter remain in force. The House of Representatives may establish with law any other grounds for divorce; such new grounds for divorce were eventually established with the promulgation of Law 46(I)/1999 and then Law 104(I)/2003.
(d) All members of the Greek Community, including members of the Greek Orthodox Church or of the three religious groups, may choose to perform a civil marriage. This became possible after the promulgation of Law 21/1990, which established a dual regime of civil and religious marriage and subsequently Law 104(I)/2003.
(e) Matters relating to betrothal, marriage and nullity of marriage continue to be governed by the law of the Greek Orthodox Church or the Church of the corresponding religious group as the case may be.

*23.* The Orthodox Church considered the First Amendment of the Constitution as an affront to the religious sentiments of its members.[39] In a decision of the Holy Synod, it was declared that: 'no one had ever imagined that one day, representatives of our people in the House of Representatives, would try to take such rights away from the Church'.[40] The Holy Synod decided that the celebration of a civil marriage by a member of the Greek Orthodox Church, or the petition to the Family Courts for the dissolution of a religious marriage, would be punished by the deprival of the participation of such persons to every aspect of religious life. However, the Holy Synod eventually mellowed, since in 1991 it acknowledged that petitioning before the Family Courts is obligatory, so as to have the religious dissolution of marriage recognized by the State; the Church therefore accepted that its members may petition the Family Courts for divorce, so long as they first petition the ecclesiastical courts and a dissolution of their marriage is granted by both courts.

*24.* In addition, in view of the fact that the Orthodox Church, as well as the Maronite and Roman Catholic Church, had not recognized the competences of the Family Courts, in essence, if a person wanted to obtain a divorce and then perform a new religious marriage according to the rites of his/her respective Church, he/she had to obtain both a divorce from the family courts which would be recognized by the State only, as well as a divorce from the ecclesiastical courts which would be recognized by the Church authorities only; if, however, a person did not wish to perform a new religious marriage, but he/she wished to perform a civil marriage, then

---

39. *See* G. Antoniou, 'Family Law: An Ecclesiastical Approach', *Cyprus Law Review* 8 (1984): 1353–1361 (in Greek), *Id.*, 'Church's Opinion on Divorce', *Cyprus Law Review* 41 (1993): 6149–6157 (in Greek), P. Mpoumis, 'Dissolution of Marriage from State Courts', *Apostolos Varnavas* 51 (1990): 43–49 (in Greek).
40. (1989) 50 *Apostolos Varnavas* 324.

he/she only had to obtain a divorce from the family courts. This peculiar situation undoubtedly caused many problems with respect to the application of family law with regard to members of the Orthodox Church and the religious groups of the Republic.[41] Eventually, with the enactment of its new Charter in 2010, the Orthodox Church impliedly recognized the jurisdiction of the Family Courts, retaining only its competences for spiritual dissolution of the marriage.[42]

*25.* The 1989 amendment of the Constitution was a step in the right direction; Cypriot family law has been modernized and its religious character might be said to have diminished. However, the Church membership of the parties remains an important criterion for the division of people for the purposes of family law; Church membership is important not only with respect to the application of the provisions of Article 111 of the Constitution but also with respect to the interpretation of the Cypriot law of marriage and divorce.[43] Thus, family matters of members of the Greek Orthodox Church or of the three religious groups continue to be treated specifically in Article 111 of the Constitution, despite the fact that the competence with respect to such family matters now belongs to the (State) Family Courts and not to the (religious) ecclesiastical court.

## §3. Sources of Family and Succession Law

### I. Constitution

*26.* The 1960 Constitution of Cyprus is a major source of Cypriot family law. No law or administrative act may be inconsistent or contrary to the Constitution. While only the Supreme Court and the Administrative Court have jurisdiction to examine the alleged unconstitutionality of administrative acts, both the Supreme Court and district courts have jurisdiction to declare a law as unconstitutional. Since the Fifth Amendment of the Constitution in 2006, EU law is considered as an integral part of the Constitution; therefore, no provision of the Constitution may invalidate the law of the EU, irrespective of whether such law arises from the Treaties, or from secondary legislation, such as an EU Regulation, or Directive. It should be noted that EU law is acknowledged as an intra-constitutional principle and not as a *supra*-constitutional principle; therefore, EU law acquires constitutional status and cannot be invalidated due to the existence of contrary constitutional provisions.[44]

41. *See* G. Serghides, 'Observations on the Cypriot Marriage Law of 2003', *Armenopoulos* 58 (2004): 677 (in Greek), E. Nicolaou, 'Family Law: Legislative and Procedural Problems', *Cyprus Law Review* 49–50 (1995): 7259ff (in Greek).
42. *See* in detail A. Emilianides, C. Katsaros (eds), *The New Charter of the Church of Cyprus* (Nicosia: Hippasus, 2013, in Greek).
43. *See* A. Emilianides, *The Cypriot Law of Marriage and Divorce* (Thessaloniki: Sakkoulas, 2006, in Greek).
44. A. Emilianides, *Beyond the Constitution of Cyprus* (Thessaloniki: Sakkoulas, 2006, in Greek), 218ff, *Id.*, 'The Constitution of Cyprus after Accession', in *Policy Proposals after the Accession of Cyprus in the EU*, ed. A. Emilianides (Nicosia: Power Publishing, 2005, in Greek), 110–118, C. Lykourgos,

*27.* Article 22 of the Constitution safeguards the fundamental right to marry and found a family.[45] Article 22 §1 provides that any person reaching nubile age is free to marry and to found a family according to the law relating to marriage applicable to such person under the provisions of the Constitution. Such constitutional right is enjoyed by all natural persons, irrespective of whether they are citizens of the Republic or foreigners, and it implies not only the right to marry but also the right not to marry; consequently, legislative provisions which imposed taxation to unmarried persons only were held to be unconstitutional.[46] Article 22 corresponds to Article 12 of the ECHR; however, it is more detailed and extensive due to the peculiarities of the Cypriot law of marriage. Such additional provisions are not inconsistent with Article 12 of the ECHR, since Article 12 specifically provides that the right is exercised in accordance with national laws. The right to marry is complemented by the right to respect for a person's private and family life safeguarded by Article 15 of the Constitution which corresponds to Article 8 of the ECHR.[47]

*28.* The right to marry is exercised in accordance with the applicable law for each person in accordance with the constitutional provisions.[48] Article 111 of the Constitution applies with respect to marriages between members of the Greek Orthodox or the three religious groups, while marriages between members of the Turkish Community are governed by the constitutional provisions establishing the Turkish Communal Chamber. Article 111 of the Constitution is of extreme importance, since it also governs the grounds for divorce applying to marriages of members of the Greek Orthodox Church, the establishment and composition of the Family Courts and the Appellate Family Courts, as well as the attempt to compromise and the spiritual dissolution of the marriage and the choice of civil marriage for members of the Greek Community. Article 22 §2 of the Constitution further governs the applicable law in case of mixed marriages.[49]

*29.* EU Regulations, which have constitutional status, apply directly in the Republic of Cyprus. The most important of such instruments with respect to Family Law are: Council Regulation (EC) 2201/2003 of 27 November 2003 concerning jurisdiction and the recognition and enforcement of judgments in matrimonial matters and the matters of parental responsibility (Brussels IIa) and Council Regulation (EC) 4/2009 of 18 December 2008 on jurisdiction, applicable law, recognition and

---

'Cyprus Public Law as Affected by Accession to the European Union', in *Studies in European Public Law: Thematic, National and Post-National Perspectives*, ed. Kombos C (Athens: Sakkoulas, 2010), 101–113. S. Laulhe-Shaelou, *EU and Cyprus* (Leiden: Martinus Nijhoff, 2010), C. Kombos, *The Impact of EU Law on Cypriot Public Law* (Athens-Thessaloniki: Sakkoulas, 2015).

45. C. Tornaritis, 'The Right to Marry and Found a Family, Especially under the Laws of Cyprus', *Mélanges Offerts à Polys Modinos* (Paris, 1968), 320–330.
46. *Panayides v. The Republic of Cyprus* [1965] 3 CLR 107.
47. C. Tornaritis, *The State Law of the Republic of Cyprus* (Nicosia: Centre for Scientific Research, 1982): 128.
48. *Venglis v. Venglis* [1982] 1 CLR 223.
49. G. Serghides, *Internal and External Conflict of Laws in Regard to Family Relations in Cyprus* (Nicosia, 1988), A. Emilianides, *The Cypriot Law of Marriage and Divorce* (Thessaloniki: Sakkoulas, 2006, in Greek). C. Tornaritis, 'On the Applicable Law in Case of Mixed Marriages', *Revue Hellenique de Droit International* 19 (1966): 293–294.

enforcement of decisions, and cooperation in matters relating to maintenance obligations. With regard to succession law the most important EU Regulation is Regulation 650/2012 of the European Parliament and of the Council of 4 July 2012 on jurisdiction, applicable law, recognition and enforcement of decisions, and acceptance and enforcement of authentic instruments in matters of succession and on the creation of a European Certificate of Succession.

## II. Legislation

*30.* Nearly all legislation relevant to Family Law was enacted following the 1989 constitutional amendment and reflects changing social structures and policy in the regulation of family law affairs. The corpus of family law legislation includes the Marriage Law 104(I)/2003, Articles 83–90 of the 2010 Charter of the Orthodox Church of Cyprus, and the Attempt to Compromise and Spiritual Dissolution of Marriage Law 22/1990 which govern marriage and divorce. The Family Courts Law 23/1990 and the Family Courts (Religious Groups) Law 87(I)/1994 set out the jurisdiction, composition, and applicable law of the Family Courts and the Family Courts of the Religious Groups respectively. Section 22 of the Courts of Justice Law 14/1960 is also relevant, since it provides for the limited jurisdiction of the President of the District Court to hear family law disputes. Law 120(I)/2003 for the application of the Marriage Law of 2003 to Members of the Turkish Community (Temporary Provisions) and the Marriage of Members of the Old Calendar Law 60(I)/1994 are also relevant with respect to the law of marriage.

*31.* With respect to parental care and maintenance the relevant law is the Relationship between Parents and Children Law 216/1990. The Children (Kinship and Legal Substance) Law 187/1991 provides for the kinship and filiation, while the Matrimonial Property of the Spouses Law 232/1991 provides for the maintenance and matrimonial property of the spouses in cases of separation or divorce. The Adoption Law 19(I)/1995 and the Adoption Procedural Regulations of 1954 govern adoption in the Republic of Cyprus. The two main Procedural Regulations are the Family Court Procedural Regulation of 1990 and the Family Court (Religious Groups) Procedural Regulation of 1995.

*32.* Contrary to the situation with respect to Family Law, legislation governing Succession Law was enacted prior to Independence. The main legislation with respect to substantive law is the Wills and Succession Law, Cap. 195 which was enacted in 1945; Cap. 195 has been modified twice with Laws 75/1970 and 100/1989 and remains:

> *a very composite statute. The sections relating to the form of the will are based upon the English law. The sections relating to intestate succession and the limitation of the disposable portion are based upon the Italian Civil Code (which in its main lines is based upon that of the Roman Law, i.e., upon the 118th*

*Novel of Justinian). In both cases the legislator has introduced numerous modifications of substance, presumably with a view to adapting the law to the circumstances of this country.*[50]

*33.* Administration of estates is governed by the Administration of Estates Law, Cap. 189 which was enacted in 1955; Cap. 189 has been modified with Laws 157/85, 45/90 and 20(I)/94. The Administration of Estates Regulations of 1955 further specify procedure provided for in Cap. 189. Cap. 195 is further complemented by the Probates (Re-Sealing) Law, Cap. 192, as well as the Probates (Re-Sealing) Rules of 1936 which provide for the sealing by Cypriot courts of probates granted by common law courts outside Cyprus.

## III. Treaties

*34.* An international treaty, convention, or agreement that has been concluded by the Republic of Cyprus shall have as from its publication in the Official Gazette of the Republic, superior force to any municipal law on condition that such a treaty, convention, or agreement is also applied by the other party thereto, in accordance with Article 169 §3 of the Constitution. The Convention on the Establishment of a Scheme of Registration of Wills (Ratification) Law 64/1974 and the Convention providing a Uniform Law on the Form of an International Will (Ratification) Law 22/1980 are the most important Treaties with respect to succession law. Also relevant for both succession and family law is the bilateral Convention for Legal Cooperation between the Republic of Cyprus and the Republic of Greece in matters of Civil, Family, Commercial, and Criminal Law ratified by Law 55/1984.[51]

*35.* The main treaties in force with respect to Cypriot Family Law are the Convention on the Civil Aspects of International Child Abduction (Ratification) Law 11(III)/1994, the Convention on the Legal Status of Children born out of Wedlock (Ratification) Law 50/1979, the Convention on the Rights of the Child (Ratification) Law 5(III)/2000, the European Convention on the Exercise of Children's Rights (Ratification) Law 23(III)/2005, the Convention on the Recovery Abroad of Maintenance (Ratification) Law 50/1978, the Convention on Protection of Children and Cooperation in respect of Intercountry Adoption (Ratification) Law 26(III)/1994, and the Convention on Consent to Marriage, Minimum Age for Marriage, and Registration of Marriage (Ratification) Law 16(III)/2002.

*36.* Of importance for both family and succession law is the ECHR which was ratified in the internal legal order by the European Convention for the Protection of

50. *Charalambous v. Demetriou* [1961] CLR 30.
51. A. Papantoniou, 'The Convention for Legal Co-Operation between the Republic of Cyprus and the Republic of Greece', *Cyprus Law Review* 18 (1987): 2831–2853.

Human Rights (Ratification) Law n. 39/1962.[52] The instrument of ratification was deposited with the Secretary of the Council of Europe on 6 October 1962. Part II of the Constitution of Cyprus which guarantees the fundamental rights and liberties is modelled on the ECHR; however, the provisions of the ECHR have been extended and enlarged in some respects with a number of social and economic rights added in order to meet the basic requirements of a modern society.[53] Consequently, to the extent that it has been incorporated in constitutional provisions and to the degree that its provisions have not been altered during incorporation, the ECHR enjoys limited constitutional status.[54] Legislation which is contrary to the provisions of the Constitution safeguarding individual human rights may be declared unconstitutional by the trial court.

*37.* Moreover, the ECHR and its Protocols have, on the basis of Article 169 §3 of the Constitution, superior force to any municipal law, either antecedent or subsequent to their ratification by Law. However, the ECHR is not superior to the Constitution; thus, the constitutional provisions shall prevail in case of any inconsistency between them and the provisions of the ECHR.[55] It should be further observed that the Cypriot courts are invoking the case law of the ECtHR, not only with respect to the interpretation of the ECHR but also with respect to the interpretation of the corresponding constitutional Articles. Therefore, the courts will try, wherever possible, to interpret the relevant constitutional provisions in a manner which is consistent with the interpretation adopted by the ECtHR.[56]

52. *See* in general A. Loizou, 'Cyprus', in *Fundamental Rights in Europe: The European Convention on Human Rights and its Member States, 1950–2000*, ed. R. Blackburn & J. Polakiewicz (Oxford: Oxford University Press, 2001), 217, *Id.*, *Cyprus and the European Convention on Human Rights* (Athens: Sakkoulas, 2003, in Greek).
53. Acknowledged in several judgments of the Supreme Court of Cyprus, such as *Attorney-General v. Ibrahim* [1964] CLR 195: 225, *Attorney-General v. Afamis* 1 RSCC 121: 125–126. *See* further P. Evangelides, *The Republic of Cyprus and its Constitution with Special Regard to Constitutional Rights* (Difo–Druck GmbH, 1996), C. Tornaritis, *The Human Rights as Recognized and Protected by Law, with Special Reference to the Law of Cyprus* (Nicosia, 1967), C. Paraskeva, *Cypriot Constitutional Law: Fundamental Rights and Freedoms* (Athens: Nomiki Vivliothiki, 2015, in Greek).
54. *See* A. Emilianides, *Beyond the Constitution of Cyprus* (Sakkoulas, Athens-Thessaloniki, 2006, in Greek).
55. *See* T. Hadjanastassiou, 'The European Convention on Human Rights applicable in Cyprus', *Cyprus Law Tribune* 3 (1976): 97–113.
56. *See* further A. Loizou, *Cyprus and the European Convention on Human Rights* (Athens: Sakkoulas, 2003, in Greek), C. Tornaritis, 'The Operation of the European Convention for the Protection of Human Rights in the Republic of Cyprus', *Cyprus Law Review* 3 (1983): 455–464, C. Clerides, 'The Operation of the European Convention on Human Rights in the Civil Courts of Cyprus', *Cyprus Law Review* 39–40 (1992): 6029–6043 (in Greek).

### IV. Jurisprudence (Case Law)

*38.* The principles of common law and equity apply in the Republic of Cyprus.[57] Previous judgments of the Supreme Court are binding for lower courts; thus, case law is of great significance with regard to the interpretation of legal provisions.[58] The legal rule which must be applied is the *ratio decidendi*, or the legal principle on which the previous decision was founded. The ratio of the case is distinguishable from *obiter* dicta, which are statements on principles of law made in the course of a decision, but on which the decision does not depend. It is noted, however, that previous case law is only binding so far as a subsequent law with different content has not been enacted. Having a substantially codified legal system, Cyprus applies common law principles where there is no Cypriot legislation in force and insofar as existing Cypriot legislation is not contradicted.[59]

## §4. The Courts Administering Family and Succession Law

### I. District Courts

*39.* There are six District Courts, one for each administrative district of the Republic of Cyprus (Nicosia, Famagusta, Limassol, Larnaca, Paphos, and Kyrenia). Since the 1974 Turkish Invasion the District Court of Famagusta is located at Paralimni and the District Court of Kyrenia is located at Nicosia. The District Courts have jurisdiction to hear and determine at first instance all civil actions, with the exception of matters that fall within the jurisdiction of the Rent Control Tribunal, the Industrial Disputes Tribunal, and the Family Court. Cases before District Courts are heard by a single judge, who may be, depending on the amount of the dispute, a District Court Judge, a Senior District Court Judge, or a President of a District Court.[60]

*40.* District Courts have jurisdiction to hear all disputes relating to the law of succession, including actions between heirs or legatees, or actions related to the validity of the will. An Administrator of the Estate or an Executor of a will fulfil their duties under the supervision of the Court. The Registrar of the District Court,

57. L. Loucaides, 'The Dependence of Cypriot Law from Common Law', *Subjects of Cypriot Law* (Nicosia, 1982, in Greek): 36–77, G. Pikis, *The English Common Law: The Rules of Equity and their Application in Cyprus* (Larnaca, 1981, in Greek).
58. C. Artemides, 'The Principle of Commitment of Courts to Case-Law in English Common Law', in *Aspects of Cypriot Law*, v. I (Nicosia: Asselia, 1981, in Greek), 219–231, S. Nikitas, 'The Principle of Judicial Precedent in English Common Law', *Corpus de Jure Cyprii*, v. I (Nicosia: Legal Studies Council, 1987), 119–133 (in Greek).
59. S. Symeonides, 'The Mixed Legal System of the Republic of Cyprus', *Tulane Law Review* 78 (2003): 441–455, A. Emilianides, 'Cyprus: Everything Changes and Nothing Remains Still' in *A Study of Mixed Legal Systems: Endangered, Entrenched or Blended*, ed. S. Farran et al (Aldershot: Ashgate, 2014).
60. *See* in detail C. Clerides, *The Cypriot Legal System* (Athens: Nomiki Vivliothiki 2018, in Greek).

while granting probate or proceeding to any other actions related to the administration of an Estate, acts under the supervision of the Court. In order for the distribution of the estate to the heirs to take place, the Court must approve the final accounts prepared by the Administrator of the Estate or the Executor of the will.

*41.* With respect to family law disputes a President of a District Court has the power, in accordance with Article 22 of the Courts of Justice Law 14/1960, to hear any marital dispute which does not fall within the jurisdiction of the Family Court or the Family Courts of the Religious Groups. Consequently, the Presidents of the District Court currently have the exclusive jurisdiction to adjudicate the matrimonial affairs of members of the Turkish Community who have celebrated their marriage in Cyprus, under the provisions of the Marriage Law 104(I)/2003;[61] no other marital disputes fall within the jurisdiction of the President of a District Court. Section 21A of the Courts of Justice Law 14/60 provides that matrimonial affairs include nullity, divorce, maintenance of children and spouses, and custody of children; however, they do not include adoption, legitimacy of children, or pecuniary relations of spouses.

*42.* Section 2 of Law 19(I)/95 provides that the Family Court of the habitual residence of the prospective adoptive parents shall have jurisdiction if the person or persons applying to adopt are members of the Greek Community; in any other case it is provided that the District Court of the petitioner's habitual residence has jurisdiction. However, Law 26(I)/98 which amended section 11 of the Family Courts Law 23/90 provided that the Family Courts have jurisdiction for adoption cases, so long as the parties or either of them habitually resides in the Republic for a continuous period of three months. In *Ajero* the Appellate Family Court held that Law 26(I)/98 has impliedly repealed any inconsistent provisions of Law 19(I)/95 and consequently the Family Courts have jurisdiction in all cases where the parties or either of them habitually reside in the Republic for a continuous period of three months as provided in section 11 of Law 23/90 and not only in cases where the parties are members of the Greek Community.[62]

*43.* In the case of *Biyikli*, the Family Court of Nicosia – Kyrenia held that it had no jurisdiction to examine an application for adoption by members of the Turkish Cypriot Community, in view of the fact that this competence constitutionally belongs to the Turkish Communal Chamber and there has been no law enacted by the House of Representatives with respect to adoption, in a manner similar to the Marriage Law 120(I)/2003.[63] While the Family Court correctly noted that this legal vacuum is unacceptable, it held that it could not exercise jurisdiction on its own, contrary to the constitutional provisions. The Appellate Family Court affirmed the approach of the Family Court; however, it was held *obiter* that while the Family Courts do not have jurisdiction with respect to adoptions made by members of the

61. Or Cap. 279 for the brief period from the enactment of Law 46(I)/2002 until the entry into force of Laws 104(I)/2003 and 120(I)/2003.
62. *Ajero* [2006] 1 CLR 1165 (in Greek).
63. *Biyikli and another* [2010] 1 CLR 71(in Greek).

Turkish Community, District Courts do have such jurisdiction in accordance with section 2 of Law 19(I)/95. The Appellate Family Court noted that a different approach would deprive members of the Turkish Community from their fundamental right to adopt and have access to court.

*44.* It is submitted that such *obiter* comments of the Appellate Family Court may not be reconciled with its other findings; if the Family Court has no jurisdiction because the Constitution, namely the supreme law of the Republic, provides that such jurisdiction belongs to the Turkish Communal Chamber, then how can the District Courts exercise such jurisdiction by virtue of Law 19(I)/95. If the Law is inconsistent with the Constitution, then such Law is unconstitutional. It is one thing for a court to interpret a law in a manner which is consistent with the ECHR or the doctrine of necessity; however, it is entirely different to arbitrarily decide that a court may exercise competences it does not enjoy.[64] In the subsequent *Sioukrou* case the Appellate Family Court correctly clarified that the District Court has no jurisdiction with respect to applications for judicial recognition of a child;[65] while it was held that the Family Courts have jurisdiction with respect to such cases, it is not sufficiently clear whether this was due to the fact that only the alleged father, and not both parties, was a member of the Turkish Community. It has further been clarified that no court in the Republic has jurisdiction with regards to matrimonial property of members of the Turkish Community.[66]

## II. Family Courts

### *A. Composition*

*45.* Article 112 §2 A of the Constitution provides that the Family Court is composed of three judges in divorce proceedings and of a single judge in any other trial. In divorce cases, the President of the Family Court is appointed by the Orthodox Church of Cyprus and should be a ranked member of the clergy with legal education, while the other two judges are appointed by the Supreme Court and should be jurists of the highest professional and moral standards who belong to the Orthodox Church. If the Orthodox Church refuses to appoint the President of the Family Court, as has been the practice since the establishment of the Family Courts, then such President is also appointed by the Supreme Court and is a jurist of the highest professional and moral standards who belongs to the Orthodox Church; thus, in practice no member of the Family Court is a member of the clergy.

*46.* In view of the refusal of the Orthodox Church to appoint the President of the Family Courts, or to recognize the Family Courts, the issue of the participation

64. A. Emilianides, 'The Case for Amending the Current Legal Framework', *Cyprus and European Law Review* 11 (2011): 135ff, G. Serghides, 'Reflection on some Aspects of the Family Law of the Turkish Community in Cyprus', *Cyprus and European Law Review* 11 (2011): 156ff.
65. *Sioukrou v. Ulrich* [2011] 1 CLR 443(in Greek).
66. *GM v. HV and another*, App. 38/2015, Judgment of 10 Sep. 2018 (in Greek).

of a clergyman in the composition of the Family Court remained of theoretical interest only. However, in 2008 and following discussions between the Church and the State, the Archbishop of Cyprus suggested to the Supreme Court that he was willing to appoint the new President of the Family Court of Larnaca–Famagusta, when the previous President retired, as provided for in Article 111 of the Constitution. Despite the fact that this right of the Orthodox Church is constitutionally provided for, the Supreme Court disregarded the submission of the Archbishop and appointed a judge as the new President of the Family Court of Larnaca–Famagusta.

*47.* Section 3 of the Family Courts Law 23/1990 provides that the Family Courts are composed in the manner provided for in Article 111 §2 A of the Constitution. However, the fact that section 3 of Law 23/1990 merely reiterates the constitutional provisions with respect to the composition of the Family Courts is a cause for concern. Article 111 §2 A of the Constitution refers to the Family Courts when they specifically adjudicate divorce cases of members of the Greek Orthodox Church. Family Courts, however, have acquired by statutory law, the additional jurisdiction to adjudicate divorce cases of persons who are not members of the Orthodox Church or disputes arising out of civil marriage. It is in our view inconsistent with the fundamental right of religious freedom safeguarded by Article 9 of the ECHR, that membership to the Orthodox Church is a prerequisite for the appointment of judges who are to adjudicate disputes arising out of a civil marriage, or a religious marriage of persons not belonging to the Orthodox Church. The relevant provision is completely unreasonable, and this is due to the fact that the legislator had failed to distinguish between the cases where the Family Court should be composed in accordance to Article 111 of the Constitution with respect to marriages celebrated according to the rites of the Orthodox Church, and all other cases.[67]

*48.* It should be noted that the Family Courts need not be composed by three judges in all stages of the divorce proceedings; the three-judge panel is required only for the hearing or proof of the divorce case, while a single judge may hear the parties during the earlier stages of the trial such as directions.[68] In all other cases, other than divorce proceedings, the Family Courts are composed by a single judge; section 3.1.b.ii of the Family Courts Law 23/1990, as amended by section 3 of Law 33(I)/1996, which provided that matrimonial property disputes over CYP 50,000 are to be adjudicated by two judges, was declared by the Supreme Court to be inconsistent with Article 111 §2 A b of the Constitution and thus unconstitutional. Law 58(I)/2000 which amended section 3 of the Family Courts Law 23/1990 now explicitly provides that the Family Court is composed in cases other than divorce proceedings by a single judge.

67. *See* A. Emilianides, *The Cypriot Law of Marriage and Divorce* (Thessaloniki: Sakkoulas, 2006, in Greek): 276ff.

68. Until 8 May 1991 the Family Court was composed of three judges even at the earlier stages of the trial. *See* G. Serghides, 'Travelling Family Court', *Cyprus Law Review* 37 (1992): 5674 (in Greek).

*B. Jurisdiction*

*49.* In addition to its competences provided for in Article 111 of the Constitution, the Family Court currently exercises all competences with respect to family law disputes previously exercised by the District Courts; thus, in accordance with the Family Courts Law 23/1990 as amended by Law 26/1998, the Family Courts have exclusive jurisdiction with respect to all disputes concerning (i) dissolution of religious marriage celebrated in accordance with the doctrine of the Greek Orthodox Church, (ii) dissolution of religious marriage of any other rite, insofar as the dissolution of such marriage does not fall within the jurisdiction of the Family Courts of the Religious Groups, (iii) dissolution of civil marriage (with the exception of civil marriages of members of the three religious groups), (iv) family law disputes in judicial proceedings commenced in accordance with the provisions of bilateral or multilateral treaties to which the Republic of Cyprus is a party, (v) parental care, maintenance, recognition of a child, adoption, matrimonial property, and any other marital or family law dispute, so long as the parties or either of them reside in the Republic for a continuous period of over three months. With regard to matrimonial property disputes the Family Courts also exercise jurisdiction if there is any property in Cyprus. Thus, the Family Courts currently have first instance jurisdiction for all marital or family law disputes, irrespective of whether the parties are citizens of the Republic or foreigners, with the exception of the cases falling within the jurisdiction of the Family Courts of the Religious Groups or the President of the District Court. It should be noted that pursuant to section 14 of Law 23/90, Cypriot courts always apply the law of the forum, i.e., Cypriot domestic law, in all cases of divorce, maintenance, distribution of matrimonial property, custody of minors, guardianship, legitimacy, child recognition, and adoption.[69]

*C. The Family Courts of Religious Groups*

1. Introduction

*50.* Only the Armenian religious group had established its own ecclesiastical courts in Cyprus when the Constitution came into force. The ecclesiastical courts of the Roman Catholic religious group were situated in Jerusalem, while the ecclesiastical courts of the Maronite religious group were situated in Lebanon. Thus, there were no ecclesiastical courts of the Maronite and Roman Catholic religious group in Cyprus, but only preparatory fact-finding committees, which then sent their report to the ecclesiastical courts situated in Lebanon and Jerusalem respectively. This awkward situation was considered to be very problematic by the Supreme Court.[70] Since the First Amendment of the Constitution, all matters relating to

69. For this and conflicts with EU Regulations *see* A. Emilianides et al, *Private International Law in Cyprus* (The Hague: Kluwer, 2015).

70. *Christodoulou v. Christodoulou* [1962] CLR 68, *HjiJovanni v. HjiJovanni* [1969] 1 CLR 207. *See* further G. Serghides, *Internal and External Conflict of Laws in Regard to Family Relations in Cyprus* (Nicosia, 1988): 300ff.

divorce, judicial separation, or restitution of conjugal rights or to family relations of the members of the three religious groups, have come under the jurisdiction of the family courts of the respective religious group.

*51.* Article 111 §3 of the Constitution which provides for the establishment of the family courts of the religious groups specifies that such courts are separate from the Family Courts referred to in Article 111 §2 of the Constitution. It is further provided that a relevant law will regulate matters relating to the establishment, composition, and jurisdiction of the family courts of religious groups, in line with the provisions for Family Courts of members belonging to the Greek Orthodox Church. The relevant law is the Family Courts (Religious Groups) Law 87 (I)/1994, which came into effect on 1 January 1995 and which established family courts for the religious groups of the Armenian, Maronite, and Latin with headquarters in Nicosia.

*52.* Article 3 of the Family Courts Law No. 231/91 provided that the ecclesiastical courts of the three religious groups would continue to serve as Family Courts of the religious groups, until the relevant law came into force. Thus for a period of five years, the ecclesiastical courts continued to perform the duties of Family Courts, despite the express constitutional provision providing for the establishment of Family Courts of Religious Groups replacing the ecclesiastical courts of such religious groups. While such transitional arrangements were not in accordance with the Constitution, this fact is now of a theoretical interest only.

## 2. Composition

*53.* The Family Courts of Religious Groups are composed of three judges in divorce proceedings and one judge in any other trial. Of particular interest is the establishment of a three-member Family Court in divorce proceedings; it is provided that the chairman and one of the two members are appointed by the Supreme Court, while the other judge is a member of the religious group to which the parties belong to and is proposed by the Representative of that religious group in the House of Representatives. If for any reason the Representative of the religious group in the House does not propose any of their members, then the Supreme Court also appoints the remaining member of the Court. In practice the Maronite and Roman Catholic religious groups do not recognize the jurisdiction of their respective family courts and thus do not propose a judge. On the contrary the Armenian religious group recognizes the jurisdiction of the Family Court of the Armenians and proposes an Armenian judge to represent their religious group in the composition of their respective family court.

*54.* It is observed that the composition of the Family Courts of the three Religious Groups provided for by Law 87(I)/94 should have been considered to be unconstitutional. Article 111 §3 of the Constitution provides that the establishment of the Family Courts of Religious Groups should be, *mutatis mutandis*, to the establishment of family courts with respect to members of the Greek Orthodox Church.

The relevant provision of the Constitution provides that the President of such Family Court of members of the Orthodox Church shall be indicated by the Orthodox Church. Why then is it not provided that the president – and not just a member – of the Family Court of Religious Groups should also be indicated by the respective religious group? The fact that from a juridical point of view it is preferable for the religious groups to be represented by a member of the court, instead of the President, is not a justification for violating constitutional provisions and differentiating arbitrarily between the Orthodox Church and the three religious groups.[71]

*55.* In *Ouzounian*, however, the majority of the Supreme Court held that the composition of the Family Courts of Religious Groups is consistent with Article 111 of the Constitution.[72] While in our view the judgment of the majority is highly problematic, it is now settled case law that the composition of the Family Courts of Religious Groups is constitutional. A more practical problem is that the Supreme Court appoints district court judges and not family court judges as members of the Family Court of religious groups. It is submitted that family court judges are more experienced with issues concerning family law and should therefore be preferred from district court judges. A final question to be considered is what happens if a marriage has been celebrated between spouses belonging to different religious groups. Which family court will have jurisdiction in such a case? The answer is: the family court of the religious group of the Church where the marriage has been celebrated.

### 3. Jurisdiction

*56.* Article 2(b) of Law No. 87 (I) / 94, as amended by Law 38 (I) / 96, provides for the jurisdiction of the Family Courts of Religious Groups to hear applications for the dissolution of religious marriages which have been celebrated in accordance with the tenets and rules of a religious group, regardless of whether such marriages are mixed or not. This arrangement is consistent with the best interpretation of Articles 22 and 111 of the Constitution, according to which mixed marriages of parties belonging to a different religious group should be heard before the respective court of the religious group where the marriage has been celebrated. In addition, Article 2(b) provides for the jurisdiction of the Family Courts of Religious Groups to consider applications for the dissolution of civil marriages which have been celebrated between persons belonging to the same religious group.

*57.* The Family Courts of the Religious Groups do not, however, have jurisdiction to hear applications for the dissolution of civil marriages between persons belonging to different religious groups or between persons belonging to a religious group and persons who do not belong to a religious group; it is the family courts which are competent over the dissolution of such civil marriages and not the family courts of the religious groups. As a result, Article 11 of the Family Law Courts

71. *See* A. Emilianides, *The Cypriot Law of Marriage and Divorce* (Thessaloniki: Sakkoulas, 2006, in Greek): 285–286.
72. *Ouzounian v. Constantinides* [2011] 1 CLR 177 (in Greek).

23/90 which provides for the competence of family courts to deal with matters relating to the dissolution of civil marriages should be interpreted as excluding from its ambit the competence over civil marriages between persons belonging to the same religious group, since such competence belongs to the family courts of the religious group, in accordance with the principle *lex specialis derogat lex generalis*.

*58.* Law 87(I)/1994, as amended by Law 29(I)/1997, provides that the Family Courts of the Religious Groups only have jurisdiction with respect to divorce cases and not with respect to any other family law matters concerning members of the respective religious groups; the Supreme Court held that the aforementioned modification of Law 87(I)/1994, by Law 29(I)/1997, does not violate the Constitution.[73] It further held that the Family Courts – and not the Family Courts of the Religious Groups – have jurisdiction over any other family matters concerning members of the religious groups.[74] It is submitted that the aforementioned judgment of the Supreme Court is highly problematic.[75] Article 111 §3 of the Constitution provides that all matters of members of a religious group concerning divorce or family relations should be adjudicated by the Family Court of the respective religious group; the term *family relations* is a term also used in Article 111 §2 with respect to members of the Greek Orthodox Church and has been interpreted by the Supreme Court as denoting all matters concerning family law in the wide sense and not restricted simply to issues concerning divorce.[76]

*59.* It is not legally correct to interpret the same term in the same Article of the Constitution, in one manner with respect to members of the Greek Orthodox Church and in a different manner with respect to the three religious groups of the Republic. Such a differing interpretation violates the equal treatment of religions safeguarded by the system of coordination of the Constitution of Cyprus and is inconsistent with the fundamental legal principle that terms should be interpreted in the same manner when used in the same context. In view of the above, it is submitted that, contrary to the view of the Supreme Court, the Family Courts of the three Religious Groups of the Republic ought to have jurisdiction with respect to all family matters concerning members of the three religious groups.[77] However, again this is a moot point in view of the fact that there is now settled case law of the Supreme Court in this area.

73. *Toumayan v. Toumayan* [2007] 1 CLR 1024 (in Greek).
74. *Damtsa v. Damtsa* [2006] 1 CLR 760 (in Greek).
75. *See* A. Emilianides, 'Jurisdiction for the Adjudication of Property Disputes between Members of Religious Groups', *Cyprus and European Law Review* 4 (2007): 153–170.
76. *Dadakarides v. Dadakarides* [1990] 1 CLR 566 (in Greek), *Ioannou v. Ioannou* [1991] 1 CLR 186 (in Greek), *Demetriou v. Demetriou* [1991] 1 CLR 1153 (in Greek).
77. *See also* G. Serghides, 'Cyprus Family Jurisdiction Ratione Personae and Ratione Materiae', *Family Law Review* 2 (2011): 6–7.

*D. Supreme Court*

*60.* The highest Cypriot court is the Supreme Court of Cyprus, which functions, following the constitutional crisis of 1963, both as the supreme constitutional court and as the supreme appellate court of the Republic. The Supreme Court is composed of thirteen judges, one of whom acts as the President. The Court has jurisdiction to hear and determine all appeals from lower courts in civil and criminal matters, including all succession law matters. Appeals are heard by a panel of three judges. The hearing of the appeal is based on the record of the proceedings kept in the lower court. The Supreme Court only hears oral evidence in exceptional and very rare circumstances. In the exercise of its appellate jurisdiction the Supreme Court may uphold, vary, or set aside the decision appealed from or it may order a retrial.

*61.* Article 144 of the Constitution provides that the Supreme Constitutional Court (now merged with the Supreme Court) has exclusive jurisdiction to decide on any questions of constitutionality of any law of the Republic which are material for the determination of any matter at issue in judicial proceedings. Whenever such question is raised before a court, it shall reserve the question for the decision of the Supreme Constitutional Court and stay further proceedings until such question is determined by the Supreme Constitutional Court. Any decision of the Supreme Constitutional Court is binding on the court by which the question has been reserved and on the parties to the proceedings. Following the constitutional crisis of 1963, the Administration of Justice Law 33/1964, invoked on the basis of the doctrine of necessity, provided that any court in the Republic has jurisdiction to hear questions on the constitutionality of laws without having to resort to the procedure provided for in Article 144 of the Constitution, or having to refer the question to the Supreme Constitutional Court. Thus, any District Court (subject to appeal), or the Supreme Court in the exercise of its appellate jurisdiction, may hear and decide on any questions concerning the constitutionality of laws in succession law disputes.[78]

*62.* The exceptional mechanism provided for in Law 33/1964 does not apply with respect to family law disputes.[79] Consequently, the Supreme Court has exclusive jurisdiction with respect to questions of constitutionality of laws in family law affairs in accordance with Article 144 of the Constitution. The decision of the Family Court or the Family Court of Religious Groups to refer should occur whenever a question of constitutionality of any law which is material for the determination of the dispute is raised; the opinion of the lower court on whether the law is prima facie constitutional or unconstitutional is not a factor on the basis of which it may decide

78. C. Tornaritis, *Constitutional Review of Laws in the Republic of Cyprus* (Nicosia, 1983), E. Venizelos, 'The Judicial Control of the Constitutionality of Laws in Greece and Cyprus: A Parallel Overview', *Cyprus Law Review* 39–40 (1992): 5845–5856 (in Greek), E. Nicolaou, *The Control of Constitutionality of Laws and Distribution of Competences of the Organs of the State in Cyprus* (Athens: A. Sakkoulas, 2000, in Greek), A. Loizou, 'The Judicial Control of Unconstitutionality of Laws and Legality of Administrative Acts', *Cyprus Law Review* 27 (1989): 4161–4173 (in Greek).
79. *Nicolaou* [1991] 1 CLR 1045 (in Greek).

whether to refer the question to the Supreme Court or not.[80] It has been held that in divorce proceedings for a valid reference to take place, this should be referred and signed by the three-judge panel and not by any single judge of the Family Court.[81]

### *E. Appellate Family Court*

*63.* The Appellate Family Court, provided for in Article 111 §4 of the Constitution, has jurisdiction to hear and determine all appeals from the Family Courts (section 21 of Law 23/1990) and the Family Courts of Religious Groups (section 25 of Law 87(I)/1994) on family law matters. Appeals are heard by a panel of three Supreme Court judges who are appointed by the Supreme Court as members of the Appellate Family Court for a period of two years. The Appellate Family Court during the hearing of a dispute is not restricted by the factual findings of the lower courts and has the power to reach its own conclusions,[82] admit, hear, or review additional evidence on any issue any decree or order that the circumstances of the case might justify, including ordering a retrial. It has been held that the Appellate Family Court is not identical to the Supreme Court, despite the fact it is composed by Supreme Court justices'.[83] Consequently, a family law appeal addressed to the Supreme Court of Cyprus may not be considered as a proper one, since the Appellate Family Court is not related to the Supreme Court.[84] The Court has declined to grant extension of time to file an appeal to the Appellate Family Court in cases where the appeal has been dismissed due it having been submitted to the Supreme Court instead.[85] Similarly, it has declined to allow amendment of the appeal so as to correct the name of the court.[86]

80. *Zeniou v. Zeniou* [2002] 1 CLR 1175 (in Greek).
81. *Paikkou v. Paikkou* [1994] 1 CLR 610.
82. *Zachariou v. Zachariou* [1993] 1 CLR 159 (in Greek).
83. *Nicolaou* [1991] 1 CLR 1045 (in Greek).
84. *Theodorou v. Theodorou* [1995] 1 CLR 200 (in Greek), *Christodoulou v. Christodoulou* [1996] 1 CLR 1244 (in Greek), *Theodorou v. Neophytou* [2013] 1 CLR 2139 (in Greek), *Petroudi v. Antoniou*, Apps 21-22/2013, Judgment of 6 Jun. 2014 (in Greek). *See*, however, the distinction drawn in *Kleitou v. Mappourou*, App. 16/2010, Judgment of 7 Jun. 2016 (in Greek).
85. *Petroudi v. Antoniou*, App. 4/2014, Judgment of 16 Dec. 2015 (in Greek).
86. *Savvides v. Pourgouridou*, App. 12/2012, Judgment of 25 Sep. 2014 (in Greek).

# Part I. Persons

## Chapter 1. The Status of a Person

### §1. Definition of a Person

*64.* Legal personality may be attached either to a human being or a legal person. Any individual human being is considered to be a natural person recognized by law; legal rights and duties are ascribed to natural persons during the span of their lifetime. In some cases a foetus may also be fictionally considered as having legal personality, so long as he/she is born alive.[87] Despite not being natural persons, legal persons are recognized by the law to have rights and responsibilities similarly to natural person; thus, legal persons may enjoy constitutional fundamental rights, or have criminal responsibility. Legal persons have a legal personality separate than that of any of their members. Dissolution of a legal person has the same function as death has for a natural person.

*65.* The most common forms of legal persons in the Cypriot legal order are the following:

(a) Companies limited by shares or by guarantee. In companies limited by shares the liability of each member is limited to the nominal value of the shares that he/she has agreed to take up, or, if he/she has agreed to take up shares at more than their nominal value, to the total amount agreed to be paid for such shares. In companies limited by guarantee the liability of each member is limited to the amount agreed in the memorandum of association to be contributed if the company goes into liquidation. Companies limited by guarantee are normally nonprofit companies. Both companies limited by shares and companies limited by guarantee are governed by the Companies Law, Cap. 113.[88]
(b) Partnerships. Partnerships of general or limited liability, consisting of between two and twenty natural or legal persons, carrying on a business in common, with a view to profit. In general every partner is liable severally and jointly with the other partners without limit for all the debts and obligations of the partnership incurred while he/she is a partner, while in limited partnerships one or more general partners are liable for all the debts and obligations of the partnership,

87. *See* for instance s. 15 of the Wills and Succession Law, Cap. 195.
88. G. Cacoyiannis, *Cypriot Company Law* (Limassol: Pilcaco, 2001, in Greek).

while one or more limited partners are liable only for a stated amount. Partnerships are registered under the Partnerships and Business Names Law, Cap. 116.[89]

(c) Cooperative societies. These may be incorporated in accordance with the provisions of the Cooperative Societies Law 22(I)/1985, which defines a cooperative society as a voluntary association of an unlimited number of persons which runs a joint business activity in the interest of its members. The most common form of a cooperative society is the cooperative credit society, namely a registered company whose activity consists in making available credit facilities and other banking services to their members in accordance with the principles of mutual help and assistance. The Cooperative Societies Supervision and Development Authority is exercising the supervision, examination and inspection of cooperative societies. It should be noted, however, that in June 2018 the Cyprus Cooperative Bank was liquidated and some of its assets and deposits were sold to the Hellenic Bank.

(d) Associations and foundations which are registered in accordance with the provisions of the Associations and Foundations and other relevant issues Law 104(I)/2017.[90] An association is the union of at least twenty persons for achieving a specific non-profit purpose, while a foundation is the dedication of property for a specific cause.

(e) Charities. Charities are incorporated in accordance with the Charities Law, Cap. 41; the purposes of the charity may be educational, literary, scientific, or other charitable purposes, while the application for registration has to be submitted before the Council of Ministers.

## §2. Capacity

*66.* A natural person has capacity to contract, in accordance with section 11 of the Contract Law, Cap. 149,[91] if he/she is not of unsound mind and has not been deprived of the capacity to contract by virtue of any law of the Republic; a contract made with a person of unsound mind is valid, but if the other party was aware that he/she was contracting with a person who could not understand the nature of the contract by reason of the unsoundness of his/her mind, then the contract is voidable at the option of the person who is of unsound mind. Defining a person of unsound mind necessitates certain distinctions. As noted in *Boughton*:

---

89. E. Neocleous et al., 'Corporate Law', in *Introduction to Cyprus Law*, ed. Andreas Neocleous & Co LLC, 3rd edn (Limassol, 2010), 341.

90. A. Emilianides, 'Certain Problems of Interpretation of the Associations and Foundations Law', *Cyprus and European Law Review* 8 (2008): 329–348 (in Greek), C. Ioannides, 'Which are the Unions of Private Law apart from Companies', *Cyprus Law Review* 10 (1985): 1605–1610 (in Greek).

91. P. Polyviou, *The Law of Contracts* (Nicosia: Chryssafinis and Polyviou, 2014, in Greek), Idem, *Contracts in Cypriot Law. Theory and Practice* (Nicosia: Chryssafinis and Polyviou, 2017, in Greek), Y. Constantinides, 'Contract Law, Cap. 149', *Aspects of Cypriot Law*, v. I (Nicosia: Asselia, 1981 in Greek), 235ff, A. Malliotis, 'Contracts', in *Introduction to Cyprus Law*, ed. Andreas Neocleous & Co LLC, 3rd edn (Limassol, 2010), 756–757.

> *A sound mind in contemplation of law does not necessarily mean a perfectly balanced mind, and large allowance must be made for the difference of individual character, habits, and mode of living. It must not he assumed that because a man acts in unaccustomed ways he is, therefore, of unsound mind.*[92]

*67.* Section 3 of the Psychiatric Hospitalization Law 77(I)/1997 provides for the issuing of orders of temporary or permanent hospitalization in the case of persons who are psychiatrically ill and suffer from a psychiatric disorder. Persons who have been adjudged as psychiatrically ill in accordance with the provisions of Law 77(I)/97 may be considered as persons not of sound mind. Furthermore, a person who has been declared as incapable in accordance with the provisions of the Administration of the Estate of Incapable Persons Law 23(I)/1996 should be considered as a person of unsound mind. Section 2 of Law 23(I)/96 defines as incapable any person who, due to a mental disorder, drug addiction, alcoholism, or due to either mental or other bodily injury, is unable to exercise his/her judgment or will and is not in a position to administer his/her property or conduct his/her own affairs.

*68.* Thus, Law 23(I)/96 extends its application not only to persons suffering from mental disorder, as is the case of Law 77(I)/97, but also to persons suffering from bodily injuries, drug addiction, alcoholism or brain injury, so long as they are unable to administer their property or conduct their affairs due to such injury. In addition to the cases referred to in the previous paragraphs, a person may be considered as a person not of sound mind, even without the existence of a prior court judgment to this effect, so long as the person has no free will, because he/she is incapable of appreciating the consequences of his/her actions due to old age, or disease.[93] If a person has a lucid interval he/she shall be considered as having a sound mind, but only for as long as the lucid interval lasts; a lucid interval understandably shall be extremely difficult to prove.[94] Specific principles governing persons of unsound mind regarding family and succession law shall be analysed in the relevant chapters.

*69.* A minor, namely a person under 18 years of age, has limited capacity to enter into contracts. Minors' contracts are voidable at the option of the minor, irrespective of whether the other party to the contract was aware of a minor's age. When a minor has paid money under a voidable contract, he/she cannot recover it, unless he/she can prove a complete failure of consideration, namely that he/she did not receive any benefit from the contract. There are certain exceptions to the rule that a minor lacks the capacity to contract. Contracts for necessaries by a minor are enforceable; necessaries are defined as goods suitable to the condition in life of the infant and to his/her actual requirements at the time of sale and delivery, such as food, clothes, educational books, medical attention or other necessities. Similarly, contracts which are for the minor's benefit, including contracts of employment,

---

92. *Boughton v. Knight* [1861–1873] All ER 40.
93. *Re Fuld* [1968] 675, *Waring v. Waring* (1848) 6 Moo PC 530.
94. *See Attorney-General v. Parnther* (1792) 3 Bro CC 441, *In the Estate of Walker* (1912) 28 TLR 466.

apprenticeship, service and for education, are valid and enforceable; trading contracts, however, are not enforceable irrespective of whether they are for the minors' benefit. It should be noted that a married minor is not considered as lacking capacity, simply because of the fact that he/she is a minor. The specific principles governing capacity regarding family and succession law shall be analysed in the relevant chapters.

*70.* A legal person has the capacity to contract once it has been incorporated. Limited companies and partnerships come into existence once they have been registered before the Registrar of Companies, while associations and foundations come into existence once they have been registered before the Registrar of Associations and Foundations. The certificate of incorporation issued by the Registrar of Companies, or the Registrar of Associations and Foundations, depending on the case, is conclusive evidence that all legal requirements have been complied with and that the legal person is duly registered under the provisions of the law. Cooperative societies are registered before the Registrar of the Cooperative Societies Supervision and Development Authority, while charities are registered following an application before the Council of Ministers; in all cases a certificate of incorporation is conclusive evidence that the legal person is duly registered in accordance with the law.

## Chapter 2. Registration of Civil Status

### §1. The Registrar

*71.* The Permanent Secretary of the Ministry of Interior is the General Registrar of the Republic in accordance with section 3 of the Population Registry Law 141(I)/02; the Director of the Civil Registry and Migration Department is the Deputy General Registrar who assists the General Registrar during the implementation of his/her duties and may substitute him/her if he/she is absent or unable to act. The Commissioner of each District shall act as the Registrar of Births and Deaths in accordance with the directions of the General Registrar, or the Deputy General Registrar as the case may be.

### §2. Registers and Certificates

*72.* The General Registrar maintains, in accordance with section 35 of Law 141(I)/02, a General Registry of all births and deaths which were registered in any District of Cyprus; such General Register shall contain the original registrations of births or deaths, or certified copies. In addition to the General Registry, each District has a District Registry of all births and deaths which were registered in the specific District. The contents of the several District Registries and of the General Registry with respect to the registration of births and deaths should coincide. Section 40 of Law 141(I)/02 stipulates that the General Registrar may direct that any registration is amended by rectifications of errors, additions, a new name or a change of name, or a change of sex and by cancelling any previous registration.

*73.* The General Registrar may further direct that any additional elements are added to any registration, including more details about an abandoned child or the father of a child, the date of a subsequent marriage between the mother of the child and the father, the findings of an inquest, any details which had not been provided when the birth or the death had been registered, as well as relevant Court decisions. If there is evidence that the registration of birth or death should be cancelled, the Registrar may cancel such registration. The General Registrar and the Registrars may issue any certificate of birth or death and provide it to any persons having legal interest.

# Chapter 3. Names

## §1. Surname

### I. Acquisition of the Surname

*74.* Parents may determine the surname of their children by a common written declaration in accordance with section 3 §1 (a) of the Relationship between Parents and Children Law 216/90; such declaration should be made before the Registrar of the place of birth of the child within three months from the date of birth. The surname of the child might be the surname of either spouse, or a combination of their surnames; such combination should, however, not include more than two surnames. The surname should be common for all children of the same couple. If the parents fail to declare the surname of their child, then the child shall have the surname of the father by virtue of section 3 §3 of Law 216/90. If the child was born out of wedlock, then such child shall have the surname of the mother; however, the mother's husband may give his surname to the child with a written declaration before the Registrar, so long as the mother consents.

### II. Change of the Surname

*75.* In case of subsequent marriage between the parents of the child, the parents may, by virtue of section 4 §2 of Law 216/90 determine the surname of the child by a common declaration within three months from the date of the subsequent marriage. If the child is recognized, either voluntarily or judicially, the parents or either of them may, within six months from the recognition add to the surname of the child the surname of the father, or, by a common declaration, determine the new surname of the child.

## §2. First Name

*76.* The parents may determine by a common declaration the first name of their child in accordance with section 5 §1 (b) of Law 216/90. It is possible that the child has more than one first names; such name or names could be Christian, Greek, or any other, and could derive from members of the family of either parent, or not. The determination of the first name of a child is an exercise of parental care and should thus aim at the best interests of the child. Any subsequent change of the first name of the child ought to be made also by a common declaration of the parents.[95] In *Pashardis* the child was named Paris-Yakinthos.[96] Following the dissolution of the parent's marriage, the mother applied before the Family Court and requested that the name be changed to Michalis-Paris; the father insisted that the child should continue to be named Paris-Yakinthos.

---

95. *Republic v. Pashardis* [1996] 3 CLR 34 (in Greek).
96. *Pashiardi v. Theodosiou* [2004] 1 CLR 338 (in Greek).

*77.* It was held that the change of name ought to be accepted, since the child had also expressed the opinion that he wanted to be named Michalis-Paris and that most of his classmates call him either Michalis or Paris. The Appellate Family Court observed that every person has a right to choose their name; if the person is a minor then the parents exercising parental care shall decide and if they disagree, it is the Family Court's duty to decide. The Court should always take into account the traditions of the parties and not discriminate between them on account of sex, religion, language, beliefs, nationality or ethnic or social background. If the child is sufficiently mature, his/her opinion on the matter ought to be taken into account.

# Chapter 4. Nationality

## §1. Introduction

*78.* From 1878 until 1914 Cypriots were considered as Ottoman subjects. Following the Cyprus Annexation Order in Council of 1914, however, and a subsequent Order in Council of 27 November 1917 it was provided that any person who was habitually resident in Cyprus on 27 November 1917 would automatically become a British subject; persons born in Cyprus who did not have their habitual residence in Cyprus could apply to the British High commissioner in order to become British subjects.[97] Following the establishment of the Republic, Annex D of the Treaty of Establishment[98] provided that any citizen of the United Kingdom and its Colonies who on the date of the entry into force of the Treaty of Establishment (namely 16 August 1960) possessed any of the qualifications specified in section 2 §2 of the Treaty shall become a citizen of the Republic if he/she was ordinarily resident in Cyprus at any time in the period of five years immediately before 16/8/1960. The qualifications specified in section 2 §2 of the Treaty of Establishment are that the person concerned: (i) became a British subject under the Cyprus Annexation Orders in Council of 1914 to 1943, (ii) was born in Cyprus on or after 5 November 1914, or (iii) descends in the male line from any of the persons referred to in (i) and (ii) above.

*79.* Any citizen of the United Kingdom and its Colonies born between 16 August 1960 and 16 February 1961 shall become a citizen of the Republic at the date of his/her birth if his/her father becomes a citizen or would, but for his death, have done so. In accordance with section 4 of the Treaty of Establishment any person who was a citizen of the United Kingdom or its Colonies before 16 August 1960 and possesses the qualifications specified in section 2 §2 of the Treaty but did not become a citizen of the Republic shall be entitled to apply to the appropriate authority of the Republic, be granted citizenship of the Republic if he/she was immediately before 16 August 1960 ordinarily resident in the United Kingdom, or in a colony, protectorate, protected State or United Kingdom trust territory or in the territory of any country within the British Commonwealth of Nations, or Greece or Turkey, or elsewhere if he/she became or may become Stateless.

*80.* A person of Cypriot origin (namely a person who was on 5 November 1914 an Ottoman subject ordinarily resident in Cyprus or who descended in the male line from such a person) who immediately before 16 August 1960 was not a citizen of the United Kingdom and its Colonies shall be entitled to apply to the appropriate authority of the Republic in order to be granted citizenship by virtue of section 4 §2 of the Treaty. A woman who was married before 16 August 1960 to a person who

97. A. Emilianides, 'The Issue of Citizenship of Cypriot from British Rule until Today', *Symmikta Streit* (Athens, 1939, in Greek): 299ff.
98. Annex D is extremely detailed; only an overview of its main provisions shall be included in this section. For an overview *see* C. Tornaritis, *The State Law of the Republic of Cyprus* (Nicosia, 1982, in Greek): 35ff.

is both entitled to and applied for citizenship of the Republic shall be entitled, to also apply, so long as the marriage is still valid, to be granted citizenship of the Republic by virtue of section 4 §3 of the Treaty; the same right is granted under certain conditions for a woman who was married before 16 August 1960 to a person of Cypriot origin or a person possessing the qualifications specified in section 2 §2 of the Treaty, if their marriage was terminated by death or divorce (sections 4 §4 and §5 of the Treaty).

*81.* The Citizen of the Republic Law 43/67 governed all questions regarding the status of a citizen of the Republic until such law was abolished by the Population Registry Law 141(I)/02.[99] It is submitted that the provisions of Law 141(I)/02 regarding citizenship remain unnecessarily complicated. Citizenship of the Republic may be acquired by birth or descent, registration or naturalization. Section 108 of Law 141(I)/02 provides that a person is considered to be a citizen of the Republic if he/she had either acquired or is entitled to acquire citizenship at the entry into force of Law 141(I)/02, or who acquire citizenship following the entry into force of Law 141(I)/02 in accordance with the provisions of such Law or under the provisions of Annex D of the Treaty of Establishment. An overview of the provisions of Law 141(I)/02 with respect to citizenship shall be presented in the subsequent paragraphs.

## §2. Citizenship by Birth or Descent

*82.* Citizenship by birth is established, by virtue of section 109 of Law 141(I)/02. Section 109 §1 of Law 141(I)/02 provides that a person born in Cyprus at or after 16 August 1960 (the date the Republic of Cyprus was established) shall be a citizen of the Republic, if either of his/her parents was a citizen of the Republic at the time of birth; if neither parent was alive at the time of birth, then the person shall be a citizen of the Republic if either parent would have been entitled to become a citizen of the Republic, had he/she not died. The above provisions do not apply if the entry into or stay in the Republic of either parent was illegal. By virtue of section 109 §1 of Law 141(I)/02 a person born in any foreign country at or after 16 August 1960 shall be a citizen of the Republic under the same conditions, as those provided for persons born in Cyprus, namely if either of his/her parents was or would be entitled (had he/she not died) to become a citizen of the Republic at the time of birth. The above provisions do not apply to a person who is a permanent resident of a foreign country unless his/her birth was registered in accordance with the provisions of Law 141(I)/02.

*83.* Section 109 §3 of Law 141(I)/02 introduces an exception to the general rule; it is provided that the relevant provisions of sections 109 §1 and §2 do not apply to any person born between 16 August 1960 and 11 June 1999 who would have been entitled to become a Cypriot citizen by virtue of the fact that his/her mother was a

99. C. Christoforou & C. Vezouvios, 'Immigration Law and Policy', in *Introduction to Cyprus Law*, ed. Andreas Neocleous & Co LLC, 3rd edn (Limassol, 2010): 132ff.

citizen of the Republic or was entitled to become a citizen of the Republic at the time of death. Such a person has to be registered as a citizen of the Republic by applying to the Minister of Interior in the manner provided in Law 104(I)/02; if the person is a minor, the application should be made by either parent. If a person was born at or after 18 June 1960 and is descended from a person who either became a British national on the basis of the Annexation of Cyprus Orders in Council of 1914 to 1943, or was born in Cyprus between 5 November 1914 and 16 August 1960, during which time his/her parents were habitually resident in Cyprus, is entitled to be registered as a citizen of the Republic by submitting an application to the Minister of Interior and so long as he/she has made an affirmation of loyalty to the Republic.

### §3. Citizenship by Registration

*84.* In accordance with section 110 §1 of Law 141(I)/02 a citizen of the United Kingdom or its Colonies or of a member of the Commonwealth, who is of Cypriot origin (namely a person who was born in Cyprus while his/her parents were habitually residing in Cyprus), may register as a citizen of the Republic by submitting an application to the Minister of Interior and by making an affirmation of loyalty to the Republic, so long as he/she: (i) resides or has resided in Cyprus for a continuous period of twelve months prior to the submission of his/her application or is a member of the Public Service of the Republic; the period of twelve months may be reduced at the discretion of the Minister, if there are special circumstances, (ii) is a person of good character, (iii) intends to continue residing in the Republic, or depending on the case, serving at the Public Service of the Republic, (iv) is a person of sound mind and over 18 years of age.

*85.* The Minister of Interior may further register as a citizen of the Republic, by virtue of 110 §2 of Law 141(I)/02 and following the submission of an application and an affirmation of loyalty to the Republic, any person who: (i) is the spouse or widower/widow of a citizen of the Republic or who would have become or would have a right to become a citizen of the Republic, but for his/her death, (ii) has resided with such spouse in Cyprus for a period of at least three years; provided that the period may be reduced by the Minister to a period of at least two years, but only so long as the spouse does not reside permanently or temporarily abroad. The period of three (or two) years need not be continuous; if the persons resided in Cyprus for at least six months a year and an aggregate of two years in the last three years, this shall be considered as sufficient, (iii) is of a good character, (iv) intends to continue residing in the Republic, (iv) is a person of sound mind and over 18 years of age. No person may be registered if he/she entered or stays in the Republic illegally. The Minister of Interior may further register the minor child of any citizen of the Republic by virtue of section 110 §3 of Law 141(I)/02. A person who has denounced or who has been deprived of citizenship may also register, but only with the approval of the Minister of Interior.

## §4. Citizenship by Naturalization

*86.* The Minister may grant a certificate of naturalization, in accordance with section 111 of Law 141(I)/02, to any foreigner who is of sound mind and over 18 years of age, following the submission of an application and an affirmation of loyalty to the Republic. The qualifications for naturalization are provided in the Third Schedule of Law 141(I)/02 and are the following: (i) residence in the Republic for a period of twelve continuous months prior to the submission of the application, (ii) residence in the Republic or being a member of the Public Service for a period of at least five years in total during the eight years preceding the submission of the application; the ambit of such provision is heavily restricted by the highly confusing proviso that students, visitors, self-employed persons, athletes, coaches, sports technicians, domestic assistants, nurses, as well as persons employed by Cypriot or foreign employers or by offshore companies who reside in the Republic in order to work, or their spouses, or children, should reside in Cyprus for at least seven years in total during the last seven years, the last twelve of which must have been continuous. Admittedly, the proviso makes no sense, (iii) good character, (iv) intention to reside in the Republic, or become or continue to be a member of the Public Service of the Republic or international organization to which the Republic is a member, or association, or company, or body which was established in the Republic.

*87.* The Council of Ministers may at its discretion: (a) consider a period of twelve continuous months which occurred not more than six months prior to the submission of the application, as having occurred immediately prior to the submission of the application, (b) consider the residence of a person of Cypriot origin in a foreign country, or the residence in the former Colony of Cyprus or service at the Government of the former Colony of Cyprus prior to 16 August 1960, as residence in the Republic, (c) take into account periods of residence or service prior to the eight years before the submission of the application, (d) allow a person who has denounced Cypriot citizenship to acquire citizenship by naturalization irrespective of the time of residence, or (e) allow the naturalization of a foreigner irrespective of the time of residence, if there are exceptional cases of providing services of the highest standard to the Republic and for the public interest, so long as the House of Representatives is informed in advance.

## §5. Denunciation and Deprivation of Citizenship

*88.* Section 112 of Law 141(I)/02 provides that any citizen of the Republic who is of sound mind and over 18 years of age, and further has citizenship of another country, may denounce citizenship of the Republic. The person is no longer considered as a citizen of the Republic from the time that such denunciation is registered by the Minister of Interior; however, the Minister may suspend the effects of such denunciation if it occurs during wartime, or if the Minister considers that the aim of such denunciation is to avoid an obligation of military service, or any criminal prosecution.

*89.* A person who acquired citizenship by registration or naturalization may be deprived of such citizenship by an Order of the Council of Ministers in accordance with section 113 of Law 141(I)/02, if such registration or naturalization was achieved by fraud, false pretences, or disclosure of any material facts. A person who acquired citizenship by naturalization may further be deprived of such citizenship if: (i) he/she showed lack of loyalty to the Republic either verbally or by his/her actions, (ii) he/she was communicating or dealing with the enemy or knowingly participated in any activities which were assisting the enemy during wartime, (iii) was sentenced to imprisonment in any country for a particularly abominable offence or for an offence showing moral turpitude within ten years of naturalization, in so far as it is also an abominable offence or an offence showing moral turpitude and providing for the penalty of imprisonment under Cypriot law, (iv) resided in foreign countries for a continuous period of seven years, and if during such time he/she did not notify every year the consular authorities of the Republic of his/her intention to remain a citizen of the Republic, or was not at any time a member at the service of the Republic or at the service of an international organization to which the Republic is a member.

# Chapter 5. Domicile and Residence

## §1. Residence

*90.* Residence is the principal connecting factor in family law legislation. In *Sayegh*[100] the Supreme Court cited with approval the following quote from an English judgment[101] concerning the interpretation of the term residence:

> *'Resident' denotes some degree of permanence. It does not necessarily mean that the applicant has a home of his own, but it means that he has his settled headquarters in this country. It seems to me dangerous to try to define what is 'resident'. It is very unfortunate that it is not possible to do so, but, in my judgment, the court must ask itself in every case: Is the applicant resident in this country? In the present case, when I ask myself that question in respect of the wife, I can only answer: 'No. She is merely a sojourner here during a period of leave. Like her husband, she is resident in Nigeria where his duties are and whether she accompanies him, in pursuance of her wifely duties.' I do not think the applicants in this case are residents in England at present, although they may be hereafter.*

*91.* It was further held that the term residence generally means actual physical presence in a particular place with a degree of permanence; temporary sojourn or casual presence in transit, even for a substantial time, does not amount to residence. The term ordinary residence which is translated in Greek and has the same meaning as habitual residence has been analysed in several judgments of the English courts which are applicable also in Cyprus.[102] A person is ordinarily resident if they are normally residing in Cyprus, apart from temporary or occasional absences, and their residence has been adopted voluntarily and for settled purposes as part of the regular order of their life for the time being; decisions about whether a person is ordinarily resident will need to be based on all the circumstances of the particular case. A person can be ordinarily resident in more than one country; therefore if a person divides their time between two different countries and can be said to live in both with a settled purpose, it shall be held as a matter of law that they are ordinarily resident in both.[103]

---

100. *Sayegh* [1990] 1 CLR 773 (in Greek), adopted by the Appellate Family Court in *Kristoffer Castardo Ajero* [2006] 1 CLR 1165 (in Greek). *See also Koraka v. Georghiou* [2004] 1 CLR 1935 (in Greek), *Antoniou v. Theodorou* [2004] 1 CLR 1944 (in Greek), *Razis v. Republic* [1979] 1 CLR 127, *Rossides v. Republic* [1984] 1 CLR 1482 interpreting the term in the context of electoral applications.
101. *Re Adoption Application No. 52/1951*[1951] 2 All ER 931: 936.
102. *Gout v. Cimitian* [1922] AC 105, *Levene v. Inland Revenue Commissioner* [1928] AC 217, *IRC v. Lysagth* [1928] AC 234, *Hopkins v. Hopkins* [1951] P 116, *Clarke v. Insurance Office of Australia Ltd* [1965] 1 Lloyd Rep 308, *Stransky v. Stransky* (1954) P 428, *Lewis v. Lewis* [1965] 1 All ER 375.
103. *Ikimi v. Ikimi* [2001] EWCA Civ 873, [2002] Fam 72, *Armstrong v. Armstrong* [2003] EWHC 777 (Fam), [2003] 2 FLR 375, FD. *See*, however, *Marinos v. Marinos* [2007] EWHC 2047 (Fam) for the interpretation of habitual residence under the provisions of Brussels IIa Regulation.

*92.* The term 'habitual residence' has also been considered by the Supreme Court for the purposes of the Hague Convention on the Civil Aspects of International Child Abduction (Ratification) Law 11(III)/1994 in *Fasarias*.[104] The majority of the Court held that the term should be understood in accordance with the ordinary and natural meaning of the two words which it contains; whether a person is or is not habitually resident in a specific country is thus a question of fact to be decided by reference to all the circumstances of the particular case.[105] The definition adopted by the Court seems to include both an element of living at a place for a period of time, as well as the element of a settled intention to live in a place. Residence need not be permanent or indefinitely; so long as there is a settled purpose, even temporary stay might qualify.[106] Factors such as professional employment, participation in cultural and social events, existence of a permanent home, family relations, inclusion in registries, etc. shall be taken into account by the Court in order to conclude whether a person has habitual residence in Cyprus.

*93.* It is noted that the CJEU has also autonomously interpreted the term 'habitual residence' for the purposes of Community legislation; it was therefore held that the concept of habitual residence must be interpreted as meaning the place where the person concerned has established the permanent or habitual centre of his/her interests.[107] However, such interpretation regarding non-family law instruments cannot be directly transposed in the context of the assessment of the habitual residence in family law cases, a fact which was observed by the CJEU itself in a 2009 case where habitual residence of children was interpreted for the purposes of Brussels IIa Regulation.[108] The CJEU held that the habitual residence of a child must be established on the basis of all the circumstances specific to each individual case. In addition to the physical presence of the child other factors must be chosen, which are capable of showing that such presence is not temporary or intermittent and the residence of the child reflects some degree of integration in a social and family environment.

*94.* Consequently, the duration, regularity, conditions and reasons for the stay on the territory of a Member State and the family's move to that State, the child's nationality, the place and conditions of attendance at school, linguistic knowledge and the family and social relationships of the child in that State must be taken into consideration by the Court in order to determine whether the child has habitual residence in a State or not. While the aforementioned judgment is binding only for the purposes of Brussels IIa Regulation, it is submitted that it is consistent with the case law of the Supreme Court as far as the interpretation of 'residence' is concerned.

104. *Fasarias v. Minister of Justice and Public Order* [2008] 1 CLR 1024 (in Greek).
105. *In Re J (A Minor) (Abduction: Custody Rights)*[1992] AC 562.
106. *In Re B (Minors Abduction)*[1993] 1 FLR 993, *In Re F (A Minor) (Child Abduction)*[1992] 1 FLR 548.
107. Case T-69/03, *W v. European Parliament*, CFI 25/5/2004, C-90/97, *Swaddling v. Adjudication Officer* [1999] ECR I-1075, Case T-90/92, *Fernandez v. Commission* [1993] ECR II-971, Case T-69/03, *W v. European Parliament*, CFI 25 May 2004, T-63/91, *Benzler v. Commission* [1992] ECR II-2095.
108. Case C-523/07, *A* [2009] ECR I-2805.

Thus, it should be considered that even habitual residence presupposes actual physical presence in a particular place with some degree of permanence.

## §2. Domicile

### I. Introduction

*95.* The connecting factor in succession law cases, until the introduction of Regulation 650/2012, was domicile.[109] Domicile still remains relevant for deaths which occurred prior to 17 August 2015. The notion of domicile is a rather complicated one. It has been accepted that domicile is a legal and not a factual notion.[110] Residence and domicile are distinct from each other; it has been held that it is by no means to be inferred from the fact of residence that domicile results;[111] domicile is the permanent home of a person,[112] and not simply the place of permanent residence. Section 6 of the Wills and Succession Law, Cap. 195 provides that there are two general categories of domicile; the domicile of origin and the domicile of choice. Every person has either a domicile of origin or a domicile of choice at any given time;[113] however, no person may have more than one domicile in accordance with section 13 of Cap. 195.[114]

### II. Domicile of Origin

*96.* A person acquires a domicile of origin at the time he/she is born. Section 7 of Cap. 195 provides that a child born in wedlock during the lifetime of his/her father, has the domicile that his/her father had at the time of birth.[115] If the child was born out of wedlock or after the death of his/her father, his/her domicile is the domicile that his/her mother had at the time of birth.[116] Cap. 195 does not provide for the case where the parent of a child is not known; it is submitted that in such a case the domicile of the child should be the domicile of the place where the child was found. Domicile is thus related to the parental domicile at the time of birth; not with the country of birth or citizenship of the child. A domicile of origin has an enduring character and is maintained until, and if, a domicile of choice is

109. A. Emilianides, 'Interpreting Domicile in Cypriot Law of Succession', *Cyprus and European Law Review* 6 (2008): 526–552 (in Greek).
110. *Schwartz v. Republic* [1995] 3 CLR 1359 (in Greek).
111. *Bell v. Kennedy* (1868) LR 1 SC & Div 307, at 320. *See also* P. Rogerson, 'Habitual Residence: The New Domicile', *International and Comparative Law Quarterly* 49 (2000): 86–107.
112. *Whicker v. Hume* (1858) 7 HLC 124.
113. *Bell v. Kennedy* (1868) LR 1 SC & Div 307, *Udny v. Udny* (1869) LR 1 SC & Div 441.
114. *Udny v. Udny* (1869) LR 1 SC & Div 441, *Garthwaite v. Garthwaite* [1964] 356, *IRC v. Bullock* [1976] 1 WLR 1178, *Lawrence v. Lawrence* [1985] Fam 106.
115. *Henderson v. Henderson* [1965] 1 All ER 179, *Re Duleep Singh* (1890) 6 TLP 385.
116. *Pottinger v. Wrightman* (1817) 3 Mer 67.

acquired.[117] If the domicile of choice is abandoned, without acquiring a new domicile, then the domicile of origin revives. If there is no sufficient evidence that a person has acquired a domicile of choice, he/she shall be presumed as maintaining his/her domicile of origin.[118]

*97.* Cypriot courts have adopted the principles of common law in interpreting the domicile of origin. In *Winans* the deceased had a domicile of origin at Baltimore, USA where he lived until 1859; he then moved to England where he lived until his death in 1896. However, the deceased disliked England and had no British friends; his sole ambition was to help the USA replace England as a world navy power. The House of Lords held that the deceased had never acquired a domicile of choice in England, despite the fact that he had lived there for the last thirty-seven years of his life; the domicile of origin had never been abandoned.[119] In *Udny* the deceased had a Scottish domicile of origin, but when he reached 18 years of age moved to England where he lived for nearly fifty years. He was then forced to abandon England and move to France in order to avoid his creditors; The Court held that while the deceased had acquired a domicile of choice in England, such was abandoned without a new domicile of choice having been acquired; thus, the Scottish domicile of origin had revived.[120]

*98.* An English judgment concerning a Cypriot, reaffirmed the principles governing domicile of origin.[121] The deceased had his domicile of origin in Cyprus but left for England in 1958. He stayed in England until 1972, when he returned to Cyprus with an intention to reside there permanently; due to the Turkish invasion of 1974 he left Cyprus again and moved to England where he stayed until his death in 2003. The English Court of Appeal observed that while the deceased resided in England for nearly forty-three years, he had still continued to live as a Greek Cypriot, speaking Greek and maintaining contacts with Cyprus and the Greek community of London; the deceased was proud to be Cypriot, bought immovable property in Cyprus and had repeatedly expressed his wish to return to Cyprus in order to die there. It was thus held that the deceased had never acquired a domicile of choice in England and had retained his Cypriot domicile of origin.

## III. Domicile of Choice

*99.* Section 6 of Cap. 195 provides that a person may acquire a domicile of choice, either only by his/her own actions. Furthermore, section 9 provides that a person may acquire a domicile of choice if he/she acquires residence in the Republic with the intention of residing there permanently or indefinitely. Thus, the domicile of choice presupposes not only the acquisition of residence in a territory, but

117. *Bell v. Kennedy* (1868) LR 1 SC & Div 307.
118. *Udny v. Udny* (1869) LR 1 SC & Div 441, *Re Fuld* [1968] 675.
119. *Winans v. AG* [1904] AC 287.
120. *Udny v. Udny* (1869) LR 1 SC & Div 441.
121. *Agulian & Anr v. Cyganik* [2006] EWCA Civ 129. *See also* P. Mc Eleavy, 'Regression and Reform in the Law of Domicile', *International and Comparative Law Quarterly* 56 (2007): 453.

also the intention to reside there permanently or indefinitely. The intention is crucial;[122] the residence must have been freely chosen and not dictated by external necessity such as professional or medical reasons.[123] Convincing proof has to be adduced for the Court to conclude that a domicile of choice has been acquired.[124] In *Ramsay* the deceased had a domicile of origin in Scotland, but in 1892 he moved to England where he lived the last thirty-six years of his life. The House of Lords held that despite such long residence in England, the deceased had never acquired a domicile of choice, because he would have abandoned England if his family members, with whom he resided, decided to move.[125]

*100.* However, a person might acquire a residence of choice even if he/she resided there for a brief period of time, so long as there is also intention to reside there permanently or indefinitely.[126] In *Christopoulou,* which is a District Court case, the Court held that the deceased had not acquired a domicile of choice in South Rhodesia despite the fact that he resided there for twenty-five years until 1961;[127] this was due to the fact that he always maintained that he wanted to return to Cyprus and live there permanently and had bought immovable property in Cyprus. However, in 1962 the deceased acquired a domicile of choice in Greece, when he bought immovable property there with the intention to reside there permanently; the mere fact that he still had a feeling of sentimental attachment to Cyprus was not sufficient for the retention of domicile of origin.

*101.* The Supreme Court considered the application of the requirements for the acquisition of a domicile of choice in *Schwartz,* which was an administrative law case regarding inheritance tax.[128] The Court observed that the deceased, a person of British origin, had resided in Cyprus in accordance with a lawful permit of residence for thirteen years; her rather old age, the fact that she was satisfied with her employment, the fact that she made a will before a Cypriot advocate and provided that her funeral expenses should be paid by the money she had in Cyprus, all pointed towards the direction that she had acquired a domicile of choice in Cyprus. Domicile of choice was also considered by the Supreme Court prior to Independence.[129] The deceased had his domicile of origin in Cyprus, but left Cyprus for Tanganyika in 1913 and stayed there until his death in 1950. During these thirty-seven years he bought immovable property in Tanganyika and filed for permanent residence there, whereas he visited Cyprus only twice. The Court held that the deceased had acquired a domicile of choice in Tanganyika.

122. *Winans v. AG* [1904] AC 287.
123. *Udny v. Udny* (1869) 1 Sc & Div 441.
124. *Re Fuld* [1968] 675.
125. *Ramsay v. Liverpool Royal Infirmary* [1930] AC 588.
126. *White v. Tennant* (1888) 31 W Va 790.
127. *Christopoulou v. Christopoulou* [1971] 1 CLR 437, District Court.
128. *Schwartz v. Republic* [1995] 3 CLR1359 (in Greek).
129. *Re Papadopoulos* (1959) 24 CLR 148. *See also Patiki v. The Firm A.G. Patiki and Co of Limassol* (1954) 20 (I) CLR 36.

*102.* A person shall abandon his/her domicile of choice if he/she leaves such domicile with the intention to never return; both physical abandonment and intention to never return must be established.[130] In *Re Lloyd Evans* the deceased had an English domicile of origin, but acquired a domicile of choice in Belgium.[131] However, he was forced to leave Belgium in 1940 during the Second World War and he returned back to England where he resided until 1944, before deciding whether he would return to Belgium or move to Australia. The Court held that the deceased had never abandoned his domicile of choice, since the physical abandonment was not accompanied by an intention to never return.

## IV. Special Cases

*103.* Minors may not acquire a domicile of choice, since the acquisition of such domicile of choice presupposes the capacity to legally act; thus, the acquisition of a domicile of choice is possible only for persons who have completed 18 years of age and do not suffer from mental illness or other incapacity. However, if a person has married before completing 18 years of age, then such person ought to be capable of acquiring a domicile of choice, since section 2 of the Relationship between Parents and Children Law 216/1990 excludes from the definition of 'children' married persons who have not yet completed 18 years of age. Section 10 of Cap. 195 provides that the domicile of origin is retained until a domicile of choice is acquired, which implies, that contrary to the position of common law the domicile of origin of minors is not altered whenever their parents change their domicile. Thus, the domicile of origin is set at birth and may not be changed before the person completes 18 years of age and acquires by his/her own actions a domicile of choice. Incapable persons also do not have the capacity to acquire a domicile of choice or abandon their domicile of origin.

*104.* Common law principles provided that the wife acquired as a domicile of choice, the domicile of her husband; this principle no longer applies in England following the statutory enactment of the Domicile and Matrimonial Proceedings Act 1973. Contrary to the position in common law, in Cyprus each person, irrespective of sex, may acquire a domicile of choice or retain the domicile of origin. Marriage might be a factor to be taken into consideration by the Court, but is not necessarily the crucial factor. Section 9 of Cap. 195 further provides that no person acquires a domicile of choice in Cyprus simply due to the fact that he/she resides in Cyprus as part of the naval, military, or public service of the United Kingdom. It is submitted that while section 9 refers only to United Kingdom (because it was enacted during British Rule), it is of a more general application. Members of foreign military forces, or of the military forces of the UN, or members of foreign diplomatic missions, do not acquire a domicile of choice in Cyprus simply because they reside in Cyprus in order to carry out their professional obligations.

130. *IRC v. The Duchess of Portland* [1982] Ch 314; All ER 784.
131. *Re Lloyd Evans* [1947] 1 Ch 695.

*105.* Persons who suffer from grave illness and move to another country for medical purposes are not normally considered as acquiring a domicile of choice in that country, even if they move there indefinitely.[132] However, if it is proven that the persons further intended to acquire a domicile of choice in that country, then the Court might conclude that such persons acquired a domicile of choice.[133] Persons who abandoned their former domicile in order to avoid being sent to prison or to avoid their creditors shall also not be considered to have acquired a domicile of choice, unless it is proven that they further intended to acquire a domicile of choice.[134] Prisoners should be considered as retaining the domicile they had prior to their imprisonment, since their imprisonment is not an exercise of free will.[135]

*106.* Cypriot displaced persons have not abandoned their domicile of choice merely because they were forced to leave Cyprus following the Turkish invasion; however, if their intention was to acquire a domicile of choice outside of Cyprus, then they shall be considered as having abandoned their domicile of origin.[136] Similarly, political refugees or asylum seekers are not considered as having acquired a domicile of choice in Cyprus, simply because they were forced to leave their country; however, a political refugee might acquire a domicile of choice in Cyprus if he/she has expressed the intention to reside permanently in Cyprus irrespective of what happens in his/her country.[137] Illegal immigrants, however, may not acquire a domicile of choice in Cyprus, because staying illegally in a country is an obstacle to acquiring a domicile of choice;[138] similarly, Turkish settlers may not acquire a domicile of choice in Cyprus since their residence in Cyprus is illegal in accordance with international law. The position is different with respect to children of Turkish Cypriots who have married Turkish settlers. If the father was a Turkish Cypriot and the mother a settler from Turkey, the child shall have Cypriot domicile. If the child was born out of wedlock and the mother was a Turkish Cypriot, the child shall also have Cypriot domicile; however, if the mother was a Turkish Cypriot and the father a Turkish settler, the children shall have the domicile of their father.

---

132. *Udny v. Udny* (1869) 1 Sc & Div 441, *Moorhose v. Lord* (1863) 10 Cas 272.
133. *Hoskins v. Mathews* (1856) 8 De GM & G 13.
134. *Re Martin* [1900] Ch 211.
135. *Burton v. Dolben* (1756) 2 Lee 312, *Burton v. Fisher* (1828) Milw 183.
136. *See also Agulian & Anr v. Cyganik* [2006] EWCA Civ 129.
137. *Re Lloyd Evans* [1947] Ch 695, *May v. May* [1943] 2 All ER 146.
138. *Puttick v. Attorney – General* (1980) Fam 1, *Solomon v. Solomon* [1912] 29 WN 68, cited with approval in *Schwartz v. Republic* [1995] 3 CLR 1359 (in Greek).

# Part II. Family Law

## Chapter 1. Marriage

### §1. The Nature of Marriage

*107.* Article 22 of the Constitution does not define marriage. Marriage is, however, defined in section 3 §1 of the Marriage Law 104(I)/2003 as the agreement between a man and a woman to unite in marriage which is celebrated by a Marriage Officer in accordance with the provisions of this law or by a registered priest in accordance with the rites of the Greek Orthodox Church or the doctrines of the three religious groups recognized by the Constitution. The above rather tautological definition (marriage is the agreement to unite in marriage) is not very helpful. For the Christian Church marriage is a sacred mystery (sacrament) consisting of the 'union between a man and a woman, an association for the whole life, a community of human and divine law'.[139] Again the above definition is not a legal one, but focuses upon the Christian ideals of the sanctity of marriage. A more legally accurate definition would be to characterize marriage as an agreement between two natural persons of different sex to unite in a lasting partnership which is recognized by the State and subject to a specific legal status.

*108.* There are two contrasting views regarding the nature of marriage; on the one hand it is argued that marriage is an institution, while on the other it is suggested that marriage is a contract. According to the first approach, while marriage is concluded as a contract, nevertheless it is an institution of the State which is governed by provisions of mandatory law; thus, marriage should be understood through its effects which aim at achieving extralegal results, such as child-bearing. It is submitted that the first approach is flawed, in the sense that it fails to give appropriate weight to party autonomy and the exercise of the free will of persons who opt to perform a marriage, focusing instead on the State provisions governing marriage. According to the second approach marriage is another contract between two persons who intend to fulfil their individual expectations by performing marriage; such approach fails to give appropriate weight to the fact that marriage is mostly governed by provisions of mandatory law and that it is considered by the State as a pillar of society.

139. Digesta 23, 2, 1: nuptiae sunt coniuctio maris et feminae et consortium omnis vitae, divini et humani iuris communication, J. Zhisman, *The Law of Marriage of the Eastern Church* (Athens, 1912, v. I).

*109.* It is therefore submitted that marriage ought to be understood both as an institution and a contract. Marriage is a unique contract of private law which is governed both by the will of the parties and the mandatory provisions of the State. Thus, while marriage is a contractual relation and an exercise of fundamental rights, it is at the same time a socially important institution which is of special interest to the State and governed by mandatory provisions. An understanding of marriage as both a contract and an institution is more consistent with the legal framework governing it.

## §2. The Capacity to Marry

### I. Determining Applicable Law

*110.* Article 22 of the Constitution safeguarding the right to marry provides that this is exercised in accordance with the applicable law for each person in accordance with the constitutional provisions. Consequently, any analysis of the Cypriot law of marriage presupposes an analysis of the peculiarities of Cypriot internal and external conflict of laws.

#### *A. The Application of Article 111 of the Constitution*

##### 1. Membership in the Greek Orthodox Church and the Case of the Old Calendar Orthodox Church

*111.* Article 111 of the Constitution refers to members of the Greek Orthodox Church and to members of the three religious groups of the Republic. The courts of the Republic of Cyprus have generally accepted that since there is no definition of membership of the Greek Orthodox in the Constitution itself, the expression 'members of the Greek–Orthodox Church' should be interpreted as referring to membership of the Church under the rules of the Church itself.[140] Article 2 of the 1980 Charter of the Church of Cyprus provided that membership of the Orthodox Church of Cyprus does not presuppose residence in Cyprus and that Orthodox of Cypriot origin residing abroad might still be considered as members of the Orthodox Church of Cyprus. Such provision was considered to be incompatible with Orthodox canon law;[141] Article 1 §2 of the new 2010 Charter provides that only Orthodox Christians with residence in Cyprus may be considered as members of the Orthodox Church of Cyprus.

*112.* It is doubtful whether membership of the Greek Orthodox Church has to be restricted to membership of the Greek Orthodox Church of Cyprus. There are no cases of the Supreme Court of Cyprus, which provide a settled answer to such a

140. *Tsivitanides v. Tsivitanides* (1956) 21 CLR 111.
141. C. Papastathis, *On the Administrative Organisation of the Church of Cyprus* (Thessaloniki, 1981, in Greek).

question. There are some cases which imply that membership of the Greek Orthodox Church in terms of Article 111 of the Constitution may only cover membership of the Greek Orthodox Church of Cyprus,[142] as well as some cases which favour the view that membership of the Greek Orthodox Church in terms of Article 111 of the Constitution may cover membership of any Greek Orthodox Church.[143] It is suggested that Article 111 of the Constitution relates only to members of the Greek Orthodox Church of Cyprus and not to members of other Orthodox Churches.[144] Article 111 should not be construed as a solitary provision, but within the context of Part V of the Constitution dealing with Communal Chambers and Article 110 of the Constitution which refers to the Autocephalous Greek Orthodox Church of Cyprus; indeed it would be quite peculiar if the Constitution referred to members of other Orthodox Churches, or if it conferred jurisdiction – before the 1989 Constitutional Amendment – to ecclesiastical courts of other Orthodox Churches.

*113.* The case of the Old Calendar Orthodox Church has to be considered in more depth. A number of Orthodox Christians have continued to adhere to the Old Julian Calendar, in both Cyprus and Greece, despite the fact that the Orthodox Churches of Cyprus and Greece respectively, had adopted the New Julian Calendar. Such Old Calendarists have separated themselves from the traditional Orthodox Churches and have formed their own Church. Cypriot and Greek Old Calendarists are not in communion with those Orthodox Churches who follow the Old Calendar, such as the Patriarchates of Jerusalem or Russia; such Churches are in communion with the Orthodox Church of Cyprus and Greece respectively. There is no doubt that Article 111 of the Constitution refers to the Autocephalous Orthodox Church of Cyprus, which is in communion with the Ecumenical Patriarchate and the other Orthodox Churches, irrespective of whether such Churches adhere to the New, or the Old Calendar. The Church of the Orthodox Christians who follow the Old Calendar may not be considered as part of the Autocephalous Orthodox Church of Cyprus, to which the great majority of the population adheres, since it has its own separate administrative organization, with its own Metropolises, bishops and priests, as well as its own Charter which differs from the Charter of the Orthodox Church of Cyprus.

*114.* Therefore, Orthodox Christians who follow the Old Calendar have opted to exercise their constitutionally safeguarded rights and to separate themselves from the Autocephalous Orthodox Church of Cyprus. In view of the above, the Church of the Orthodox Christians who follow the Old Calendar is not the Church provided

142. *Cosgrove v. Cosgrove* [1961] CLR 221; [1964] CLR 77, *Papasavvas v. Johnstone* [1984] 1 CLR 38. *See also* C. Tornaritis, *The Law of Marriage, as Applied in Cyprus* (Nicosia, 1986): 13.
143. *Christodoulou v. Christodoulou* [1962] CLR 68, *Antoniou v. Antoniou* [1969] 1 CLR 307. *See also* G. Serghides, *Internal and External Conflict of Laws in Regard to Family Relations in Cyprus* (Nicosia, 1988): 142.
144. *See* A. Emilianides, *The Cypriot Law of Marriage and Divorce* (Thessaloniki: Sakkoulas, 2006, in Greek): 159ff.

for in Article 111 of the Constitution.[145] The Family Court in the case of *Onisiphorou* correctly observed that the Church of the Orthodox Christians who follow the Old Calendar has its own administrative organization, Charter, clergy, and temples and does not consider itself bound by the provisions of the Charter of the Orthodox Church of Cyprus.[146] The Family Court thus held that:

> *Since a person belonging to the Church of the Orthodox Christians who follow the Old Calendar does not consider himself as a member of the Orthodox Church who follows the New Calendar, it may not be considered that such a person belongs to the latter Church. A person who resides in Cyprus, and yet has not been baptized, nor perform marriage, nor participated in any ecclesiastical ceremonies, in temples belonging to the Greek Orthodox Church of Cyprus, but rather he has been baptized and participated in ecclesiastical ceremonies in temples belonging to the Church of the Orthodox Christians who follow the Old Calendar, may not, even presumably, be considered as belonging to the Greek Orthodox Church of Cyprus, or any other Church which follows the New Calendar. A different result would be contrary to the principles of religious freedom, as well as the right to liberty, and the right to marry and found a family, which are all fundamental freedoms safeguarded by Articles 18, 11 and 22 of the Constitution respectively.*[147]

## 2. Membership of a Religious Group

*115.* A *religious group* in the constitutional sense is, according to Article 2 §3 of the Constitution, a group of persons, ordinarily resident in Cyprus, professing the same religion and either belonging to the same rite or being subject to the same jurisdiction thereof. As already mentioned, the three constitutionally recognized religious groups are the Armenians, the Maronites and the Roman Catholics (Latins). Article 2 §3 of the Constitution does not provide who may be considered to be a member of each specific religious group. There is therefore no provision which stipulates who the State should consider to be a member of a religious group. This is due to the fact that being a member of a Church should depend upon the law of such a Church and not upon a State's law. This was the position of the Supreme Court of Cyprus prior to Independence in the case of *Tsivitanides*, where it was held that: *whether a church admits a person to its membership, no doubt depends on the*

145. A. Emilianides, *The Status of the Old – Calendar Church of Cyprus* (Nicosia: Cyprus Institute of Church and State Relations, 2008, in Greek).
146. *Onisiphorou v. Onisiphorou Cyprus Law Review* 49–50 (1995): 7439 (in Greek).
147. *Ibid.* This is consistent with the case law of the ECtHR. *See Serif v. Greece*, Judgment of 4 Dec. 1999; (2001) 31 EHRR 561, *Agga v. Greece*, Judgment of the European Court of Human Rights of 17 Oct. 2002.

*ecclesiastical law of that church.*[148] Thus, whether a person is a member of a specific religious group depends primarily upon the law of such group, and not upon any State legal provisions.[149]

*116.* The only criteria which the State law may apply, apart from ecclesiastical law, in order to specify whether a person should be considered as a member of a specific religious group, are: whether such person is a citizen of the Republic and whether he/she resides ordinarily in Cyprus.[150] Such criteria are contained in the definition of religious groups provided for, in Article 2 §3 of the Constitution. Accordingly, it was held in *Achcar v. Saad* that a person may not be a member of a religious group, defined as *a group of persons ordinarily resident in Cyprus*, if such person is not ordinarily resident in Cyprus.[151] Furthermore, a person may not be considered to belong to the Greek Community, unless such person is a citizen of the Republic, since members of the Greek or the Turkish Community are by definition citizens of the Republic of Cyprus.

*117.* According to one view, initially supported by the Government, members of the three religious groups were fixed in 1960 and following such date, no new members may be added. The above view exempts only descendants of persons who were members of the three religious groups in 1960. This approach is not only misguided, but it is also not based upon any legal provisions. The drafters of the Constitution were perfectly aware that a great number of members of the three religious groups had not acquired citizenship of the Republic by the time of the coming into force of the Constitution. Such persons, ordinarily resident in Cyprus, could of course acquire citizenship of the Republic of Cyprus at any later stage and would thus, become members of their respective religious group. Nevertheless, any person has the right, at any given time, to opt to become a member of a religious community. Such a right is safeguarded by Article 18 of the Constitution, as well as by Article 9 of the ECHR. If a person considers that he/she is a member of one of the three religious groups of the Republic and further the respective religious group considers that such person is indeed a member of such religious group, it would be unconstitutional and in violation of fundamental human rights, should the State refuse to recognize such person as member of the relevant religious group, simply due to the fact that such person became a member of the religious group at a later stage.

*118.* Consequently, if a person, who is a member of the Orthodox Church or the Protestant Church, or indeed any other Church, opts to change his/her religious

148. *Tsivitanides v. Tsivitanides* [1956] 21 CLR 111.

149. *See* G. Serghides, *Internal and External Conflict of Laws in Regard to Family Relations in Cyprus* (Nicosia, 1988): 147.

150. *See* A. Emilianides, *The Cypriot Law of Marriage and Divorce* (Thessaloniki: Sakkoulas, 2006, in Greek): 173ff.

151. *Achcar v. Saad* [1979] 1 CLR 627.

beliefs, then the State must accept the change. Otherwise, the right to religious freedom would be fettered.[152] Similarly, if Roman Catholics or Maronites or Armenians, acquire Cypriot citizenship and ordinarily reside in Cyprus at any given time, they should properly be considered members of the respective religious group; otherwise, not only would the constitutional provisions be inaccurately applied, but also there would be a violation of the right of non-discrimination, which is safeguarded by Article 28 of the Constitution and Article 14, as well as Protocol twelve, of the ECHR.

3. Is Cypriot Citizenship a Requirement for the Application of Article 111?

*119.* It is not clear from the wording of Article 111 of the Constitution whether the family courts have jurisdiction only if the parties are both Cypriot citizens. The view that Article 111 relating to jurisdiction, applies only to Cypriot citizens was first adopted in the case of *HjiJovanni*[153] where the Supreme Court held that:

> *Considering that Article 111(1) should be read in conjunction with Article 2 (3), in which express reference is made to citizens of the Republic and having regard to the exclusion of the competence of the Communal Chambers, which have competence only on citizens of the Republic, I am of the view that Article 111 should be construed as being applicable to citizens of the Republic only, that is to say, where both parties to the cause are citizens of the Republic.*

The view expressed in *HjiJovanni* was adopted by the Supreme Court in a series of matrimonial cases.[154] According to the above view, it is immaterial whether the parties have their residence or their domicile in Cyprus. The only important criterion is whether they are Cypriot citizens and members of the Greek Orthodox Church.

*120.* A different approach, however, was adopted by the Supreme Court in a subsequent series of cases, where it was held that the nationality of the parties was immaterial and that the only requisite for the application of Article 111 of the Constitution was the domicile of the parties in Cyprus.[155] In *Papasavvas* the Supreme Court held that the application of Article 111 of the Constitution is not confined to members of the Greek Community, but extends to all members of the Greek Orthodox Church, provided that they are domiciled in Cyprus. It was held that any other interpretation 'would defy the rule of private international law that the laws of the

152. *Tsivitanides v. Tsivitanides* [1956] 21 CLR 111.
153. *HjiJovanni v. HjiJovanni* [1969] 1 CLR 207.
154. *Achcar v. Saad* [1979] 1 CLR 627, *Dokidhou v. Dokidhes* [1970] 1 CLR 124, *Papa Alexandrou v. Andreou* [1970] 1 CLR 297.
155. *Medjel v. Medjel* [1983] 1 CLR 944, *Papasavvas v. Johnstone* [1984] 1 CLR 38, *Tooley v. Tooley* [1984] 1 CLR 279.

country of domicile define personal status'. Also in *Tooley* it was held that the application of the provisions of Article 111 is confined to cases where both parties are not only members of the Greek Orthodox Church, but also domiciled in Cyprus.

*121.* The view adopted in *HjiJovanni* according to which nationality and not domicile is the important factor for the application of Article 111 of the Constitution, was, however, once again adopted by the Supreme Court in the subsequent cases of *Chahine*[156] and *Televantos*[157] where it was held that the application of Article 111 of the Constitution was confined to Cypriot nationals. Domicile or residence of the parties was not considered to be a factor in order for the Cypriot courts to accept jurisdiction. The same view also seems to have been adopted by the House of Representatives, since the introductory report of Law 95/1989, which amended Article 111 of the Constitution, held that: 'Article 111 of the Constitution refers to matters of personal status of citizens of the Republic, who are members of the Greek Community'. The view according to which Article 111(2)(a) applies only with regard to matters of personal status of citizens of the Republic who are members of the Greek Community, was also adopted in a series of cases, subsequent to the amendment of Article 111 of the Constitution with law 95/1989.[158] However, two other cases of the Supreme Court have adopted the approach in *Tooley*, according to which domicile and not nationality of the parties is the important factor in order to determine whether Article 111 of the Constitution should apply.[159]

*122.* The question whether Article 111 applies only to citizens of the Republic has been the subject of much debate; however, it is suggested that the initial position of the Supreme Court in *HjiJovanni* was undoubtedly correct, and that subsequent case law simply perplexed a rather straightforward issue.[160] Article 111 intended to remove from the competence of the communal chambers those matters of family status which concerned members of the Orthodox Church or of the three religious groups. Article 111 is therefore part of Part V of the Constitution which concerns Communal Chambers and relates to competences otherwise belonging to the Greek Communal Chamber; it therefore concerns members of the Greek Communal Chamber, namely Cypriot citizens. If Article 111 was intended to apply with respect to parties who were not Cypriot citizens, then Article 111 ought to also exclude competences otherwise exercised by the House of Representatives and not simply competences otherwise exercised by the Communal Chambers.[161]

---

156. *Chahine v. Chahine* [1984] 1 CLR 167.
157. *Televantos v. Televantou* [1985] 1 CLR 412.
158. *Demetriou v. Demetriou* [1991] 1 CLR 1153 (in Greek), *Elia* No. 3 [1995] 1 CLR 412 (in Greek). *See* further *Mantzafou v. Demetriades* [1995] 1 CLR 762 (in Greek).
159. *Koupparis v. Koupparis* [1996] 1 CLR 670 (in Greek), *Markitanis v. Moutzouri* [1997] 1 CLR 314 (in Greek).
160. *See* A. Emilianides, *The Cypriot Law of Marriage and Divorce* (Thessaloniki: Sakkoulas, 2006, in Greek): 174ff.
161. *See* G. Serghides, *Internal and External Conflict of Laws in Regard to Family Relations in Cyprus* (Nicosia, 1988): 201ff and 488ff.

*123.* In addition it is noted that if the approach in *Tooley* was to be adopted this would essentially imply that members of the Orthodox Church who are not citizens of the Republic may not perform a valid civil marriage, contrary to members of the Orthodox Church who are citizens of the Republic. This is due to the fact that in 1977 the Supreme Court of Cyprus held that a civil marriage between members of the Orthodox Church is null, to begin with, wherever it has been celebrated.[162] While the Constitutional Amendment of 1989 provided for the right of citizens of the Republic, and members of the Greek Community, to perform civil marriage, such a right is not provided for members of the Orthodox Church who are not citizens of the Republic. It emerges that the House of Representatives considered that Article 111 only applies to citizens of the Republic. It is submitted that this is the correct view.

### *B. The Application of Article 22 of the Constitution*

#### 1. Article 22 §2 (a) of the Constitution

*124.* Article 22 §2(a) of the Constitution provides that if the law relating to marriage applicable to the parties as provided under Article 111 is not the same, the parties may elect to have their marriage governed by the law applicable to either of them under such Article; such paragraph refers to mixed marriages between (i) persons who are members of the Greek Orthodox Church and to any of the three religious groups, or (ii) persons belonging to different religious groups (a marriage of an Armenian with a Roman Catholic or a Maronite, or a marriage of a Maronite with a Roman Catholic). In accordance with Article §2 (a) the persons about to be married may elect to have their marriage governed by the law applicable to either of them.

*125.* The Supreme Court has held in several cases that the application of Article 111 of the Constitution is restricted to cases where both parties are member of the Greek Orthodox Church (or of the same religious group).[163] It is submitted that such approach is flawed; Article 22 §2 (a), as well as Article 22 §2 (c), expressly provide for the right of a person to elect to have his/her marriage governed by the law applicable under Article 111 of the Constitution.[164] Thus, it is submitted that Article 111 may well apply with respect to marriages of parties who are not both members of the Greek Orthodox Church, or of the same religious group, so long as the parties have elected in accordance with the provisions of Article 22 §2 of the Constitution to have their marriage governed by the law applicable to either of them under 111

162. *Metaxa v. Mita* [1977] 1 CLR 1.
163. *Tooley v. Tooley* [1984] 1 C.L.R 279, *Televantos v. Televantos* (1985) 1 C.L.R 412, *Elias* (n. 3) [1995] 1 CLR 412 (in Greek), *Mantovani v. Mantovani* [1962] CLR 336, *Theocharides v. Theocharides* [1965] 1 CLR 1.
164. *Michael v. Michael* [1971] 1 CLR 211, *HjiHanna v. HjiHanna* [1973] 1 CLR 186, *De Stefano v. De Stefano* [1982] 1 CLR 367.

of the Constitution. Article 111 may not be read in isolation, but should be read in conjunction with Article 22 of the Constitution.[165]

*126.* Article 22 §2 (a) aims at facilitating the celebration of mixed marriages by persons who are members of the Orthodox Church and of the three religious groups; otherwise, the parties would have to celebrate a dual marriage in accordance to the law applicable for each of them, instead of simply one marriage in accordance to the law applicable for either of them. The choice of applicable law is, however, optional; thus, the persons about to be married may still choose to celebrate their marriage in accordance to the law applicable for each of them, namely to celebrate two marriages (one in accordance, for instance, with the rites of the Greek Orthodox Church), while the other in accordance with the rites of the Roman Catholic Church). In the latter case, the parties may still choose after celebrating both marriages, either law as applicable for their marriage; such election is not so important following the 1989 constitutional amendment, as it was prior to such amendment.

### 2. Article 22 §2 (b) of the Constitution

*127.* Article 22 § 2(b) of the Constitution stipulates that if the provisions of Article 111 are not applicable to any of the parties to the marriage and neither of such parties is a member of the Turkish Community, the marriage shall be governed by a law of the Republic which the House of Representatives shall enact and which shall not contain any restrictions other than those relating to age, health, proximity of relationship and prohibition of polygamy. This provision applies in cases where neither of the parties is a member of the Orthodox Church, or of a religious group, or a member of the Turkish Community. It applies to both citizens of the Republic and foreigners. Thus Article 22 §2 (b) refers to marriages between: (i) persons belonging to a religion or rite other than the five constitutionally recognized, such as Jews, Protestants, Orthodox Christians who follow the Old Calendar, or Jehovah's Witnesses,[166] (ii) persons belonging to the Orthodox Church, but who are not citizens of the Republic, or who are not members of the Greek Orthodox Church of Cyprus and (iii) persons belonging to the Armenian, Roman Catholic or Maronite Church who are not citizens of the Republic, or do not have their habitual residence in the Republic.

*128.* Following the entry into force of the Constitution, the House of Representatives did not enact the law provided for in Article 22 §2 (b). However, in *Malkiel*[167] the Supreme Court held that the Marriage Law, Cap. 279, could be considered as the law provided for in Articles 22 §2 (b) and 22 §2 (c), despite the fact that such

165. A. Emilianides, *The Cypriot Law of Marriage and Divorce* (Thessaloniki: Sakkoulas, 2006, in Greek): 188ff, G. Serghides, *Internal and External Conflict of Laws in Regard to Family Relations in Cyprus* (Nicosia, 1988): 175.

166. *See* C. Tornaritis, 'Is Chiliasm a Religion? Is it Allowed by the Constitution and which Measures are Provided against It?', *Cyprus Law Tribune* 1–2 (1981): 3–5 (in Greek), *Minister of Interior v. The Jehovah's Witnesses Congregation (Cyprus) Ltd* [1995] 3 CLR 78 (in Greek).

167. *Mihael v. Malkiel* [1976] 8 JSC 1223.

law had been enacted prior to Independence in accordance with Article 188 §1 of the Constitution; Article 188 §1 provides that laws existing prior to the entry into force of the Constitution should remain in force, subject to their modification and adaptation to the provisions of the Constitution. This approach was confirmed in the subsequent judgment of *Karanikki*.[168] The issue is now moot in view of the enactment of the Marriage Law 104(I)/2003 which abolished Cap. 279 and which is the law provided for in Article 22 §2 (b) of the Constitution.

### 3. Article 22 §2 (c) of the Constitution

*129.* Article 22 §2 (c) of the Constitution stipulates that if the provisions of Article 111 are applicable only to one of the parties to the marriage and the other party is not a member of the Turkish Community, the marriage shall be governed by the law of the Republic as provided for in 22 §2 (b), provided that the parties may elect to have their marriage governed by the law applicable under Article 111 to one of such parties, insofar as such law allows such marriage. This provision applies in cases where one of the parties is a member of the Greek Orthodox Church or one of the three religious groups of the Republic, while the other (i) belongs to a religion or rite other than the five constitutionally recognized, or (ii) belongs to the Orthodox Church but is not a citizen of the Republic or is not a member of the Greek Orthodox Church of Cyprus, or (iii) belongs to the Armenian, Roman Catholic or Maronite Church but is not a citizen of the Republic, or does not have habitual residence in the Republic.

## *C. Marriage of Members of the Turkish Cypriot Community*

*130.* Article 2 of the Turkish Family Courts Law, Cap. 338 defined the term *religious matters* for which the Turkish Family Courts have exclusive competence, as covering any matters concerning marriage, divorce, alimony and registration of wakfs, but not matters concerning hereditary succession or wills. Following the enactment of the Constitution of Cyprus, the Turkish Family Courts essentially functioned as Turkish Communal Courts under the relevant constitutional provisions and continued to have exclusive competence with regard to marriage and divorce of Turkish Muslims, according to the provisions of the Turkish Family (Marriage and Divorce) Law, Cap. 339.[169] The Turkish Family Law applied to all marriages of parties, at least one of whom was a Turkish resident in Cyprus professing the Muslim faith. In the case of a Muslim male, he could marry any woman, irrespective of the latter's religion. Muslim women, however, were prohibited from marrying a non-Muslim man.

---

168. *Karanikki v. The Police* [1984] 2 CLR 144.
169. *See* more generally A. Emilianides, *Annotated Legal Documents on Islam in Cyprus* (Leiden: Brill, 2014).

*131.* As a result of the 1974 Turkish invasion and the subsequent occupation of the northern part of the Republic of Cyprus, it became impossible for any Turkish Muslim to perform marriages in the areas controlled by the Republic of Cyprus; this was due to the fact that Article 34 of the Marriage Law, Cap. 279 provided that the provisions of that law could not apply to marriages of parties, one of which was a Turk, professing the Muslim faith. In addition, there was no court which had competence with regard to the matrimonial affairs of Turkish Muslims. The right of Turkish Muslims to perform legal marriages in the Republic was eventually recognized by Law 46(I)/2002, which extended to members of the Turkish Community the application of the marriage Law Cap. 279. When the Marriage Law, Cap. 279, was replaced by the Marriage Law 104(I)/2003, Law 120(I)/2003 provided that the provisions of Law 104(I)/03 would also apply with respect to the marriages of members of the Turkish Community on the basis of the doctrine of necessity. The Presidents of the District Courts have the exclusive competence to adjudicate the matrimonial affairs of members of the Turkish Community who have performed their marriage under the provisions of either Cap. 279, or Law 104(I)/03.

*132.* It was therefore provided, that the application of Caps. 338 and 339 in the Republic of Cyprus would be suspended for as long as the Republic is prevented to exercise effective control over the occupied territories. The law was enacted on the basis of the doctrine of necessity and was the result of an application to the ECtHR by the Turkish Cypriot Kemal Selim.[170] Selim complained under Articles 8, 12 and 13 of the ECHR that he had been denied the right to marry and found a family. The ECtHR declared the application admissible, and the Government of the Republic of Cyprus submitted a formal declaration accepting a friendly settlement of the case. Law 46(I)/02 provided for the temporary application of the Marriage Law, Cap. 279 to members of the Turkish Community, for as long as the abnormal situation prevailing on the island continued.[171]

*133.* It has been submitted that Law 120(I)/03 only applies with respect to marriages celebrated by persons who are both members of the Turkish Community, under the proviso that if the husband is a member of the Turkish Community and the wife a member of the Greek Community, then automatically by the celebration of their marriage both parties become members of the Turkish Community by virtue of Article 2 §7 of the Constitution; thus, the Family Court should have jurisdiction in cases where only one party is a member of the Turkish Community.[172] Such an approach, while based in the alleged intention of the legislator, is, however, inconsistent with the clear wording of section 3 of Law 120(I)/03 which provides that all the provisions of Law 104(I)/03 with regards to all topics and subjects for which there is a provision in the said Law, are applicable also to the case where *either* or *both* parties belong to the Turkish Community.

---

170. *Selim v. Cyprus*, Judgment of 16 Jul. 2002.

171. A. Emilianides, 'The Case for Amending the Current Legal Framework', *Cyprus and European Law Review* 11 (2011): 135ff.

172. G. Serghides, 'Reflection on some Aspects of the Family Law of the Turkish Community in Cyprus', *Cyprus and European Law Review* 11 (2011): 156ff.

*134.* With respect to marriages of members of the Turkish Community which were performed outside the Republic, the Appellate Family Court held in the case of *Holubova* that the Family Courts which were established under the Family Courts Law 23/1990 have jurisdiction on the matter.[173] The Appellant was a Czech Catholic who performed a civil marriage in the former Czechoslovakia with a Muslim, member of the Turkish Community. Both spouses were thus members of the Turkish Community, since according to the anachronistic and discriminatory Article 2 §7 of the Constitution (which, however, continues to be valid) the wife belongs to the Community of her husband. The Appellate Family Court held that since the marriage had been celebrated in Czechoslovakia and not in Cyprus, the Family Court should have jurisdiction, since the intention of the legislator was to transfer to the Family Courts all competences previously enjoyed by the District Courts and the Supreme Court with respect to family law matters.

*135.* While the result of *Holubova* might be correct from a sociopolitical point of view and de *lege ferenda*, it is submitted that it is not consistent with the constitutional provisions. It is of course correct that the Family Courts have, on the basis of Article 11 (2) (c) of Law 23/1990 jurisdiction with respect to the dissolution of civil marriages; however, such competences may not include also civil marriages performed by members of the Turkish Community abroad, since neither the District Courts nor the Supreme Court ever had such competences in the first place. The Turkish Communal Chambers have jurisdiction with respect to all marriages of members of the Turkish Cypriot Community, in accordance with Article 87 of the Constitution, irrespective of whether the marriage was celebrated in Cyprus or abroad. Consequently, the Family Courts could have acquired jurisdiction only if the legislator had enacted a relevant law on the basis of the doctrine of necessity; otherwise, the exercise of such competences is incompatible to the Constitution. The fact that the Appellate Family Court reached a correct result *de lege ferenda* in this case, does not change the fact that its decision is not a proper interpretation of the constitutional provisions.[174]

### *D. The Regime for Solemnization of Marriages in Cyprus*

*136.* The First Amendment of the Constitution introduced a dual system for the solemnization of marriage, with respect to members of the Greek Community; hence, members of the Greek Orthodox Church or of the three religious groups may choose to perform either a civil marriage, or a religious marriage according to the rites of their respective Church. A person may further perform both a civil and a religious marriage with the same person. Article 111 of the Constitution, however, provides that matters relating to betrothal, marriage, and nullity of marriage of members of the Greek Orthodox Church continue to be governed by the law of the

173. *Holubova v. Mehmet Ali* [2003] 1 CLR 643 (in Greek).

174. A. Emilianides, 'The Case for Amending the Current Legal Framework', *Cyprus and European Law Review* 11 (2011): 135ff, G. Serghides, 'Cyprus Family Jurisdiction: Ratione Personae and Ratione Materiae', *Family Law Review* 2 (2011): 7–8.

Greek Orthodox Church or of the respective religious group. Consequently, in case that the members of the Greek Orthodox Church opt to perform a religious marriage, such marriage shall be solemnized according to the relevant provisions of the Charter of the Orthodox Church and so long as all requirements provided by the Charter are complied with.[175] Similarly religious marriages of members of the three religious Churches must be solemnized according to the canon law provisions of the respective religious group.

*137.* The Marriage Law 21/1990 provided for the celebration of civil marriages of members of the Greek Community, in accordance with the provisions of the Constitution. It should be noted that a marriage could be celebrated on the basis of the provisions of Law 21/1990 only so long as both spouses-to-be were members of the Greek Community; civil marriages between members of the Greek Community and members of the Turkish Community, or non-Cypriots could not be celebrated in accordance with the provisions of Law 21/1990. Civil marriages between members of the Greek Community and non-Cypriots or between non-Cypriots could be celebrated in Cyprus only in accordance with the provisions of the pre-existing Marriage Law Cap. 279; Cap. 279 was held to be in force in accordance with the provisions of Article 188 of the Constitution.

*138.* Cap. 279 did not only provide for the celebration of civil marriages, but also for the solemnization of religious marriages between members of the Greek Community and non-Cypriots, as well as between non-Cypriots. In addition Cap. 279 provided for the solemnization of religious marriages between members of the Greek Community who were not members of the Greek Orthodox Church or of a religious group. Such religious marriages could be solemnized, so long as the respective Church had registered its marriage officers in accordance with the provisions of Cap. 279. In a case concerning Jehovah's Witnesses, the Supreme Court held that Law 21/1990 and Cap. 279 had an entirely different content and intention and thus, the registered ministers of a Church should continue to solemnize religious marriages of members of their respective Church, irrespective of whether such members belong to the Greek Community.[176]

*139.* In 2003 the House of Representatives enacted the new Marriage Law 104(I)/2003, which replaced both Law 21/1990 and Cap. 279. It has been debated whether the new Marriage Law provides only for the celebration of civil marriages, or whether it also provides for the celebration of religious marriages, similarly to the pre-existing Cap. 279. It has been noted that the explicit reference to marriages solemnized by registered religious ministers in accordance with the rites of the Greek Orthodox Church or the three religious groups in the definition of marriage in section 3 of Law 104(I)/2003 might imply that the solemnization of religious

---

175. *See* in detail A. Emilianides, *The Cypriot Law of Marriage and Divorce* (Thessaloniki: Sakkoulas, 2006, in Greek): 306ff.

176. *The Minister of Interior v. The Jehovah's Witnesses Congregation (Cyprus) Ltd.*[1995] 3 CLR 78 (in Greek). *See* comments in A. Emilianides, *The Cypriot Law of Marriage and Divorce* (Thessaloniki: Sakkoulas, 2006, in Greek): 212–213.

marriages by registered religious ministers of other religions is no longer permitted.[177] It is suggested that this should not be the case.[178] Section 40 §2 of Law 104(I)/2003 provides that religious ministers who had been registered in accordance with the provisions of Cap. 279 shall continue to have the right to solemnize marriages, also in accordance with the provisions of Law 104(I)/2003; moreover, section 40 §3 of Law 104(I)/2003 provides that the Minister of Interior is authorized to register any new ministers of any religion or creed.

### *E. The Applicable Law Concerning Nullity of Marriage*

*140.* It has been debated whether following the 1989 amendment of the Constitution, the Family Courts, or the Family Courts of Religious Groups, have jurisdiction with respect to nullity of marriage of marriages celebrated in accordance with the provisions of Article 111 of the Constitution. Law 95/89 which amended the Constitution provides no explicit reference to the Family Courts having jurisdiction regarding nullity of marriage; furthermore, the applicable law for matters relating to marriage or nullity of marriage continues to be the Charter of the Orthodox Church (or the internal canon law of the three religious groups, depending on the case). It has been argued that the Family Courts do not have jurisdiction for nullity of marriage and that the ecclesiastical courts continued to enjoy jurisdiction with respect to such matters.[179] It is submitted that this is not the case.

*141.* Law 95/1989 has deleted the words: 'and shall be cognizable by a tribunal of such Church' from the wording of Article 111 of the Constitution; this in our view shows that the intention of the legislator was to abolish the jurisdiction of the ecclesiastical courts regarding nullity of marriage and to retain only the provisions concerning applicable law. Thus, Article 112 §2(A) of the Constitution which refers to the jurisdiction of the Family Courts with respect to 'divorce, judicial separation or restitution of conjugal rights or family relations' should be interpreted as including nullity of marriage. Such an interpretation is consistent with the interpretation adopted by the Supreme Court in *Dadakarides* where the Supreme Court held that the term 'family relations' refers to all issues relevant to Family Law.[180] When adjudicating cases related to nullity of marriage, the Family Court shall apply the law provided for in the Charter in force of the Orthodox Church of Cyprus.[181]

*142.* It should be noted that Law 104(I)/2003 stipulates that its provisions regarding nullity of marriage apply also to religious marriages which were celebrated according to the rites of the Orthodox Church or the three religious groups

177. *See* G. Serghides, 'Observations on the Cypriot Marriage Law of 2003', *Armenopoulos* 58 (2003): 661ff (in Greek).
178. *See* in detail A. Emilianides, *The Cypriot Law of Marriage and Divorce* (Thessaloniki: Sakkoulas, 2006, in Greek): 214ff.
179. K. Chrysostomides, 'The Validity of Marriage and the New Legislation', *Cyprus Law Review* 25 (1989): 3893–3905 (in Greek).
180. *Dadakarides v. Dadakarides* [1990] 1 CLR 566 (in Greek).
181. *Papacharalambous v. Papacharalambous* [1998] 8 JSC 243 (in Greek).

of the Republic. However, such provisions of Law 104(I)/2003 are inconsistent with Article 111 of the Constitution, since Article 111 explicitly provides that matters relating to betrothal, marriage, and nullity of marriage continue to be governed by the law of the Greek Orthodox Church or the Church of the corresponding religious group as the case may be. Therefore, a State law, such as Law 104(I)/2003, may not provide for the requirements of celebrating a religious marriage according to the rites of the Orthodox Church or the three religious groups of the Republic, or for the grounds for declaring such a religious marriage null and void; such requirements and grounds of nullity have to be considered on the basis of the internal canon law of the Orthodox Church and of the three religious groups.[182]

*143.* There are astonishingly many circumstances where the applicable law concerning nullity of marriage shall be the English Law as it applied in Cyprus prior to Independence, namely the English Law of 1959, despite the fact that such law is outdated and anachronistic and has nothing to do with the Cypriot legal system.[183] The applicable law governing the nullity of all civil or religious marriages celebrated abroad, including marriages between persons who are both members of the Greek Orthodox Church and are citizens of the Republic, or between persons who are both members of the same religious group and are citizens of the Republic, or members of the Turkish Community, is essentially the English Law of 1959. Similarly, the English Law of 1959 shall be applicable for civil or religious marriages which were celebrated in Cyprus in accordance with Cap. 279, as well as religious marriages of Orthodox Christians who follow the Old Calendar celebrated in accordance with Law 60(I)/94.

## II. Rules Governing Capacity to Marry

### *A. Capacity to Marry in Accordance with Law 104(I)/2003*

*144.* A marriage may only be celebrated between a man and a woman; difference of sex is considered to be part of the definition of a marriage in accordance with section 3 of Law 104(I)/03 which defines marriage as the union between a man and a woman. In *Schalk and Kopf,*[184] a case recently examined by the ECtHR, the applicants were a same-sex couple living in a stable partnership. They petitioned the Austrian authorities for permission to marriage, albeit their request was denied on the ground that marriage could only be celebrated between persons of the opposite

182. *See* A. Emilianides, 'What is the Legal Status with Regard to the Adjudication of Cases of Nullity of Marriage?', *Cyprus and European Law Review* 1 (2006): 113–127 (in Greek).

183. G. Serghides, 'Observations on the Cypriot Marriage Law of 2003', *Armenopoulos* 58 (2003): 661ff (in Greek), A. Emilianides, *The Cypriot Law of Marriage and Divorce* (Thessaloniki: Sakkoulas, 2006, in Greek): 240.

184. *Schalk and Kopf v. Austria*, Judgment of 24 Jun. 2010, *Gas and Dubois v. France*, Judgment of 15 Mar. 2012. *See also* A. Emilianides, 'Homosexuality and Human Rights in the Cypriot Legal Order' in *Sexualities: Views, Studies and Experiences in the Cypriot and Greek Space* eds C. Phellas et al (Athens: Polyxromos Planitis, 2014): 130-151 (in Greek).

sex. The ECtHR held that the ECHR does not oblige a State to grant access to marriage to a same-sex couple. It was further held that the national authorities were best placed to assess and respond to the needs of society in this field, given that marriage had deep-rooted social and cultural connotations differing greatly from one society to another. Consequently, the ECtHR held that there was no violation of Article 12 of the ECHR safeguarding the right to marry.

*145.* The approach of the ECtHR with respect to transsexuals, however, differs. The phenomenon of transsexuality applies to individuals who psychologically feel that they belong to a different sex than the one they physically belong and therefore, seek *to adapt their physical characteristics to their psychological nature*[185] through medical treatment and surgical operations. Transsexuals are not homosexuals; transsexuals demand that their post-operative sex is recognized by the law and ask to be treated in the same manner as other individuals belonging to their new sex.[186] In the landmark *Goodwin*[187] and *I*[188] judgments, the ECtHR unanimously held that the United Kingdom's refusal to recognize the post-operative sex of the applicant violated Articles 8 and 12 of the ECHR. The Court observed that in light of the present-day conditions, the extent of the positive obligations of the United Kingdom towards transsexuals under Article 8 of the ECHR ought to be reinterpreted. The Court observed that there was something of a paradox to the fact that although the applicant's gender reassignment was lawfully provided and indeed carried out by the National Health Service, the result of such gender reassignment was not completely recognized by law.

*146.* It is striking that the Court disregarded the lack of European consensus on the subject; the Court observed that such lack of a common European approach should be attached less significance, than *to the clear and uncontested evidence of a continuing international trend in favour not only of increased social acceptance of transsexuals, but of legal recognition of the new sexual identity of post-operative transsexuals.*[189] The Court also held that the inability of transsexuals under English law to conclude a valid marriage with persons of their pre-operative sex constituted a breach of Article 12 of the ECHR. It was held that the social changes which occurred since the adoption of the ECHR, as well as the medical developments regarding transsexuality, could justify a wider interpretation of the terms 'man' and 'woman' in order to include post-operative transsexuals. A different view would lead to the undesirable conclusion that post-operative transsexuals may not marry at all, since they would be unable to marry any persons belonging either to their former, or to their post-operative sex. In view of the above, it is submitted that, in

---

185. *Rees v. United Kingdom*, Judgment of 17 Oct. 1986, Series A, No. 106; (1987) 9 EHRR 56.
186. *See* generally S. Whittle, *Respect and Equality: Transsexual and Transgender Rights* (London: Cavendish Publishing Ltd, 2002), A. Bradney, 'Transsexuals and the Law', *Family Law* 17 (1987): 350.
187. *Goodwin v. United Kingdom*, Judgment of 11 Jul. 2002; (2002) 35 EHRR 447. *See also* the analysis of A. Campbell and H. Lardy, 'Transsexuals: The ECHR in Transition', *Northern Ireland Legal Quarterly* 54 (2003): 209.
188. *I v. United Kingdom*, Judgment of 11 Jul. 2002; (2003) 36 EHRR 967.
189. *Goodwin v. United Kingdom*, para. 85, *I v. United Kingdom*, para. 65.

accordance with the case law of the ECtHR, the marriage between transsexuals should be considered as legally permitted in Cyprus.

*147.* Section 14 of Law 104(I)/03 provides that both persons who wish to conclude a marriage should be of a marriageable age which is set at 18 years. However, in accordance with section 15 of Law 104(I)/03, a person might be allowed to celebrate a marriage even if he/she is below 18 years of age, provided that he/she is over 16 years of age, there is an important ground (e.g., pregnancy) and the persons having parental responsibility consent in writing. If the persons who have parental responsibility unreasonably refuse to consent, or there are no persons having parental responsibility, the Family Court of the district where the person is residing, may waive such requirement. Furthermore, a person intending to conclude a marriage has to be capable of forming free will, as well as understanding and appreciating such act; thus, persons who are incapable due to mental disorder or intoxication, or brain injury or other illness, are not capable to celebrate a marriage.[190]

*148.* For a person to celebrate a valid marriage all previous civil or religious marriages, if any, must have already been irrevocably dissolved or annulled by a competent court; in addition bigamy is a criminal offence in accordance with section 179 of the Criminal Code, Cap. 154 which provides that any person performing bigamy is subject to a five-year imprisonment.[191] Section 18 provides that for a marriage to be considered as irrevocably dissolved or annulled, the period within which a person may appeal the judgment for dissolution or annulment should have lapsed; if an appeal is filed, then the effect of the dissolution or annulment of the marriage is suspended until a judgment is issued in the appeal proceedings. If a person is married prior to the lapse of the period within which the other party may appeal, albeit no appeal is filed, the marriage is not annulled. It is further provided that the judgment of a Court annulling or dissolving either of the religious or civil marriages shall simultaneously effect the annulment or dissolution of the other marriage as well.

*149.* Furthermore, the parties may not perform a valid marriage if they are within the prohibited degrees of relationship, either in blood or from affinity; a marriage between parties related up to the fifth degree in blood, or third degree in affinity is prohibited. This includes, in accordance with sections 3, 4 and 5 of the Children (Kinship and Legal Substance) Law 187/91, any direct ascendants or descendants of either of the parties, as well as the siblings, uncles, aunts, nephews, nieces of either of the parties (up to the third degree in blood or affinity), or the first cousins, children of nephew or niece, great uncles or aunts, children of first cousins, or children of great uncles or aunts of the party intending to perform the marriage (up to the fifth degree in blood). It is noted that in accordance with section 5 §2 of

190. *See also* the Convention on Consent to Marriage, Minimum Age for Marriage and Registration of Marriage (Ratification) Law 16(III)/2002.

191. *See also* A. Pantelides, *Some Aspects of the Offence of Bigamy in Cyprus* (Nicosia, 1967, in Greek).

Law 187/91 the kinship in affinity is maintained even after the dissolution or annulment of a marriage. Marriages between adoptive parents and their kin with the adopted child are also prohibited, as are marriages between a child born out of wedlock on the one hand and his/her father and his/her father's relatives.

### *B. Capacity to Marry in Accordance with the Charter of the Orthodox Church*

*150.* The requirements for celebrating a religious marriage in accordance with the rites and doctrine of the Orthodox Church are set out in Articles 83 and 84 of the 2010 Charter of the Orthodox Church.[192] Such marriage may only be celebrated between persons of the opposite sex. Both parties must further be of marriageable age which is set at 18 years in accordance with section 83 of the 2010 Charter of the Orthodox Church; however, parties may be allowed to celebrate a marriage even if they are below 18 years of age, so long as they have completed 16 years of age, there is an important ground (such as pregnancy) and the consent is given both by the persons having parental responsibility, as well as of the Archbishop or bishop of the place of solemnization of the marriage. The Archbishop or bishop of the place of solemnization of the marriage may waive the consent of the persons having parental responsibility if such persons may not be found. In addition to the above, it is provided that the age difference between the husband and the wife should not exceed 25 years; the Archbishop or bishop of the place of solemnization of the marriage may waive such requirement.

*151.* Both parties must in principle be members of the Orthodox Church; nevertheless, the competent Archbishop or bishop may permit a marriage to be celebrated between a member of the Orthodox Church and a member of another Christian Church, so long as the non-Orthodox party declares that he/she shall not interfere with the exercise of the religious duties of the Orthodox spouse and that he/she shall not be opposed to the children being baptized and raised in accordance with the rites of the Orthodox Church. An Orthodox religious marriage between a member of the Orthodox Church and a member of a non-Christian Church is prohibited. Furthermore, members of the clergy who have been consecrated, or monks, may not perform a marriage according to the rites of the Orthodox Church. While it is not explicitly provided for, persons who wish to solemnize a marriage should be mentally capable of understanding the consequences of their decision.

*152.* A person may not celebrate a valid religious marriage according to the rites of the Greek Orthodox Church, unless all previous marriages, if any, have already been dissolved or annulled by a competent court. Furthermore, a person may not

192. For a detailed analysis *see* A. Emilianides, 'The Family Law Provisions of the Charter of the Church of Cyprus', *Family Law Review* 2 (2011): 21ff (in Greek), S. Liasides, 'Comments – Observations on the New Charter of the Church of Cyprus', *Family Law Review* 1 (2011): 23ff (in Greek). *See* further A. Emilianides, *The Cypriot Law of Marriage and Divorce* (Thessaloniki: Sakkoulas, 2006, in Greek), 309ff.

celebrate a marriage if he/she has already celebrated three valid marriages. In addition to the above, the parties may not perform a valid marriage if they are within the prohibited degrees of relationship, either in blood or from affinity; a marriage between ancestors and descendants is always prohibited irrespective of the degree of relationship between the parties, as is the marriage between parties related up to the fifth degree in blood, or third degree in affinity. Marriages between godparents and godchildren are also prohibited, as are the marriages between the siblings of two spouses. It is further provided that neither party may celebrate a marriage within ten months from the date that the decree of dissolution or annulment of a previous marriage becomes final; such requirement may be waived in an appropriate case.

## §3. Formalities of Marriage

### I. Formalities of Marriage in Accordance with Law 104(I)/2003

*153.* Any Mayor, or Vice-Mayor of any Municipality in Cyprus, or any member of a Municipal Council who has been authorized in writing by the Mayor, or any person who has been so designated by the Minister of Interior, is considered as a registered Marriage Officer in accordance with section 3 §2 of Law 104(I)/2003. Persons who purport to marry should appear before the registered Marriage Officer of the Municipality of their choice and provide a relevant notice which sets out their personal data in accordance with section 4 and Form A of the First Schedule of Law 104(I)/03. The Marriage Officer keeps the notice on record in accordance with section 5 of Law 104(I)/03 and issues a certificate which sets out the date and place of the marriage to be celebrated (section 6 and Form B of the First Schedule of Law 104(I)/03).

*154.* In order for the Marriage Officer to arrange for a date and place of marriage, the parties intending to marry should appear before the Marriage Officer, or any other person authorized by the Marriage Officer and officially declare and confirm in writing, in accordance with section 8 of Law 104(I)/2003, that they are not aware of the existence of any impediment or legal obstacle for the marriage, and that all necessary consents have been given or that no such consent is needed. The Marriage Officer may request for any additional certificates in order to ascertain that the declarations of the parties, or their personal data, are true. The Marriage Officer may decline to allow for a marriage to be celebrated, in accordance with section 10 of Law 104(I)/03, if he/she considers that the conditions for the celebration of a valid marriage are not met, or if there is any legal impediment to marry; in such a case the interested parties may apply before the Family Court challenging the decision of the Marriage Officer.

*155.* The date and place of the marriage are determined, after taking into account the wishes of the parties. The date of the marriage should not be earlier than fifteen days and no later than three months from the date the certificate is issued; however, the Marriage Officer has the discretion to arrange for the marriage to take place even earlier than fifteen days from the date the certificate is issued, if the parties so wish and provided that an increased levy is paid. Civil marriages are concluded, in accordance with section 9 of Law 104(I)/03, by the simultaneous declaration of the parties that they consent to marry and the reading of the text set out in the Second Schedule of Law 104(I)/03 by the Marriage Officer; such declaration has to be given personally by the persons intending to marry before at least two witnesses and has to be final and unconditional.

*156.* After the conclusion of the marriage, the Marriage Officer issues a certificate of marriage in accordance with section 12 and Form C of the First Schedule of Law 104(I)/03, signed by him/her, the married couple and at least two witnesses; a copy of the certificate is then given to the parties, while a second copy is sent within seven days to the Registrar who keeps a record of all marriages in the Republic, while a third copy is kept on record by the Marriage Officer. If either of the parties is a subject of a third country which has an Embassy or a Consulate in the Republic, the Marriage Officer sends a certified certificate of marriage to such Embassy or Consulate. It is provided that the marriage certificate may be issued in English if the parties so wish. If the parties have opted to solemnize a religious marriage, the Registrar has to be informed of such marriage by the registered religious minister within forty-five days from the solemnization of such marriage.

*157.* The solemnization of a marriage by a person who is not a registered Marriage Officer or a registered religious minister is a criminal offence, in accordance with section 36 of Law 104(I)/03 punishable with imprisonment up to five years or a fine up to EUR 8546,98 (CYP 5,000), or both imprisonment and a fine. Subject to imprisonment up to five years or a fine of up to EUR 8.546, or both imprisonment and a fine, is also, in accordance with section 35 of Law 104(I)/03, any person who forges any certificate of a Marriage Officer or knowingly circulates such a forged certificate. Any Marriage Officer who solemnizes a marriage despite the fact that he/she is aware that any provision of Law 104(I)/03 has not been complied with is, in accordance with section 33 of Law 104(I)/03, subject to imprisonment up to two years or a fine up to EUR 3418,79 (CYP 2,000) or both imprisonment and a fine; subject to imprisonment of up to two years or a fine up to EUR 3418,79 or both imprisonment and a fine is also, in accordance with section 34 of Law 104(I)/03 any person who wilfully makes a false statement in any declaration, certificate or other documents provided by Law 104(I)/03. Any religious minister or person who celebrates a religious marriage without informing the Registrar is subject to a fine of up to EUR 3418,79 in accordance with section 32 of Law 104(I)/03.

## II. Formalities of Marriage in Accordance with the Charter of the Orthodox Church

*158.* In order to solemnize a religious marriage according to the rites of the Greek Orthodox Church, both parties have to state their consent in writing before a member of the clergy of the Greek Orthodox Church; their consent must be genuine and complete in accordance with section 83 §1 of the 2010 Charter of the Orthodox Church. For a marriage to be performed the parties have to provide a certificate of birth, a certificate that they have not been married before and a marriage license by the Archdiocese or the Metropolis in the area of which the marriage shall be solemnized. If the future wife, or her mother, is a displaced person who resides in an Episcopal region different than the one where she stayed prior to 1974, two marriages licenses need to be issued; the future wife has to first receive a marriage license from the Archdiocese or the Metropolis where she resided prior to 1974 and present it to the offices of the Episcopal Region where the marriage is to be solemnized in order to receive the second marriage licence. The marriage is solemnized in the Orthodox Church before an Orthodox priest in accordance with the doctrines and rites of the Orthodox Church.

*159.* On 1 June 1983 the Church of Cyprus took an extremely important initiative for the premarital regulation of the health of future spouses, something that most Churches in other countries, disapprove of. In Cyprus several incidents of sickle cell anaemia are reported each year. The Holy Synod has decided that the spouses-to-be are also required to submit to the Church for the issuing of a license for the solemnization of a religious wedding ceremony, a certificate from a State-appointed doctor proving that they had been examined for sickle cell anaemia. Even when the test shows that the disease is present, the marriage can still be celebrated. The test aims exclusively at assisting the prospective spouses in making grave decisions, concerning the family that they will create.[193]

## §4. Effects of Marriage

*160.* Surprisingly the celebration of a marriage does not significantly change the legal status of a person. It could be argued that marriage presupposes cohabitation of the parties, although there are no legal provisions to this effect.[194] It is true that two married persons have a mutual obligation to maintain each other in accordance with section 3 of the Matrimonial Property of the Spouses Law 232/1991; however, marriage does not alter the independence of the property of the spouses. Furthermore, differences in the imposition of tax between married and unmarried persons have been declared as unconstitutional by the Supreme Court.[195] While Article 2 §7 of the Constitution somewhat anachronistically provides that the married woman shall belong in the Community of her spouse, such provision is of limited importance, since it has been held that Article 2 §7 applies only with respect to women who are citizens of the Republic,[196] and interracial marriages between members of the Greek and the Turkish Community have been extremely rare since 1960. There is a custom that many Cypriot women adopt the surname of their husbands; however, this is by no means legally required, nor universally adopted.

193. *Apostolos Varnavas* 44 (1983), 63–64.
194. S. Liasides, *Textbook of Family Law* (Nicosia, 2010, in Greek), 60.
195. *Panayides v. The Republic of Cyprus* [1965] 3 CLR 107.
196. *Demetriou v. Demetriou* [1991] 1 CLR 1153 (in Greek).

*161.* Section 14 of Evidence Law, Cap. 9 further provides that the spouse is competent but not compellable witness for the prosecution against the other spouse and both a competent and compellable witness for the prosecution against any other co-defendant of the other spouse A spouse is never a compellable witness with respect to anything that was communicated to him/her by his/her spouse during the marriage.[197]

## §5. Void and Voidable Marriages

### I. Void and Voidable Marriages in Accordance with Law 104(I)/2003

#### A. *Voidable Marriages*

*162.* Section 13 of Law 104(I)/03 provides that a marriage is defective and is subject to annulment, if it is void, voidable or void *ab initio*. In accordance with section 14 of Law 104(I)/03 a marriage is voidable if there is no free consent of any of the parties who intend to marry, namely if any of the parties: (i) have not completed 18 years of age (or exceptionally 16 years of age in accordance with the provisions of section 15 analysed above), (ii) are incapable of understanding and assessing the consequences of their actions due to a mental disorder or unsoundness of mind or due to a brain or other disease or illness or intoxication, (iii) married due to a mistake as to the identity of the other party; a mistake as to the attributes of the other party, for instance that he/she was rich or a well-known athlete, are not a ground of annulment or (iv) was forced to marry by duress. Duress is defined in section 14 §4 as any act or omission which may cause fear to an average reasonable person that either his/her life, honour, liberty, limb, or property or the life, honour, liberty, limb, or property of members of his/her family shall be subject to imminent and serious danger, or any legal, illegal or contrary to prevailing moral standards, acts or statements which cause fear to an average reasonable person, so long as he/she consents to marry because of such fear.

*163.* A voidable marriage may be annulled in accordance with section 21 §1 of Law 104(I)/03 by a judgment of the Family Court. The action for annulment may be filed by either of the parties if the grounds for annulment are that either of the parties had not completed the marriageable age, or was incapable of understanding the consequences of his/her actions within a limitation period of three years from the date that the marriage was celebrated. If the grounds for annulment are the mistake as to the identity of the other party, or duress, then the action for annulment may be filed by the party who was mistaken as to the identity of the other party or who was coerced into marrying, but not by such party's heirs; such an action must be filed before the lapse of six months from the date that the mistake is determined or duress ceased to exist.

---

197. N. Santis and T. Eliades, *The Law of Evidence: Substantial and Procedural Aspects* 2nd Edn (Nicosia: Hippasus, 2016, in Greek).

*164.* A voidable marriage may subsequently become a valid one, even prior to the lapse of the limitation periods, in accordance with section 16 of Law 104(I)/03, so long as: (i) the party who initially had concluded the marriage without free consent, subsequently freely and fully consents to the marriage, (ii) the incapable or underage person subsequently recognizes the marriage once it is capable or of marriageable age, (iii) the persons having parental responsibility who had not provided their consent to the marriage of a person over 16 years, but under 18 years, subsequently provide their written consent, or (iv) the party who was mistaken or coerced recognizes the validity of the marriage after the mistake is determined or duress ceased to exist, or the incapable person.

### *B. Void Marriages*

*165.* A marriage may be declared as void, in accordance with section 17 of Law 104(I)/03 if either party has already been validly married at the time of concluding the marriage, or if the parties are related within the fifth degree of consanguinity or the third degree of affinity, or if an adoptive child was married to either of the adoptive parents or their kin, or if the child born out of wedlock was married to his/her father and his/her father's relatives. A void marriage may be annulled by a judgment of the Family Court. The action for annulment may be filed by either of the parties or any other person having direct legal interest or the Republic of Cyprus; the action has to be filed before the lapse of a three-year limitation period from the date that the marriage was celebrated. Persons having direct legal interest to file an action for annulment are, in accordance with section 22 §4 of Law 104(I)/03, the parents, guardian or commissioner or administrator of the estate of a minor, as well as any person having the care and control of a person and his/her property, or the spouse from a pre-existing valid marriage, as well as any legitimate children from such a marriage, and any persons whose hereditary rights are being affected.

### *C. Null and Void ab Initio Marriages*

*166.* A marriage is further considered to be null and void *ab initio*, in accordance with section 19 of Law 104(I)/03, if: (i) it has not been solemnized by a registered Marriage Officer or religious minister, or (ii) if the parties had never read the declaration provided for in section 9 §1 of Law 104(I)/03 that they consent to the marriage, or (iii) if the marriage was celebrated despite the fact that a competent court had issued a prohibitive decree, or (iv) if the marriage was a marriage of convenience (sham marriage). A marriage of convenience is defined in section 9 §1 of Law 104(I)/03 as a marriage celebrated between a citizen of the Republic or a foreigner lawfully residing in the Republic on the one hand and a foreigner on the other hand, with the sole purpose that the foreigner enters and stays in the Republic.

*167.* A null and void *ab initio* marriage may be declared as such by a judgment of the Family Court. The action for annulment may be filed by either of the parties or any other person having direct legal interest or the Republic of Cyprus; the action has to be filed before the lapse of a three-year limitation period from the date that the marriage was celebrated. Persons having direct legal interest to file an action for annulment are, in accordance with section 22 §4 of Law 104(I)/03, the parents, guardian or commissioner or administrator of the estate of a minor, as well as any person having the care and control of a person and his/her property, or the spouse from a pre-existing valid marriage, as well as any legitimate children from such a marriage, and any persons whose hereditary rights are being affected.

### D. *Effect of Annulment*

*168.* Void and voidable marriages which are annulled by a judgment of the Family Court cease to have any legal effect whatsoever from the date of issue of the judgment annulling them in accordance with section 24 of Law 104(I)/03; thus, the effect of annulment is not retroactive. On the contrary, null and void *ab initio* marriages are considered to be null and void and to not have produced any effect retroactively. However, section 26 provides that the declaration of a null and void *ab initio* marriage shall not produce its effects retroactively with respect to the party who at the time of conclusion was unaware of the defectiveness of the marriage, or with respect to both parties if they both were unaware of the defectiveness of the marriage. If only one of the parties was unaware of the defectiveness of the marriage at the time of conclusion, such bona fide party is entitled to the rights he/she would have if a decree of divorce (instead of a declaration of annulment) had been issued; such rights may be enforced against the heirs of the deceased in case of death of the latter after the judgment for annulment is issued. Similarly, a party who was forced to conclude a marriage by duress, illegally or contrary to the prevailing morality, is entitled to the rights he/she would have if a decree of divorce had been issued in case that the other party died after the annulment of the marriage. In any event, children born out of a marriage that has either been annulled or declared null and void *ab initio*, maintain, in accordance with section 25 of Law 104(I)/03, the status of a child born in wedlock.

*169.* It should be noted that the provisions of section 23 §1 of Law 104(I)/03 which provides for a limitation period in case of void and null and void *ab initio* marriages, as well as section 18 §2 of Law 104(I)/03 which provides that the parties may declare before the Family Court that they consider their marriage as valid before such is annulled, are particularly problematic. Validating a marriage which has been concluded in violation of mandatory provisions, such as the prohibition of bigamy, or the prohibition of marriage between near members of kin, or marriages which had never been concluded before a registered Marriage Officer or a registered religious minister, is not, in our view, consistent with Cypriot public order. It is therefore submitted that the aforementioned provisions ought to be amended.[198]

198. G. Serghides, 'Observations on the Cypriot Marriage Law of 2003', *Armenopoulos* 58 (2003): 663 (in Greek), A. Emilianides, *The Cypriot Law of Marriage and Divorce* (Thessaloniki: Sakkoulas, 2006, in Greek), 240.

## II. Void and Voidable Marriages in Accordance with the Charter of the Orthodox Church

*170.* Since the requirements to perform a valid religious marriage according to the rites of the Greek Orthodox Church are provided in the Charter of the Orthodox Church, the grounds of nullity of such marriages are also provided in the Charter. Any marriage performed in violation of the provisions of the Charter concerning the religion on the parties, the existence of previous marriages, or the prohibited degrees of marriages, is null and void *ab initio.*[199] On the contrary, a marriage performed in violation of the provisions concerning marriageable age, or due to duress, or due to a mistake as to the identity of the person, is voidable; consequently, such a marriage will be considered valid, if the minor spouse becomes an adult without seeking the annulment of the marriage, or if the party who performed the marriage due to duress or lack of consent, subsequently recognizes the effect of the marriage.

199. For a detailed analysis of void and voidable marriages in accordance with ecclesiastical law *see* A. Emilianides, *The Cypriot Law of Marriage and Divorce* (Thessaloniki: Sakkoulas, 2006, in Greek): 313–321.

# Chapter 2. Divorce

## §1. Grounds

### I. Introduction

*171.* A marriage may be dissolved either by a decree of divorce,[200] or by the death of one of the parties. If the death occurred prior to the issue of the divorce decree, then the petition for divorce becomes moot. An interesting example of the interrelation between death and divorce is the first instance judgment of the Family Court in *Papaloizou*.[201] The Family Court had granted a decree of divorce; however, the defendant filed an appeal before the Appellate Family Court. While the appeal was pending, the Defendant-Appellant died. It was held that the marriage of the petitioner had been dissolved by the death of her husband which occurred on 17 August 1995 and not with the decree of divorce granted on 19 July 1995, in view of the fact that the decree had never become final.

*172.* The amended Article 111 §2 B of the Constitution provides that the ten grounds for divorce mentioned in the 1980 Charter of the Orthodox Church remain in force with respect to marriages of members of the Greek Orthodox Church; such grounds for divorce are the following: (a) adultery of the other party, (b) immoral or otherwise unacceptable conduct of the other party, so that the petitioner may no longer be expected to live with him/her, (c) intention of the other party to murder the petitioner, (d) insanity of the other party for at least three years, (e) conviction of the other party to imprisonment for a term of at least seven years, (f) disappearance of the other party for at least three years, (g) incapacity of the other party to consummate the marriage for at least six months after the celebration of the marriage, (h) desertion of the petitioner by the other party for at least two years, (i) change of religion by the other party, or (j) for insistently preventing child-bearing, despite the will of the petitioner. Thus, all grounds for divorce stipulated in the Charter of the Orthodox Church require that the defendant is at fault and that the petitioner is an innocent party.[202]

*173.* It is expressly stipulated that the grounds for divorce provided in the 1980 Charter of the Orthodox Church remain in force only to the extent that they are not

---

200. For an in-depth analysis of Cypriot divorce law *see* G. Serghides, *Grounds for Divorce* (Nicosia, 2007, v. I-II, in Greek), A. Emilianides, *The Cypriot Law of Marriage and Divorce* (Thessaloniki: Sakkoulas, 2006, in Greek): 243ff.

201. *Papaloizou v. Ioannou* [1998] 8 JSC 298 (in Greek), judgment of the Family Court of First Instance.

202. *See* in detail A. Emilianides, *The Cypriot Law of Marriage and Divorce* (Thessaloniki: Sakkoulas, 2006, in Greek): 250ff. *See* further Society of Lawyers of Northern Greece, *The Grounds for Divorce in accordance with Greek and Cypriot Law* (Thessaloniki: Sakkoulas, 1993 in Greek), L. Loucaides, 'Grounds for Divorce', *Cyprus Law Review* 4 (1983): 681–696 (in Greek), C. Tornaritis, *Divorce* (Nicosia, 1979, in Greek).

inconsistent with other provisions of the Constitution. Article 111 of the Constitution further introduced the ground of irretrievable breakdown rendering the continuation of the marital relationship intolerable for the petitioner, with respect to marriages of members of the Greek Orthodox Church. Irretrievable breakdown may occur, either due to the conduct of the defendant, or due to the conduct of both parties. Thus, contrary to what is provided in the Charter of the Orthodox Church, the ground of irretrievable breakdown may be proven even if both parties are at fault; however, divorce will not be granted if the only party who is at fault is the petitioner.[203]

*174.* It is further provided that the House of Representatives may establish any other grounds for divorce after hearing the views of the Orthodox Church of Cyprus;[204] it is accepted that the House of Representatives may enact the new grounds for divorce, even if the Orthodox Church disagrees. The House of Representatives eventually established new grounds for divorce with the promulgation of Law 46(I)/1999, which introduced as a ground for divorce the fact that the parties have lived apart for a period of at least five years immediately preceding the petition. The ground of the five-year separation of the parties does not depend upon proof of fault of either party, and was deemed to be constitutional in the case of *Zenios*.[205] Law 104(I)/2003 further introduced four other grounds for divorce, namely: (a) change of sex of the other party, (b) desertion of the petitioner, (c) intention of the other party to murder the petitioner, and (d) four-year separation, which, however, do not apply to marriages of members of the Orthodox Church of Cyprus.[206]

*175.* In view of the introduction of the ground for divorce of the irretrievable breakdown of the marriage, the separate existence of the ten grounds for divorce provided for in the 1980 Charter of the Orthodox Church was unnecessary, since such grounds for divorce are contained in the essence of the ground for divorce due to the irretrievable breakdown of the marriage. It has been correctly suggested that this dual existence of the ground of the irretrievable breakdown of the marriage and of the grounds of the 1980 Charter is a sign of legislative ambiguity between the intentions for a radical revision of Cypriot family law on the one hand and the political cost of such a radical revision on the other.[207] In practice, less than 1% of divorces are based upon the grounds provided for in the Charter of the Orthodox Church, while more than 90% of divorces are based upon the ground of the irretrievable breakdown of the marriage; the rest are mostly based upon the ground of

203. *See* G. Serghides, 'Grounds for Divorce under the Law of Cyprus: The Road to Europe', *Paneuropean Law Review* 1 (1997): 31–43.
204. *Ibid.*
205. *Zenios v. Zenios* [2002] 1 CLR 1175 (in Greek).
206. For criticism *see* G. Serghides, 'Observations on the Marriage Law of 2003', *Armenopoulos* 58 (2004): 674 (in Greek), A. Emilianides, *The Cypriot Law of Marriage and Divorce* (Thessaloniki: Sakkoulas, 2006, in Greek): 267–269.
207. E. Nicolaou, 'The Grounds for Divorce in Cypriot Family Law and recent Cypriot Case-Law', in Society of Lawyers of Northern Greece, *The Grounds for Divorce in Accordance with Greek and Cypriot Law* (Thessaloniki: Sakkoulas, 1993 in Greek): 127.

the five-year separation of the parties. However, despite the modernization of Cypriot divorce law, divorce by consent is still prohibited; this causes the parties to resort to mock adversary proceedings, whereby the defendant either defaults to appear or defaults to file a Defence, so that the petitioner may prove his/her case.[208]

## II. Grounds for Divorce before the Family Courts

*176.* The ten grounds for divorce of the Charter of the Orthodox Church, the ground of the irretrievable breakdown of the marriage and the ground of the five-year separation apply not only with respect to religious marriages of members of the Orthodox Church, but also with respect to civil marriages of members of the Orthodox Church, celebrated in Cyprus or abroad. This is due to the fact that Article 111 §2 B of the Constitution does not distinguish between civil and religious marriages of members of the Orthodox Church, but instead refers to all matters related to divorce of members of the Orthodox Church.[209] The aforementioned grounds for divorce further govern marriages celebrated in accordance with the doctrines and rites of the Greek Orthodox Church, if one of the parties is a member of the Greek Orthodox Church (and a citizen of the Republic) in accordance with the conjunction of Articles 22 §2 (a) and (c) and 111 of the Constitution.

*177.* Section 27 §3 of Law 104(I)/03 provides for four rebuttable and one irrebuttable presumption of the ground of irretrievable breakdown of the marriage; the ground of irretrievable breakdown is provided for in section 27 §2 of Law 104(I)/03 which is identical to Article 111 §2 B of the Constitution. It is particularly provided that the relations between the spouses shall be presumed to have been irretrievably broken down with the defendant being at fault, in cases of: (i) bigamy, (ii) adultery, (iii) desertion of the petitioner or (iv) intention of the other party to murder the petitioner. It is further provided that the four-year separation of the spouses forms an irrebuttable presumption that the marital relations have been irretrievably broken down, even if the claimant is at fault. It is noted that Law 104(I)/03 excludes from its scope religious marriages of members of the Greek Orthodox Church which were celebrated prior to the enactment of Law 104(I)/03, as well as religious marriages which were celebrated abroad. It is submitted that insofar as these presumptions refer to marriages of members of the Greek Orthodox Church, they are inconsistent with Article 111 §2 B of the Constitution; the ground of irretrievable breakdown is provided for in the Constitution and therefore it cannot be interpreted or amended with an ordinary law, but only with a law amending the Constitution.[210]

208. E. Nicolaou, 'Divorce: The Procedure', *Cyprus Law Review* 37 (1992): 5568–5569 (in Greek).
209. G. Serghides, 'Observations on the Marriage Law of 2003', *Armenopoulos* 58 (2004): 674 (in Greek) 673.
210. *See also* the reasoning in *Zenios v. Zenios* [2002] 1 CLR 1175 (in Greek), G. Serghides, 'Observations on the Marriage Law of 2003', *Armenopoulos* 58 (2004): 674 (in Greek) 672–673.

*178.* The grounds for divorce provided for in section 27 of Law 104(I)/03, namely the ground of irretrievable breakdown and its four rebuttable and one irrebuttable presumptions, as well as the four new grounds for divorce introduced by Law 104(I)/03 (change of sex of the other party, desertion of the petitioner, intention of the other party to murder the petitioner, and four-year separation) apply with respect to civil or religious marriages celebrated in accordance with the provisions of Law 104(I)/03 between persons who are not members of the Greek Orthodox Church or of a religious group. On the contrary the grounds provided for in section 14 of the Family Courts Law 23/90, namely the grounds provided for in Article 111 §2 B of the Constitution and the ground of the five-year separation of the spouses do not apply with respect to such marriages, since section 27 of Law 104(I)/03 is a subsequent and more specific provision compared to section 14 of Law 23/90 and thus, the principle *lex posterior specialis derogat lex anterior generalis* applies.[211]

*179.* The grounds for divorce provided for in section 27 of Law 104(I)/03 further apply with respect to civil marriages which had been celebrated in accordance with the Marriage Law 21/90 or Cap. 279 prior to the enactment of Law 104(I)/03. However, section 27 of Law 104(I)/03 does not apply with respect to religious marriages which had been celebrated in accordance with Cap. 279, or civil or religious marriages celebrated abroad; Law 104(I)/03 only applies with respect to marriages celebrated in Cyprus. Furthermore, the grounds of divorce provided for in section 27 of Cap. 104(I)/03 do not apply with respect to marriages between members of the Old Calendar Orthodox Church which were celebrated in accordance with the doctrines and rites of such Church pursuant to the provisions of the Marriage of Members of the Old Calendar Law 60(I)/94. The dissolution of religious marriages celebrated in accordance with Cap. 279 or Law 60(I)/94 or marriages celebrated abroad is governed by section 14 of the Family Courts Law 23/90; consequently, the grounds for divorce in such cases are the ten grounds of divorce provided for in the 1980 Charter, the ground of irretrievable breakdown of the marriage provided for in Article 111 §2 B of the Constitution (with no presumptions) and the ground of five-year separation of the spouses.

*180.* The application of the ten grounds for divorce of the Charter of the Orthodox Church with respect to the aforementioned cases, is of a purely theoretical nature, since the parties will most likely rely upon the grounds of either irretrievable breakdown or the five-year separation; however, providing that civil marriages between members of the Greek Orthodox Church, or civil or religious marriages of members of other religions or creeds, may be dissolved on the basis of grounds provided in the Charter of another religion, namely the Greek Orthodox Church, is undoubtedly not a sound approach.[212] In essence the application of the Cypriot law of marriage and divorce has become extremely complicated due to the attempt to regulate such a law on the basis of the religion of the parties. It is noted that the

211. G. Serghides, 'Observations on the Marriage Law of 2003', *Armenopoulos* 58 (2004): 674 (in Greek) 670.

212. *See* A. Emilianides, *The Cypriot Law of Marriage and Divorce* (Thessaloniki: Sakkoulas, 2006, in Greek): 248.

grounds provided in the 1980 Charter continue to apply as part of Cypriot divorce law, despite the fact that such Charter is no longer in force and has been replaced by the 2010 Charter which does not contain any grounds for divorce.

## III. The Grounds for Divorce of the Charter of the Orthodox Church

*181.* The amended Article 111 §2 B of the Constitution stipulates that the grounds for divorce which are provided for in the Charter of the Orthodox Church 'as such are in force at the date that the House of Representatives enacted the First Amendment of the Constitution Law of 1989' remain in force to the extent that they are not inconsistent with the Constitution. The Charter in force when Law 95/89 enacted was the 1980 Charter; therefore, the grounds for divorce referred in Article 111 §2 B are those contained in Article 225 of the 1980 Charter, as well as Articles 226–232 to the extent that such Articles contain provisions of substantive law and not procedural law.[213] All grounds for divorce stipulated in the 1980 Charter require that the defendant is at fault and this should always be taken into account while interpreting the ambit of such grounds.[214] The ten grounds of the 1980 Charter are briefly analysed in the subsequent paragraphs.

### *A. Adultery*

*182.* The first ground for divorce provided in Article 225 of the Charter is the adultery of the other spouse. Adultery is the willing sexual intercourse between a married person and a person of the opposite sex, thus violating marital faith.[215] Intercourse with another person as a result of rape, or while someone could not mentally appreciate his/her actions, is not a ground for divorce; consent and necessary capacity to form the intent to commit adultery are necessary elements of the notion of adultery. Sexual intercourse means penetration of the female by the male, however briefly. Sexual relations with a homosexual person or artificial insemination do not constitute adultery. The petition for divorce on grounds of adultery shall be dismissed if the petitioner continued to have marital relations with the adulterer even after the adultery was committed.

### *B. Immoral, Disgraceful or Otherwise Unacceptable Conduct*

*183.* The second ground for divorce provided in the Charter is the immoral or disgraceful or otherwise repeatedly occurring unacceptable conduct of the other

213. *See Thoma v. Thoma* [2001] 8 JSC 393 (Family Court, in Greek)and C. Melas, 'Grounds for Divorce in Cypriot Family Law', in Society of Lawyers of Northern Greece, *The Grounds for Divorce in accordance with Greek and Cypriot Law* (Thessaloniki: Sakkoulas, 1993 in Greek): 112.
214. *See Meittanis v. Charalambous* [1996] 7 JSC 434 (Family Court, in Greek).
215. Adultery was a criminal offence until 1 Jan. 1929 when the Criminal Law, Cap. 154 was enacted.

spouse so that the marital relation is gravely affected and it becomes unbearable for the petitioner to continue living with the spouse who is at fault. If the conduct of the defendant is immoral or disgraceful it need not be repeated; if, however, the conduct is only unacceptable, a notion which is morally less loaded, it should have occurred repeatedly. Grave insults, beatings, and attacks, as well as extramarital affairs which do not constitute adultery, might be considered as falling within the ambit of this ground for divorce. There needs to be causation between the immoral, disgraceful, or otherwise unacceptable conduct of the defendant and the deterioration of the marital relation. In order to determine whether it has become unbearable for the petitioner to continue living with the spouse who is at fault, the Court should take the personal conditions of the petitioner (education, lifestyle, character) into account.

*184.* The Charter further provides two presumptions which may be considered as gravely affecting the marital relation.[216] The first is if the wife stayed overnight at a house of a person who is not a relative without justification and without the consent of her husband, if this causes reasonable suspicions that the marital faith has been betrayed; if the husband also stayed overnight outside the matrimonial home, he may not rely upon such presumption. The second presumption is if the husband had accused the wife before a Court for adultery, if such adultery was not proved. It could be considered that the two presumptions are inconsistent with the principle of equality of the sexes safeguarded by Article 28 of the Constitution, since the first presumption might only be relied upon by the husband, while the second presumption might only be relied upon by the wife. The two presumptions might be considered as constitutional only if they applied both for the husband and the wife.

### C. *Intention to Murder*

*185.* The third ground for divorce provided in the Charter is the intention of the other spouse to murder the petitioner. Clearly, no actual murder should take place, because otherwise there would be no need for divorce. Any act or omission of a spouse with the aim of murdering the other spouse, such as an attempt, or preliminary acts like buying a gun or hiring a third party to murder the petitioner, would suffice; however, mere threats or inner thoughts would not be considered as an intention to murder. Only intentional acts are covered by this ground; thus, negligent acts are not a ground for divorce. It is further irrelevant whether the defendant intended to commit suicide after murdering the petitioner. Repeated grave bodily harm might be considered as falling within the ambit of this ground of divorce, if it may cause bodily or mental incapability to the other spouse. The divorce petition

216. T. Papazisi, 'The Reservation of Public Order in the Recognition of Decrees of Divorce between the Greek and Cypriot Legal Order', in Society of Lawyers of Northern Greece, *The Grounds for Divorce in accordance with Greek and Cypriot Law* (Thessaloniki: Sakkoulas, 1993 in Greek), 221.

shall be dismissed if the spouses resumed their normal marital life after the intention to murder took place, or if one year went by without any action on behalf of the petitioner.

### D. *Insanity*

*186.* The fourth ground for divorce provided in the Charter is the insanity of the other spouse if it continues for a period of at least three years and makes marital life unbearable; brief lucid intervals do not interrupt the three-year period. A spouse shall be considered to suffer from insanity if he/she suffers from permanent mental illness which makes it impossible for him/her to communicate and appreciate his/her marital obligations; the spouse may plead that the other spouse is insane even if there is no court decision to this effect. It is immaterial whether the insanity of the other spouse is curable or not.

### E. *Conviction to Imprisonment*

*187.* The fifth ground for divorce provided in the Charter is conviction of the other spouse to imprisonment for a term of at least seven years. While the offence committed by the other spouse is immaterial, a person may be imprisoned for seven years only if he/she has committed a felony; thus, the offence committed should have been a grave one. The imprisonment should be final and not subject to appeal. In accordance with Article 226 of the Charter, the petition for divorce may be filed only after two years from the conviction and so long as the other spouse still remains imprisoned.

### F. *Death in Absentia*

*188.* The sixth ground for divorce provided in the Charter is death *in absentia*. According to the prevailing view, death *in absentia* does not presuppose a judgment of the District Court to that effect;[217] however, if the missing person has been declared as dead *in absentia* by a judicial decree, such decree is binding upon the Family Courts and proves that the person has died *in absentia*.[218] In accordance with section 226 of the Charter, the petition for divorce may not be filed, unless three years have passed from the date that the other spouse disappeared and no news has been heard since about him/her.

217. C. Tornaritis, *Divorce* (Nicosia, 1979, in Greek): 18–19. However, the majority of the Family Court held in *Thoma v. Thoma* [2001] 8 JSC 393 (in Greek) that death *in absentia* should have been declared by a competent court.

218. L. Loucaides, 'Grounds for Divorce', *Cyprus Law Review* 4 (1983): 681–696 (in Greek).

### G. Incapacity to Consummate

*189.* The seventh ground for divorce provided in the Charter is the incapacity of the other spouse to consummate the marriage, so long as the other spouse is incapable to consummate the marriage at the time of celebration of the marriage and such incapacity continues for at least six months and until the time the petition is filed. Incapacity to consummate at any time after the marriage was celebrated does not constitute a ground for divorce.

### H. Desertion

*190.* The eighth ground for divorce provided in the Charter is the unreasonable desertion of the petitioner by the other spouse for at least two years; repeated unreasonable lengthy acts of desertion which are over two years fulfil the requirements for desertion to occur. Desertion may consist of desertion of the matrimonial home, refusal to move to the new matrimonial home which was jointly decided by the parties, or constructive desertion in the sense that the petitioner is essentially forced to leave the matrimonial home through the use of physical or psychological force.[219] If both parties work or have earning capacity in order to maintain their family, deserting the matrimonial home in order to work in another place might be justified only if the other spouse consents in accordance with Article 229 of the Charter.

*191.* If, however, only one of the spouses work or has earning capacity, deserting the matrimonial home might be justified without the consent of the other spouse, but only in cases of compulsory transfer or where the income of the spouses is not sufficient and the new place of work offers more and better chances for maintaining the family (Article 230 of the Charter). Desertion shall not be considered as unreasonable if the treatment of the other spouse by the petitioner has been humiliating.[220] The provision of the Charter according to which the deserted spouse should have called the other spouse at least once, through the competent bishop, to return to the matrimonial home, in order for the divorce petition to be filed, refers to a matter of procedural law and thus is not applied by the Family Courts; in any event, the attempt for reconciliation is exclusively governed by the provisions of Law 22/90.[221]

219. For example. *Meittanis v. Charalambous* [1996] 7 JSC 434 (Family Court, in Greek).
220. For example *Coullouros v. Coullourou* [1989] 1 CLR 50 (in Greek).
221. *Solonos v. Charalambous*, *Cyprus Law Review* 43–44 [1993]: 6599 (in Greek). *See*, however, the opposite views expressed by C. Melas, 'Grounds for Divorce in Cypriot Family Law', in Society of Lawyers of Northern Greece, *The Grounds for Divorce in accordance with Greek and Cypriot Law* (Thessaloniki: Sakkoulas, 1993 in Greek), 105ff.

### *I. Change of Religion*

*192.* The ninth ground for divorce provided in the Charter is the change of religion or doctrine by the other spouse, or the exercise of violence and the attempt of the other spouse to proselytize the petitioner or their minor children to another religion or rite, or to force them to renounce Orthodox faith. In accordance with the prevailing view this ground for divorce is unconstitutional, since it is inconsistent with Article 18 §4 of the Constitution which safeguards the right to change one's religious beliefs and more generally to Article 18 which safeguards the right to religious freedom. While the change of one's religion might be an element of the ground for divorce of the irretrievable breakdown of the marriage, it is not accepted that it could form an independent ground for divorce.[222]

### *J. Preventing Child-Bearing*

*193.* The tenth and final ground for divorce provided in the Charter is if the other spouse insistently prevents child-bearing despite the will of the petitioner.[223] If, however, such prevention is only for a limited period of time, or is due to the fact that the spouses have already given birth to a number of children, it is accepted that there is no ground for divorce.

## IV. The Ground of Irretrievable Breakdown of the Marriage

*194.* In accordance with Article 111 §2 B b of the Constitution, there is a ground for divorce if the marital relationship between the spouses has been irretrievably broken down due to the conduct of the defendant or due to the conduct of both parties, so that the continuation of the marital relationship has been rendered intolerable for the petitioner. The ground of irretrievable breakdown thus consists of the following elements: (i) the existence of an event which causes the breakdown which is due to the conduct of the defendant or of both spouses, (ii) causation between the event and the irretrievable breakdown of the marriage and (iii) the continuation of the marital relationship has been rendered intolerable for the petitioner because of the irretrievable breakdown.[224]

*195.* The first element of the ground for divorce is the existence of an event which causes the breakdown which is due to the conduct of the defendant or of both

---

222. T. Papazisi, 'The Reservation of Public Order in the Recognition of Decrees of Divorce between the Greek and Cypriot Legal Order', in Society of Lawyers of Northern Greece, *The Grounds for Divorce in accordance with Greek and Cypriot Law* (Thessaloniki: Sakkoulas, 1993 in Greek), 223.
223. E. Nicolaou, 'The Grounds for Divorce in Cypriot Family Law and recent Cypriot Case-Law', in Society of Lawyers of Northern Greece, *The Grounds for Divorce in accordance with Greek and Cypriot Law* (Thessaloniki: Sakkoulas, 1993 in Greek), 129.
224. A. Emilianides, *The Cypriot Law of Marriage and Divorce* (Thessaloniki: Sakkoulas, 2006, in Greek), 259ff.

spouses: such event may be, depending on the circumstances, an act such as a beating, an omission such as the unreasonable omission to contribute to the family burdens, or even a situation such as incapacity to consummate. An indicative list of such events might include the ten grounds for divorce of the 1980 Charter of the Orthodox Church of Cyprus, as well as bigamy, abortion, refusal to consummate, mutual distrust and contempt of the spouses for each other which was expressed by grave insults,[225] incompatibility of temperaments, violence, grave insults which are offensive for the personality and dignity of the spouse,[226] the unreasonable jealousy of the other spouse who tends to consider that there are immoral intentions to every act of the petitioner,[227] the behaviour of the other spouse who returned late to the matrimonial home from work so as to cause suspicions that he/she has extramarital relations,[228] sexual disharmony of the couple,[229] etc.

*196.* While the overreaction of a spouse to the behaviour of the other spouse should in principle be avoided, however, it is not by itself an event which causes the breakdown of the marital relationship, unless the spouse overreacted to such an extent and form that his/her overreaction might cause the breakdown separately from the event that caused such (over)reaction. In the case of *Koufallides* it was held that the fact that the Appellant engaged in disputes with the Respondent was a reaction towards the behaviour of the Respondent and could not be considered on its own as an event causing the breakdown, even if such reaction might be considered as excessive.[230] The event which causes the breakdown should be due to the conduct of the defendant or both spouses. If the event is due to the conduct of the petitioner[231] (such as the petitioner's extramarital affair), or of third parties (such as the behaviour of the relatives of the defendant who are not directed by him/her), then the divorce cannot be granted. The percentage or degree of fault of each spouse, if they are both at fault, is immaterial; the only thing that matters is that they should be both (or only the defendant) at fault for the event which causes the breakdown.[232]

*197.* The second element of the ground for divorce is that there has to be causation between the event and the irretrievable breakdown of the marriage. A breakdown is considered to be irretrievable if it undermines the foundations of the marriage, namely the 'belief of the spouses to the aims of the institutions of marriage, their commitment to the pursuit of such objectives and their mutual respect'.[233] When from the evidence presented before the Court, there are events

225. *Zachariou v. Zachariou* [1993] 1 CLR 159 (in Greek).
226. *Ibid.*
227. *Leonidou v. Leonidou* [1993] 1 CLR 986 (in Greek).
228. *Ibid.*
229. *Lambrianides v. Lambrianides* [1996] 7 JSC 477 (Family Court, in Greek).
230. *Koufallides v. Koufallides* [1994] 1 CLR 782 (in Greek).
231. *Neocleous v. Sofocleous* [1994] 1 CLR 707 (in Greek).
232. *Christoforou v. Christoforou* [1998] 8 JSC 378 (Family Court, in Greek) and *Charalambous v. Charalambous* [1996] 7 JSC 452 (Family Court, in Greek).
233. *Zachariou v. Zachariou* [1993] 1 CLR 159 (in Greek).

which might have caused the breakdown which is due to the conduct of the defendant, and events which are due to the conduct of both spouses, the Family Court should decide as a matter of fact which event was the actual cause of the irretrievable breakdown of the marriage.[234] In the case of *Loucaides* the Appellate Family Court held that the disclosure by the Respondent to the Appellant that she was an adopted daughter of her parents could not be considered as the event which caused the irretrievable breakdown of the marriage, because the Appellant had already requested from the Respondent to leave the matrimonial home; consequently the event which caused the breakdown could not logically be such disclosure.[235]

*198.* The Court should determine whether there is causation between the event and the irretrievable breakdown by examining the principal event which is claimed to have caused the breakdown and not by attempting to evaluate the entire marital relationship of the parties. In the case of *Orthodoxou* it was held that the first instance Family Court ought to restrict itself at the determination of the principal event which was claimed to have caused the breakdown, namely the allegation of the Respondent that his wife threw him out of the matrimonial home and that this caused the breakdown. Since the Family Court had dismissed such allegation, it should not have additionally evaluated the full range of the marital relations of the spouses.[236] An isolated event may be so important so as to cause the irretrievable breakdown of the marriage; however, it might be that irretrievable breakdown is not due to an event which happened instantly, but to a continuous situation, as in the case where the event consists of incompatibility of temperaments.[237]

*199.* The third element of the ground for divorce is that the continuation of the marital relationship should have been rendered intolerable for the petitioner because of the irretrievable breakdown. The Supreme Court has held that the reasonable third person is the standard for evaluating the behaviour of the spouses and whether the event causing the irretrievable breakdown of the marriage could have reasonably rendered the marital relationship intolerable for the petitioner.[238] It is probably more accurate if one considers the standard as both a subjective and an objective one. The character, education, professional and social relations and other personal characteristics of the claimant have to be considered by the Court in order to decide whether the event causing the irretrievable breakdown could objectively have rendered the marital relationship intolerable for a reasonable third person who has the personal characteristics of the claimant.[239]

234. *Ibid.*
235. *Loucaides v. Petropoulos* [2000] 1 CLR 1619 (in Greek).
236. *Orthodoxou v. Orthodoxou* [1997] 1 CLR 501 (in Greek).
237. *Sofroniou v. Pantazis* [1998] 1 CLR 805 (in Greek).
238. *Ibid.*
239. A. Emilianides, *The Cypriot Law of Marriage and Divorce* (Thessaloniki: Sakkoulas, 2006, in Greek), 262.

## V. The Ground of the Five-Year Separation

*200.* The House of Representatives introduced the ground for divorce of the five-year separation of the spouses by Law 46(I)/1999, which amended section 14 (a) of the Family Courts Law 23/90. The amended section 14 (a) of Law 23/90 stipulates that the Family Court shall apply in the adjudication of divorce petitions the law which is provided in Article 111 §2 (B) of the Constitution:

> *provided that the continuous separation of the spouses for at least five years constitutes an irretrievable breakdown of the marital relationship and the divorce may be issued, even if the event which caused the irretrievable breakdown is due to the conduct of the claimant. The completion of the five year period is not affected by brief intervals which took place as part of the attempt to reconcile the spouses if such intervals do not exceed six months in total.*

*201.* The ground of the five-year separation of the spouses is a no-fault ground for divorce; the objective fact of the separation of the spouses for a period of five years amounts to an irrebuttable presumption that the marriage has irretrievably broken down and that a decree of divorce should be granted.[240] The only crucial element to be proven is that the parties have separated in the sense that they no longer live together as spouses. It is generally accepted that there are cases where a married couple cohabitates, but does not live together because the spouses have no psychological or physical relationship, in which cases the spouses shall be considered as having separated despite the cohabitation;[241] of course at some point the parties simply shall have to stop cohabitation, since it would be unreasonable to claim that the parties have been separated for five years if they have been cohabitating during this entire period.

*202.* In the case of *Zenios* it was argued that Law 46(I)/99 is unconstitutional, because its purpose was not to introduce a new ground for divorce, but rather to amend the ground for divorce of the irretrievable breakdown of the marriage which is provided in Article 111 of the Constitution; if its purpose was to amend the ground of irretrievable breakdown, then a constitutional amendment ought to have taken place. It was therefore suggested that the fact that the relevant provision of Law 46(I)/99 begins with the term 'provided' should lead to the conclusion that the purpose of the legislator was to authentically interpret Article 111 of the Constitution and not to introduce a new separate ground for divorce.[242] The Supreme Court rejected such arguments and held that the House of Representatives had clearly expressed its legislative intention of introducing a new ground for divorce, irrespective of the manner in which such intention was expressed. Consequently, it was held that Law 46(I)/99 was constitutional.

---

240. *Zenios v. Zenios* [2002] 1 CLR 1175 (in Greek).
241. *Pichides v. Pichides* [1997] 1 CLR 1612 (in Greek).
242. *Zenios v. Zenios* [2002] 1 CLR 1175 (in Greek).

## VI. Grounds for Divorce and Presumptions in Law 104(I)/03

*203.* Section 27 §4 of Law 104(I)/03 stipulates four new grounds for divorce. The first three, namely (i) change of sex of the other spouse, (ii) desertion of the petitioner by the other spouse and (iii) intention of the other spouse to murder the petitioner, require that the defendant is at fault, while the fourth, namely the ground of the four-year separation of the parties, is a no-fault ground for divorce. The grounds of desertion and intention to murder essentially reiterate the grounds provided in the Charter of the Orthodox Church and are contained in the ground of the irretrievable breakdown of the marriage. Thus, it is difficult to understand the reasoning for their introduction. The ground of change of sex clearly intends to cover the cases of transsexuals, namely of persons who have changed their sex following surgical operation; however, again such ground is contained in the ground of the irretrievable breakdown of the marriage and it is difficult to appreciate why there was a need for it to be introduced also as a separate ground for divorce.

*204.* The fourth ground of the four-year separation of the spouses essentially reiterates the provisions of Law 46(I)/99 concerning the five-year separation of the spouses. It is provided that it is irrebuttably presumed that the relationship between the spouses has irretrievably broken down due to the conduct of both spouses and that the continuation of the marital relationship has been rendered intolerable for the claimant, if the spouses have been separated for a period of four years; the completion of the four-year period is not affected by brief intervals which took place as part of the attempt to reconcile the spouses if such intervals do not exceed six months in total. Notwithstanding the fact that the legislator defines a ground for divorce by referencing an 'irrebuttable presumption', as well as the fact that it unnecessarily provided that the four-year separation would amount to irretrievable breakdown due to the conduct of both spouses, what is highly perplexing is why the legislator introduced two separate grounds for divorce, one providing for a ground of four-year separation, and the other providing for a ground of five-year separation.[243]

*205.* Even more perplexing is the fact that the legislator has introduced with section 27 §3 of Law 104(I/)/03 four rebuttable and one irrebuttable presumption of the ground of irretrievable breakdown of the marriage. The rebuttable presumptions are: (i) bigamy, (ii) adultery, (iii) desertion of the claimant, and (iv) intention of the other spouse to murder the claimant, while the irrebuttable presumption is the four-year separation of the parties. What was the need of introducing such rebuttable presumptions of the ground for divorce of the irretrievable breakdown of the marriage, especially when two out of the four rebuttable presumptions, namely intention to murder and desertion have been also introduced with section 27 §4 of Law 104(I)/03 as separate grounds for divorce and when adultery is a separate ground for divorce in accordance with the Charter of the Orthodox Church? What was the need

243. G. Serghides, 'Observations on the Marriage Law of 2003', *Armenopoulos* 58 (2004): 674 (in Greek) 674, A. Emilianides, *The Cypriot Law of Marriage and Divorce* (Thessaloniki: Sakkoulas, 2006, in Greek), 267ff.

of introducing the irrebuttable presumption of the four-year separation of the parties when Law 46(I)/99 introduced the five-year separation as a separate ground of divorce and when section 27 §3 of Law 104(I)/03 introduced the identical ground of the four-year separation as a separate ground for divorce (using also the term irrebuttable presumption)? It is submitted that the drafting of Law 104(I)/03 is highly problematic.

## VII. Grounds for Divorce before the Family Courts of Religious Groups

*206.* The grounds for divorce with respect to marriages for which the Family Courts of Religious Groups have jurisdiction (religious marriages which have been celebrated in accordance with the tenets and rules of a religious group, regardless of whether such marriages are mixed or not, and civil marriages which have been celebrated between persons belonging to the same religious group) are provided for in Annex A of the Family Courts (Religious Groups) Law 87(I)/94. These include the ground of irretrievable breakdown of the marriage, as well as eight of the grounds provided in the Charter of the Orthodox Church, not including the grounds of change of religion and immoral or otherwise unacceptable conduct. It should be noted that there are some minor changes in the application of the eight grounds provided in the Charter of the Orthodox Church: (i) the period during which the petitioner must have continued to have marital relations with the defendants for the petition for adultery to be dismissed is set at six months after adultery was committed, (ii) instead of the ground of the intention to murder the petitioner, it is provided that repeated violence against the petitioner or his/her children is a ground of divorce, (iii) conviction to imprisonment for six months is a sufficient ground of divorce if the offence was the act of violence against the petitioner, (iv) the ground of incapacity to consummate the marriage presupposes that the petitioner was unaware of the incapacity prior to the conclusion of the marriage, v) repeated unreasonable lengthy acts of desertion which are over two years, should have occurred within a period of four years.

*207.* The ground of five-year separation of the parties may not be pleaded before the Family Courts of the Religious Groups. In addition to the above, grounds of nullity according to the canon law of the three religious groups are also – inexplicably – treated as grounds for divorce. The four rebuttable and one irrebuttable presumption of the ground of irretrievable breakdown of the marriage introduced with section 27 §3 of Law 104(I)/03 may be relied upon in cases where a civil marriage has been celebrated between persons belonging to the same religious group in Cyprus after the enactment of Law 104(I)/03; the presumptions do not apply in civil marriages celebrated abroad, or in religious marriages, or in civil marriages celebrated in Cyprus prior to the enactment of Law 104(I)/03.[244]

244. G. Serghides, 'Observations on the Marriage Law of 2003', *Armenopoulos* 58 (2004): 674 (in Greek) 674–675.

## VIII. Grounds for Divorce before the District Courts

*208.* In those cases where the Presidents of the District Court have jurisdiction to adjudicate divorce petitions, namely with respect to divorce proceedings of marriages of members of the Turkish Cypriot Community celebrated in Cyprus in accordance with the provisions of Law 104(I)/03 (or Cap. 279), the grounds for divorce are those provided in English law which applied in Cyprus prior to Independence in accordance to sections 19 (b), 29 §2 (b) and 29 §3 of the Courts of Justice Law 14/60 and section 33 §2 of the Courts of Justice Law, Cap. 8; thus, the provisions of the English Matrimonial Causes Act, 1950 and the common law principles apply.[245] There are four grounds for divorce which may be relied upon by either of the spouse and three additional grounds which may be relied upon only by the wife. The grounds for divorce which may be relied upon by either of the spouse are: (i) adultery, (ii) desertion, (iii) legal cruelty and (iv) insanity, while the grounds which may be relied upon only by the wife are: (i) rape, (ii) sodomy and (iii) bestiality. There is admittedly no justification why such anachronistic English law of 1950 ought to apply to divorce proceedings which are adjudicated more than sixty years later. The aforementioned grounds for divorce have been considered in several cases of the Supreme Court and some additional comments are cited below.

*209.* With respect to adultery it has been held that the testimony of the petitioner by itself is not sufficient to prove adultery and that corroborative evidence is needed, either by producing an eyewitness or circumstantial evidence.[246] The fact that the other spouse refused to accompany his/her spouse to professional trips and was indifferent towards him/her,[247] the fact that the defendant cohabitated with another person of the opposing sex,[248] and the fact that the other spouse has given birth to a child whose parent could not possibly be the petitioner,[249] have all been considered as sufficient corroborative evidence of adultery. The Court should be satisfied that there is no collusion between the parties;[250] however, the mere fact that both spouses wish for the marriage to be dissolved does not amount to collusion. One interesting case that has to be noted is *Solomou* in which the Supreme Court held that a divorce decree should be granted both due to the adultery of the wife and cruelty of the husband.[251]

245. For a detailed analysis *see* A. Emilianides, *The Cypriot Law of Marriage and Divorce* (Thessaloniki: Sakkoulas, 2006, in Greek), 269ff, G. Serghides, 'Civil Substantive Law with Respect to the Dissolution of Marriage', *Kypriaki Martyria* 8 (1989): 54–58 (in Greek).
246. *Moring v. Moring* [1967] 1 CLR 256, *Nicou v. Nicou and Wood* [1966] 1 CLR 106, *Holroyd v. Holroyd and Zisimos* [1979] 1 CLR 206, *Bailie v. Bailie and Filippou* [1966] 1 CLR 283, *Cosgrove v. Cosgrove* [1964] 1 CLR 77.
247. *Branco v. Branco* [1967] 1 CLR 302.
248. *Mouzouris v. Mouzouris and Piotrowska* [1981] 1 CLR 1.
249. *Holroyd v. Holroyd and Adonis* [1981] 1 CLR 122.
250. *Nicou v. Nicou and Wood* [1966] 1 CLR 106. *Simonds v. Simonds and Harbottle* [1969] 1 CLR 596, *Betts v. Betts and Antoniou* [1983] 1 CLR 227.
251. *Solomou v. Solomou* [1979] 1 CLR 101.

*210.* Desertion should continue for a period of three years prior to the filing of the divorce petition.[252] Such desertion should have been unreasonable.[253] The notion of desertion includes constructive desertion whereby the petitioner is forced to desert the matrimonial home due to the conduct of the other spouse, as in cases where the petitioner was humiliated by the other spouse.[254] Legal cruelty should have been such so as to cause injury or danger to life or limb or health of either spouse or reasonable fear or apprehension for cause of such injury or danger.[255] For the behaviour of a spouse to be considered as cruel, it should be such that the other spouse should not reasonably be expected to tolerate; isolated acts of violence might be sufficient for divorce to be granted on the ground of cruelty[256] The persistent prevention of child-bearing,[257] false and persistent allegations that the petitioner had committed adultery,[258] or dangerous behaviour by the drunk spouse[259] have all been considered, depending upon the circumstances, to cause legal cruelty. With respect to insanity, this should have continued for a period of five years prior to the filing of the divorce petition. Rape, sodomy or bestiality may be proven even if the other spouse has not been convicted by the Assize Court for criminal offence.

## §2. Procedure

### I. Attempt of Reconciliation of Religious Marriages

*211.* Article 111 §1 of the Constitution stipulates that a law shall provide for the spiritual dissolution of the marriage and for the attempt of reconciliation before a bishop; such Laws are the Attempt of Reconciliation and Spiritual Dissolution of the Marriage Law 22/1990 with respect to religious marriages celebrated according

252. *Kaprielian v. Kaprielian* [1963] 2 CLR 143, *Keondjian v. Keondjian* [1964] CLR 93, *Theocharides v. Theocharides* [1965] 1 CLR 1, *Koutsoftides v. Koutsoftides* [1970] 1 CLR 356, *Eliades v. Eliades* [1965] 1 CLR 387, *Lunn v. Lunn* [1968] 1 CLR 247, *Tellalian v. Tellalian* [1967] 1 CLR 320, *Makrides v. Makrides* [1968] 1 CLR 241, *Wright v. Wright* [1968] 1 CLR 34, *Andrew v. Andrew* [1968] 1 CLR 237, *Krzentz v. Krzentz* [1971] 1 CLR 211.
253. *Hadjiyiannis v. Hadjiyiannis* [1979] 1 CLR 227, *Merheb v. Merheb* [1980] 1 CLR 531, *Eleftheriou v. Charalambous* [1980] 1 CLR 600, *Abul – Hawa v. Abul – Hawa* [1980] 1 CLR 135, *Avraam v. Avraam* [1979] 1 CLR 661, *Catlin v. Catlin* [1982] 1 CLR 117, *Papa Alexandrou v. Andreou* [1970] 1 CLR 297, *Ioakim v. Lopex Orihuels* [1981] 1 CLR 357.
254. *Nearchou v. Nearchou* [1974] 1 CLR 124, *Benjafield v. Benjafield* [1979] 1 CLR 665, *Tourian v. Tourian* [1965] 1 CLR 127, *Christodoulou v. Christodoulou* [1981] 1 CLR 531, *Petrides v. Petrides* [1965] 1 CLR 252.
255. *See Levonian v. Levonian* [1965] 1 CLR 339, *Soteriou v. Soteriou* [1966] 1 CLR 200, *Peratikos v. Peratikos* [1979] 1 CLR 41, *Terezopoulou v. Terezopoulos* [1979] 1 CLR 165, *Orphanides v. Michael* [1980] 1 CLR 527, *Morphi v. Mashini* [1981] 1 CLR 253, *Jabbour v. Jabbour* [1981] 1 CLR 315, *Economides v. Economides* [1979] 1 CLR 610, *Tooley v. Tooley* [1984] 1 CLR 279, *Skoullou v. Skoullos* [1983] 1 CLR 865.
256. *Dunne v. Dunne* [1966] 1 CLR 164, *Lazarou v. Lazarou* [1968] 1 CLR 334, *Darmanin v. Darmanin* [1962] CLR 264, *Iacovou v. Iacovou* [1984] 1 CLR 350, *Charalambous v. Charalambous* [1968] 1 CLR 347, *Bastadjian v. Bastadjian* [1962] CLR 308.
257. *Sibirzeff v. Sibirzeff* [1984] 1 CLR 172.
258. *Benjafield v. Benjafield* [1979] 1 CLR 665.
259. *Joseph v. Riviere* [1982] 1 CLR 95.

to the rites of the Orthodox Church and sections 13–19 of the Family Courts (Religious Groups) Law 87 (I)/1994 with respect to religious marriages celebrated according to the rites of the three religious groups of the Republic. There is no need of attempt of reconciliation or of a spiritual dissolution of civil marriages, or religious marriages which were not celebrated according to the rites of the Orthodox Church or the three religious groups; persons who have celebrated marriages other than religious marriages according to the rites of the Orthodox Church or the three religious groups may thus directly file an action for divorce before the Family Court.

*212.* According to Law 22/1990, the person who intends to file a petition for the dissolution of a religious marriage celebrated according to the rites of the Orthodox Church must first notify the bishop of the habitual residence of either party of such an intention; the notification should be sent by double-registered letter and should be in accordance with Form A of Law 22/90 or Form B of Law 87(I)/94 and provide the personal details of the spouses, when and where their marriage was celebrated and all or some of the grounds of divorce that the person sending the notification intends to rely upon. The dispatch of the notification may be proved by the submission to the Registrar of the Family Court of the proof of the receipt of the double-registered letter by the bishop. There is, however, no need to send a notification if the grounds of divorce relied upon are the fact that the other spouse has died *in absentia*, or is insane, since in such cases there can be no attempt of reconciliation.

*213.* No petition for a divorce may be filed unless the competent bishop provides the petitioner with a certificate that there has been an attempt of reconciliation which has failed, or if three months have lapsed from the date when the notification was received by the bishop. After the lapse of the three-month period, any party (including the party who did not send a notification) may file the petition for a divorce. In case where a party has not complied with the requirements of Law 22/1990, the petition shall be dismissed as premature.[260] If the notification had not been sent to the bishop of the habitual residence of either party, but to a different bishop, it is considered that the requirements of Law 22/1990 have not been complied with; in the case of *Papapetrou* the petition was dismissed because the notification had been sent to the bishop of Salamis, despite the fact that the bishop of the habitual residence of the parties was the Metropolitan of Limassol.[261] The Appellate Family Court held that the criterion of the habitual residence of either party is not legal and abstract, but a factual and practical matter, and held that the bishop of Salamis was not competent in accordance with Articles 2 and 3 of Law 22/90.

*214.* The geographical limits of the Archdiocese, as well as the Metropolises of Paphos, Kition, Kyrenia, Limassol, Morphou, Constantia and Famagusta, Kykkou and Tylliria, Tamasou and Oreinis and Trimythountos, are determined in Annex A of the 2010 Charter of the Orthodox Church. Upon receiving the notification the

260. *Zeniou v. Zeniou* [2002] 1 CLR 1175 (in Greek).
261. *Papapetrou v. Papapetrou* [2001] 1 CLR 1578 (in Greek).

bishop should invite by written notification both spouses to appear in person before him and then attempt to reconcile them with all the appropriate, at his discretion, spiritual means, in accordance with section 4 of Law 22/90; the means employed by the bishop may not be judicially reviewed. In practice the Orthodox Church of Cyprus was not attempting any reconciliation of the marriage up to 2010, since it did not recognize the jurisdiction of the Family Courts; instead it was sending a formal letter whose text was determined by the Holy Synod on 2 May 1991 and which informed the parties that the Family Courts have no jurisdiction to dissolve a marriage which was celebrated in accordance with the rites of the Orthodox Church.

*215.* Ever since the enactment of its new Charter in 2010, however, the Orthodox Church attempts the reconciliation of all religious marriages celebrated according to its rites. Section 87 of the 2010 Charter provides that prior to the spiritual dissolution of the marriage and consequently the petition for divorce, there should be an attempt of reconciliation of the spouses before the bishop of the habitual residence of either spouse in Cyprus; no attempt of reconciliation should take place if the ground for divorce is the death *in absentia* or insanity of the other party. If due to exceptional circumstances it is impossible for one of the spouses to participate in the attempt for reconciliation, the bishop may waive it. Attempt for reconciliation is not considered by the Church as a judicial or legal act, but rather a demonstration of the pastoral care and responsibility of the Church. A person has to appear in person before the bishop, or an experienced priest who has been authorized by the bishop to conduct the attempt for reconciliation. The attempt for reconciliation has to be completed within a period of three months.

*216.* It has been disputed whether a new notification is required in cases where a second petition of divorce is filed, presumably after the withdrawal or dismissal of the first. In the *Zenios* case the petitioner requested that his marriage be dissolved on the grounds of a five-year separation of the spouses in accordance with the provisions of Law 46(I)/99.[262] The Family Court held that the requirements of Law 22/90 have been complied with in view of the notification sent to the bishop with regard to a previous petition for divorce, which had been dismissed by the Family Court, and in accordance to which the petitioner claimed that his marriage should be dissolved due to irretrievable breakdown. The Appellate Family Court reversed the first instance decision and held that the notification sent to the bishop referred to different grounds of divorce than the ones on the basis of which the decree for dissolution of the marriage was granted; while it is true that Form A of Law 22/90 provides that the notification may include simply certain of the grounds on which the petition for divorce is based, it could not be claimed that the ground of five-year separation of the spouses, introduced with the subsequent Law 46(I)/99, could be covered by the notification which was sent at a time when Law 46(I)/99 had not been yet enacted. Consequently, a second notification ought to have been sent to the competent bishop; the petition for divorce had been prematurely filed.

262. *Zeniou v. Zeniou* [2002] 1 CLR 1175 (in Greek).

*217.* It is disputed whether *Zenios* has introduced a requirement that the petition for divorce must necessarily rely upon the grounds of divorce mentioned in the notification sent to the bishop in accordance with the provisions of Law 22/90. In the first instance case of *Gregoriou*, which was decided prior to *Zenios*, it was held that the party to the divorce proceedings is not obliged to rely upon the grounds of divorce mentioned in the notification, since in any event it would be unreasonable to bind the advocate who is to represent the case before the Family Court by a notification sent by the party himself/herself who does not necessarily have legal knowledge.[263] It is submitted that the approach of *Gregoriou* should be adopted. If the legislator intended for the petitioner to rely upon the grounds of divorce mentioned in the notification, it would be required to present a copy of the notification before the Family Court, instead of simply a proof of the receipt of the registered letter by the bishop; in addition Form A of Law 22/90 would not expressly refer to the possibility of including only certain of the grounds of divorce in the notification. *Zenios* should therefore be restricted to cases where the grounds of divorce relied upon were enacted subsequently to the receipt of the notification by the bishop.[264]

*218.* With respect to the three religious groups of the Republic sections 13–19 of Law 87(I)/1994 provide that the notification must be sent to the competent religious leader of the respective religious group of the parties. However, no notification needs to be sent in cases where a decree of divorce is not recognized by the canon law of the respective religious group; thus, no notification needs to be sent in cases of dissolution of marriages of members of either the Roman Catholic religious group or the Maronite religious group. No notification needs to be sent if the ground of divorce to be relied upon is death *in absentia*, or insanity of the other spouse, or a ground for annulment of the marriage. In view of the above, a notification need only be sent in the case of marriages celebrated according to the rites of the Armenian religious group; such notification should be sent to the Prelate of the Armenian Church. The Prelate may attempt to reconcile the parties within the period of three months; once the three-month period has lapsed, any party may file the petition for a divorce before the Family Court of the Armenian Religious Group. The means employed by the Prelate may not be judicially reviewed.

## II. An Overview of the Procedure before the Family Court in Divorce Proceedings

*219.* The procedure before the Family Court, not only for divorce petitions but also for other family law petitions, is set out in the Family Courts Procedural Regulation of 1990 which was enacted in accordance with section 15 of the Family

263. *Gregoriou v. Pippa* [1994] 7 JSC 438 (Family Court, in Greek).
264. A. Emilianides, *The Cypriot Law of Marriage and Divorce* (Thessaloniki: Sakkoulas, 2006, in Greek): 225–226.

Courts Law 23/90; the Civil Procedure Rules apply by analogy for issues not covered in the Family Courts Procedural Regulation.[265] With respect to petitions for dissolution of marriage, the Matrimonial Causes Rules of 1950 also apply by analogy. Proceedings in any action for divorce before a Family Court shall be commenced by filing a petition in accordance with Form A of the Family Courts Procedural Regulations of 1990; the petition should state the material facts of the case, including the place and date of the marriage, the personal data of the parties, the principal permanent address where the parties cohabited prior to the dissolution of the marriage, the place where the parties currently reside, whether there is living issue of the marriage and if so their names and dates of birth or ages, the grounds for divorce with full particulars, as well as the particulars of the relief claimed. The petition has to be signed by the petitioner or his/her advocate and should be served to the other party; three extra copies of the petition are needed in divorce petitions.

*220.* The petitioner has the burden of proving the grounds which have irretrievably broken down the marital life.[266] It has been held that while the petition for divorce should contain a detailed account of the grounds on which it is based, it should not further include the evidence to be presented during the trial. In *Danou* it was held that the Respondent should not have particularly stated in the petition for divorce the several insults spoken by the Appellant or the fact that the Appellant changed the locks of the matrimonial home, since such particulars were simply evidence of the ground of the irretrievable breakdown of the marriage and the attempt of the Appellant to throw the respondent out of the matrimonial home.[267] After the petition is filed the Registrar of the Family Court sets out a date for the first appearance of the parties before the Court. The set date should allow for sufficient time so that the defendant has a chance to file the pleading of Defence; such pleading may be filed within fifteen days from the service of the petition and should be signed by the defendant or his/her advocate. A copy of the Defence should be served to the petitioner; three extra copies of the Defence are needed in divorce proceedings.

*221.* In practice the Family Court may extend the period within which the defendant is supposed to file a Defence, following a request from the defendant. After the Defence is filed, the petitioner may file the pleading of Reply to the Defence. Where the defendant has filed a Counterclaim with his/her Defence, the petitioner is allowed to file a Defence to such Counterclaim with his/her Reply. The Family Court may direct the Parties, following an application by any party, to proceed to

---

265. For an overview of civil litigation in Cyprus *see* C. Satolias, *Judicial Practice* (Paphos, 2014, in Greek), S. Liasides, *The Civil Procedure Rules* (Nicosia, 2017, in Greek), v. I-IV, A. Markides, *Lectures of Civil Procedure* (Nicosia, 2003, in Greek), E. Odysseos, 'Civil Procedure in Cyprus', in *Symposium on Cypriot Juridical Issues* (Thessaloniki, 1974): 39–58 (in Greek), M. Nicolatos, 'Civil Procedure and Jurisdiction in Cyprus', *Cyprus and European Law Review* 9 (2009): 435–444 (in Greek), S. Nathanael, 'An Overview of Civil Litigation as Practiced in Cyprus and Enforcement of Foreign Judgments', *Cyprus Law Review* 26 (1989): 4034–4046, N. Koulouris, *Cypriot Civil Procedure* (Athens: Nomiki Vivliothiki, 2017, in Greek), C. Tsirides, *Pleadings and Issues Arising from them* (Limassol, 2013, in Greek).

266. *Loucaides v. Petropoulos* [2000] 1 CLR 1619 (in Greek).

267. *Danou v. Danou* [1998] 1 CLR 829 (in Greek).

discovery or inspection of documents, amend their pleadings, give further and better particulars, limit the issues at stake and in general may exercise any of the powers that a District Court has in accordance with the Civil Procedure Law, Cap. 6 and sections 31–47 of the Courts of Justice Law 14/60 (section 16 of the Family Courts Law 23/90). The Family Court may postpone or adjourn the case as it seems expedient for the interests of justice and further make any order with respect to costs it considers as reasonable under the circumstances of the case.

*222.* Whenever there is default of appearance by the defendant, or the defendant is in default of delivering a Defence, or the defendant does not question the material facts pleaded by the claimant, the petition may be fixed for proof; the petition shall be considered as proven if the claimant provides oral testimony confirming the truth of his/her allegations and if such evidence given in the form of oral testimony satisfies the statutory requirements for concluding that there are grounds for granting a decree of divorce. If the petition is set for trial and on the day fixed for trial the claimant does not appear, then the petition is subject to dismissal and shall not subsequently be heard unless upon application the Court considers that it is equitable in view of the circumstances of the case to order reinstatement of the petition. If it is the defendant who does not appear, then the petition may be fixed for proof; any judgment obtained where a party does not appear at the trial may, however, in a proper case be set aside by the Court.

*223.* If both parties appear, then the proceedings at the trial shall be as follows: the party on whom the burden of proof lies, namely the claimant, shall open his/her case and adduce his/her evidence and call witnesses; the defendant shall then adduce his/her own evidence and call witnesses, if he/she so wishes. Each witness, when his/her examination in chief is completed, is liable to be cross-examined by the opposite party and to be re-examined by the party calling him/her and shall not be recalled or further questioned save through and by leave of the Court. The general rules of evidence apply with respect to the procedure before the Family Court. Finally, each party shall address the Court summing up the evidence and stating their legal arguments. At the conclusion of the trial the Family Court shall give judgment for the petitioner or the defendant as the case may be and shall include in its judgment a direction as to the costs of the action. Since in divorce cases the Family Court is composed of three judges, the judgment may be given by majority, in accordance with section 13 of Law 23/90, in which case the judge who is in the minority may give his/her own dissenting judgment. The Family Court shall keep detailed minutes of any procedure held before it in accordance with section 22 of Law 23/90.

*224.* The judgments of the Family Court are subject to appeal, within forty-two days from the date the judgment was delivered, bçfore the Appellate Family Court. The Family Courts (Religious Groups) Procedural Regulation of 1995 provide that the Family Courts Procedural Regulation of 1990 applies also with respect to procedure before the Family Courts of Religious Groups. Matters concerning the evaluation of evidence and the credibility of witnesses shall be considered by the first instance Family Court which has the opportunity to hear and evaluate the entirety of the evidence.[268] The Appellate Family Court shall not interfere with the evaluation of evidence, unless such evaluation is objectively unsubstantiated, unreasonable, or arbitrary.[269] The primary findings of the Court refer to the facts of the case, while the secondary findings refer to those issues which may be determined as a matter of common sense. If the first instance Family Court fails to determine the primary findings of the case, and evaluate the evidence presented by each party, then the Appellate Family Court is not in a position to determine whether the first instance judgment is a correct one and to finally determine the dispute.[270]

*225.* The Court may take into account the way in which the spouses present their case during the trial. In the case of *Zachariou* the Appellate Family Court held that the fact that the defendant had not disputed during cross-examination the allegations of the petitioner that she had insulted him by claiming that he was homosexual, in conjunction with the manner in which the defendant presented her case by submitting to the petitioner that he was indeed a homosexual, raised serious doubts for the findings of the first instance Family Court in accordance to which the defendant had never claimed that the petitioner is a homosexual.[271] Furthermore, in *Moschatou* the Appellate Family Court held that the fact that the witnesses of either party have not been cross-examined on material facts should imply that such facts have been admitted by the other party.[272] Similarly, the facts which have not been disputed in the pleadings of the parties should be considered as having been admitted.[273] The Court should evaluate documents prepared by the parties by taking into account the circumstances under which such documents were prepared and the true intentions of the parties.[274]

*226.* It should be observed that there has been some confusion as to whether the Family Courts may dismiss the petition for divorce if it is satisfied that such petition has been filed in collusion with the other spouse. In the first instance judgment in *Panteli* it was held that if the petition has been filed in collusion with the other spouse, this should be considered by the Family Court while evaluating the credibility of witnesses, and only insofar as the entire testimony proves to be fabricated.[275] In another first instance judgment in *Yiannaki*, however, it was held that the collusion by the parties in order to be granted a divorce, essentially by consent, is contrary to the *jus cogens* nature of Cypriot family law.[276] It is submitted that the reasoning of *Panteli* should be adopted; the fact that the Cypriot legislator has not yet introduced divorce by consent is not sufficient for rejecting a petition for divorce whenever there are sufficient grounds for divorce to be granted, simply because the other party consents to the divorce being granted.

268. *Savvides v. Savvides* [1997] 1 CLR 497 (in Greek).
269. *Aradipioti v. Aradipiotou* [2002] 1 CLR 143 (in Greek).
270. *Kyprianou v. Kyprianou* [1994] 1 CLR 145 (in Greek).
271. *Zachariou v. Zachariou* [1993] 1 CLR 159 (in Greek).
272. *Moschatou v. Moschatou* [1999] 1 CLR 785 (in Greek).
273. *Charalambous v. Solonos* [1994] 1 CLR 716 (in Greek).
274. *Danou v. Danou* [1998] 1 CLR 829 (in Greek).
275. *Panteli v. Panteli* [1994] 7 JSC 514 (Family Court, in Greek).
276. *Yiannaki v. Yiannaki* [1994] 9 JSC 502 (Family Court, in Greek).

§3. Effects

*227.* Whenever there is a final judgment of the Family Court dissolving the marriage, the marriage is considered as dissolved and the parties are no longer legally considered as spouses. The judgment of the Family Court becomes final after the end of the forty-two-day period within which a party has a right to appeal. If an appeal is filed, then the execution of the judgment of the Family Court is suspended until the judgment of the Appellate Family Court is issued. Section 7 of the Attempt of Reconciliation and Spiritual Dissolution of the Marriage Law 22/90 provides that when the judgment dissolving a religious marriage celebrated according to the rites of the Orthodox Church becomes final, the Registrar of the Family Court shall send a copy of the judgment to the bishop of the habitual residence of the parties, in order for the bishop to spiritually dissolve the marriage. The bishop should spiritually dissolve the marriage within fifteen days. If for any reason the bishop fails to spiritually dissolve the marriage, the divorce decree issued by the Family Court is not affected.

*228.* Until the enactment of its new Charter of 2010, the Orthodox Church did not spiritually dissolve the marriage in accordance with the procedure provided for in section 7 of Law 22/90; this was due to the fact that the ecclesiastical courts of the Orthodox Church continued to function and issue divorces even after the amendment of Article 111 of the Constitution by Law 95/89, contrary to the provisions of the Constitution. However, the new Charter of 2010 no longer provides for the functioning of ecclesiastical courts, but only for the spiritual dissolution of the marriage. Section 88 of the 2010 Charter provides that the bishop who undertook the attempt to reconcile the parties, or if that could not take place the bishop of the place where the petitioner habitually resides, may spiritually dissolve the marriage. The petition for spiritual dissolution is not subject to a specific form and can be filed either personally or through a proxy, or even through the priest of the petitioner's parish.

*229.* The petitioner ought to personally, or if there are exceptional circumstances by a proxy, appear before a Council of Spiritual Dissolution of the Marriage composed of the three clergymen appointed by the bishop. It is provided that the Council should make every effort, if of course there is such a possibility, to maintain the marriage; if this is not possible then the Council should propose to the bishop the spiritual dissolution of the marriage. If the marriage has objectively or subjectively dissolved and its spiritual dissolution shall not further burden the established legal and factual situation, the spiritual dissolution shall be granted. There is no time limit for submitting a petition for a spiritual dissolution of the marriage. It has been suggested that the procedure set out by Article 88 of the 2010 Charter is incompatible with section 7 of Law 22/90 which provides that the bishop should spiritually dissolve the marriage within fifteen days.[277] This is correct; however, it should be noted that the spiritual dissolution is part of the ecclesiastical legal order

277. S. Liasides, 'Comments – Observations on the New Charter of the Church of Cyprus', *Family Law Review* 1 (2011): 33–34 (in Greek), G. Serghides, 'Cyprus Family Jurisdiction: Ratione Personae and Ratione Materiae', *Family Law Review* 2 (2011): 14–16.

and not of the State legal order. The Orthodox Church has set out a procedure in accordance with which the spiritual dissolution of the marriage is a condition for celebrating a second religious marriage and not as a precondition for the dissolution of the marriage by the Family Courts.

*230.* The new Charter has abolished the ecclesiastical courts and the dual, unconstitutional, divorce proceedings; the role of the Church is now only to spiritually dissolve the marriage in accordance with the Constitution. The aim of the procedure for spiritual dissolution is not to replicate the divorce proceedings held before the Family Courts, but rather to force the parties to attend before the bishop for the attempt of reconciliation. By providing that the appearance for the attempt of reconciliation is a prerequisite for the marriage to be spiritually dissolved, the Orthodox Church has ensured that the parties would have to attend for the attempt of reconciliation; otherwise, the spouses would simply wait for the lapse of the three-month period in order to file a petition before the Family Court. It is of course regrettable that the new Charter does not expressly refer to the Family Courts and the procedure held before them; however, the Holy Synod did not wish to recognize the Family Courts. Taking that into account the provisions of the new Charter safeguard that if the Family Court has granted a decree of divorce, then the marriage shall be considered as having been objectively dissolved and the spiritual dissolution shall be granted. Any practical problems may be solved by the relevant Directions of the Holy Synod.[278]

278. A. Emilianides, 'The Family Law Provisions of the Charter of the Church of Cyprus', *Family Law Review* 2 (2011): 21ff (in Greek).

## Chapter 3. Civil Union/Cohabitation without Marriage

*231.* Until recently there was no legislation governing civil partnerships since Cypriot family law referred exclusively to married couples. The right to celebrate a civil union instead of a marriage was eventually recognized by the enactment of the Civil Union Law 184(I)/2015. The right to a civil union or partnership is recognized not only for heterosexuals but also for homosexual couples. A civil union has the same legal validity and consequences as if a marriage, either religious or civil, had been celebrated,[279] with the exception of the right to adoption which is precluded as it was deemed to be highly controversial. It should be noted, however, that the ECtHR has already recognized the right of adoption to single homosexual parents,[280] and hence its exception from the ambit of Law 184(I)/2015 might well be inconsistent with the principle of non-discrimination.

*232.* A civil union presupposes the free consent of the intended partners. This is not deemed to exist, by virtue of section 5 of Law 184(I)/2015, if any of the partners lacks the capacity to conclude a civil union, i.e., if they have not completed 18 years of age, or if they are incapable of understanding and assessing the consequences of their actions due to a mental disorder or unsoundness of mind or due to a brain or other disease or illness or intoxication. Free consent is further not deemed to exist if any of the partners concluded the civil union due to a mistake as to the identity of the other partner, or due to fraud or misrepresentation, or was forced to conclude a civil union because of duress or undue influence; the latter is defined as any act or omission which may cause fear to an average reasonable person that either his/her life, honour, liberty, limb, or property or the life, honour, liberty, limb, or property of members of his/her family shall be subject to imminent and serious danger, or any legal, illegal, or contrary to prevailing moral standards, acts, or statements which cause fear to an average reasonable person. If a civil partnership was concluded with either partner lacking free consent as defined above, then the civil partnership is voidable.

*233.* Persons intending to conclude a civil union should, by virtue of section 6 of Law 184(I)/2015, appear in person before the Registrar (i.e., the District Commissioner) of the district either of them resides, or, if neither resides in the Republic, of a district of their choice, and submit completed and signed the Civil Union Form of Table I of Law 184(I)/2015. They should also submit an identity card or passport in force, a certificate from the competent authorities of the country of origin that they are not currently married or civil partners in another civil union and an affidavit that: (a) they have not concluded other marriage or civil union in force, (b) that they are not aware of any impediments or legal obstacle to the conclusion of

279. *See* S. Liasides, *Civil Union (Law 184(I)/2015). Legal Aspects* (Nicosia, 2016, in Greek), A. Tryfonidou, 'The Legal Position of LGBT Persons and Same-Sex Couples in Cyprus' *The Cyprus Review* 29 (2017): 183-213. *See also Valianatos v. Greece*, Judgment of 7 Nov. 2013, *Oliari v. Italy*, Judgment of 9 July 2016.

280. *E.B. v. France*, Judgment of 22 Jan. 2008.

the Civil Union and that they have secured all necessary consents, or that no consents are needed. The Registrar calls the potential partners to read a statement that they agree to the conclusion of the Civil Union and then reads to them a text as per Table II of Law 184(I)/2015 and signs the Civil Union Form. The Civil Union Form is also signed by two witnesses who have completed 18 years of age and are of a sound mind. A certificate is then issued by the Registrar and is proof of the validity of the Civil Union before any court, authority, or other authorized persons.

*234.* A Civil Union may be declared as void, in accordance with section 11 of Law 184(I)/15 if: (a) either party has already been validly married or in a civil union at the time of concluding the marriage, or (b) the parties are within the prohibited degrees of relationship, i.e., any degree between ancestors and descendants in a direct line and between parties related up to the fifth degree in blood, or third degree in affinity, or c) between an adoptive child and their kin and the adoptive parents or their kin, or d) to a person having not concluded 18 years of age,[281] or if the formalities of concluding a civil union before the Registrar have not been followed. A void or voidable civil union may be annulled by a judgment of the Family Court. Pursuant to section 13 of Law 184(I)/15, a petition for annulment may be filed by either of the partners or the administrator of the estate of a person who is not of sound mind, or the Deputy General Registrar, i.e., the Director of the Civil Registry and Migration Department. The petition has to be filed before the lapse of a three-year limitation period from the date that the civil union was celebrated by virtue of section 14 of Law 184(I)/15. If a civil union is declared as void by the Family Court, it no longer has any legal effect (section 15 of Law 184(I)/15); however, by virtue of section 16 of Law 184(I)/15, a child born by the partners shall maintain the status of a child born in a civil union.

*235.* A civil union is dissolved, in accordance with sections 17 and 18 of Law 184(I)/15, in the following ways: (i) by a joint written declaration of the partners which is signed in person before the Registrar and in the presence of at least two witnesses who have completed 18 years of age and are of a sound mind. This dissolution by consent shall take effect within 60 days from the date the joint written declaration is made unless the partners withdraw such declaration by a subsequent joint written declaration; (ii) by an order of the Family Court of the district where the civil union had been concluded. The Court takes into account the wishes of any of the partners to dissolve the civil partnership; (iii) automatically, if the partners celebrate a marriage; or (iv) with the death of either partner. It is clear that a civil union may be dissolved quite easily, contrary to what is the case with regard to divorce.

*236.* Whereas until a few years ago cohabitation without marriage was negligible, in recent years the number of persons who cohabitate without marriage has

281. It is somewhat paradoxical that a person having not concluded 18 years of age is considered as both grounds for a civil union to be declared as void and as voidable.

increased.[282] Where there is no law governing cohabitation, it is accepted that the law of equity concerning constructive trusts applies to cohabitants. In the case of *Clerides*, the claimant and the deceased Clerides were cohabitating in an apartment legally owned by Clerides for seven years.[283] When Clerides died, the executor of the will of the deceased asked the claimant to vacate the premises. When she refused, the executor sought an eviction order against her; she counterclaimed that the deceased was the legal owner of the department for the only reason that she had an unpaid mortgage debt in her name and further claimed that there was an express common intention that she had beneficial interest in the apartment, indicated also by the fact that Clerides has written her name under the doorbell and had told third parties that the apartment belonged to her.

*237.* The Supreme Court held that the apartment was held on a trust and that she was the sole beneficiary of such trust; it was further held that she had solely dealt with the interior design of the apartment and additionally had contributed to the deceased's business affairs. Consequently there was express common intention coupled with detriment. In the subsequent case of *Reckendorfer*, the application of the claimant for a declaration that the defendant was a trustee of his estate in favour of both of them in equal shares was rejected by the Supreme Court. It was held that where the contribution to the estate is minimal, this does not create a right under a trust. The claimant's contribution to the marriage was considered to be simply accompanying the defendant to social commitments and mutual love and appreciation; there was no minimal financial contribution.[284]

---

282. For the issue *see* the analysis of S. Loizidou, 'The Witch's Brew: Cohabitation and its Property Implications on Relationship Breakdown in Cyprus', in *Matrimonial Property of the Spouses and Partners and Various Legal Issues*, ed. G. Serghides (Nicosia, 2010): 30ff.
283. *Clerides v. Stavrides* [1998] 1 CLR 521 (in Greek).
284. *Reckendorfer v. Reckendorfer* [2004] 1 CLR 1132 (in Greek).

# Chapter 4. Filiation

## §1. Children Born in Wedlock

### I. The Identity of the Mother: Surrogacy

*238.* Traditionally, the identity of the mother was established by birth and this remains the position under Cypriot law, despite the fact that in cases such as surrogacy the issue is much more complicated than what the traditional approach might imply. Surrogacy is an arrangement in which a woman (the surrogate mother) carries and delivers a child for another person or couple, so that she may have no genetic relationship with the child; the biological mother may thus differ from the surrogate mother. Until recently no legislation was in force with regards to surrogacy. Surrogacy agreements were not prohibited so long as the surrogate mother received no compensation for carrying and delivering the child; in the latter case the surrogacy agreements were void. In view of the fact that the carrying mother was always defined as the legal mother, the biological mother would not be recognized as the mother of a child born by a surrogate mother. The only available option for the biological mother would be to adopt the child, provided that the surrogate mother consents to such an adoption.[285]

*239.* The Application of the Medically Assisted Reproduction Law 69(I)/2015 introduced for the first time specific provisions with regards to surrogacy.[286] However, the application of Law 69(I)/2015 was suspended immediately and whereas it was decided by the Council of Ministers that the suspension would end at September 2017, until now the provisions of Law 69(I)/2015 have not been applied in practice. Whereas section 25 § 5 introduces the possibility of both the commissioning mother and the surrogate filing a petition contesting motherhood within six months from the birth of the child, the Family Courts Law 23/90 has not been amended so as to explicitly provide that Family Courts have jurisdiction in cases of surrogacy. This has led to the Family Court declining to hear a case on the determination of motherhood following birth by surrogacy and referring the case to the District Court on the grounds that it lacked jurisdiction.[287] It is submitted that such a finding of the Family Court was clearly incorrect since the Family Court has jurisdiction for all family law disputes and the determination of motherhood is clearly a family law dispute and accordingly the Family Court should have jurisdiction without any need for amendment of Law 23/90. It should be noted that the surrogate mother may contest maternity and petition to be declared as the mother of the child only if it is proven that she is the genetic mother.

---

285. A. Emilianides, 'Introduction', in *Surrogacy: In Search of a Legal Framework*, ed. A. Emilianides et al. (Nicosia: Dikaionomia, 2010 in Greek), 5–10.

286. T. Trokanas, *The Cypriot Law of Medically Assisted Reproduction* (Athens: Nomiki Vivliothiki, 2016, in Greek).

287. *Mirimskaya v. Bezpiataia*, Case 4/2015, Judgment of 26 Feb. 2016 (Family Court, in Greek). For the general reluctance of Cypriot courts towards surrogacy *see also Mirimskaya*, App. 173/2015, Judgment of 8 Feb. 2016 (in Greek).

*240.* Pursuant to sections 22-27 of Law 69(I)/2015 surrogacy can take place so long as there is: (i) a surrogacy agreement, (ii) a court order issued prior to the embryo transfer procedure, and (iii) the written consent of the Council for Medically Assisted Reproduction is secured prior to the court order being granted. The surrogacy agreement should at a minimum specify that the surrogate mother shall not be the mother of the child and shall deliver the child immediately after birth to the commissioning couple. The commissioning couple shall be considered from the beginning as the parents of the child. It should be noted that Law 69(I)/2015 does not provide for the right of a single mother to apply for surrogacy, but only of a 'couple'; this is defined as a man and woman who have lawfully celebrated a marriage, or maintain a steady and permanent relationship. Persons who have filed a civil partnership should in principle also be considered as a 'couple' for the purposes of Law 69(I)/2015, pursuant to section 4 of the Civil Union Law 184(I)/2015 which provides that a civil partnership should be treated, *mutatis mutandis*, in the same manner and as having similar consequences as a marriage.

*241.* The surrogacy agreement should not provide for consideration to the surrogate mother; however, the commissioning couple should pay the expenses necessary for the pregnancy and birth of the child, as well as compensation for the leave of the surrogate mother from her work due to the pregnancy and birth may be covered. The Council of Ministers may determine the maximum amount of expenses and compensation that can be paid. It should be noted that the right of the commissioning mother to maternity leave does not arise directly from Directive 92/85/EEC[288] and accordingly it should be enacted by domestic legislation.[289] Law 116(I)/2017 amended the implementing Protection of Maternity Law 100(I)/97 so as to provide that the surrogate mother has a right to fourteen consecutive weeks of maternity leave in addition to the right of the commissioning mother to maternity leave. The right of the commissioning mother to maternity leave is the same as for any other mother.[290]

*242.* A bank guarantee for eleven months, i.e., until the birth of the child, should be issued. It is expressly stipulated that the genetic parents and not the surrogate mother shall be the parents of the child. The surrogacy agreement should further provide that the surrogate mother shall be a resident of the Republic from the twenty-eighth week of pregnancy until the birth of the child. Negotiating surrogacy agreements of a commercial nature, i.e., receiving any monetary compensation for surrogacy, or acts so as to receive any monetary sum for the conclusion or negotiation or facilitation of a surrogacy agreement is prohibited and constitutes a criminal offence liable to imprisonment of one year and/or a fine not exceeding EUR 50.000. Furthermore, advertising that a person is willing to conclude or negotiate or

288. Council Directive 92/85/EEC of 19 October 1992 on the introduction of measures to encourage improvements in the safety and health at work of pregnant workers and workers who have recently given birth or are breastfeeding.
289. *See* Case C-167/12, *CD v. ST* EU, C-2014: 169.
290. *See* A. Emilianides and C. Ioannou, *Labour Law in Cyprus* (The Hague: Kluwer, 2016).

facilitate a surrogacy agreement, or that persons seek for a surrogate mother, is prohibited and constitutes a criminal offence liable to imprisonment of six months and/ or a fine not exceeding EUR 35.000.

*243.* The Council for Medically Assisted Reproduction consents to the surrogacy, provided that it is convinced that: (a) it is medically impossible for the commissioning mother to get pregnant, (b) that the surrogate mother is suitable for becoming impregnated considering her general health status, (c) that the embryos to be transferred belong to the commissioning mother or a donor, (d) that a surrogacy agreement has been signed and that there is no consideration involved, and (e) that both the commissioning mother and the surrogacy mother are domiciled or habitually resident in the Republic. However, if it is practically impossible to find a surrogate mother domiciled or habitually resident in the Republic, the Council may approve a surrogate mother who is not domiciled or habitually resident in so far as she resides in the Republic from the twenty-eighth week of pregnancy until the birth of the child, (f) that there is a positive medical and psychiatric evaluation of the commissioning couple and the surrogate mother, and (g) that the commissioning couple and the surrogate mother have not been convicted of offences relating to child pornography or sexual harassment or exploitation of children.

## II. Determining Parentage

### *A. Presumptions*

*244.* Section 6 of the Children (Kinship and Legal Substance) Law 187/1991 provides that if a child was born in wedlock or within a period of 302 days from the dissolution or annulment of such wedlock, then it is presumed that the husband of the mother is the father of the child. The presumption applies if the parties have separated, but a decree of divorce has not yet been issued, or even if a decree has been issued but has not been yet finalized because an appeal is pending. If the decree of divorce is final, then the presumption still applies for a period of three hundred and two days, a period which roughly corresponds to the period within which the child would have been born if the mother was pregnant at the time the divorce or annulment was issued or at the time the mother's spouse – and presumed father – died. The presumption is rebuttable; thus, it might be rebutted so long as the Family Court is satisfied that the mother had not conceived the child by her husband or that during the crucial period of conception it was impossible for the child to have been conceived by the husband of the mother.[291]

*245.* If a child is conceived in wedlock by the sperm of a man other than the spouse and with the written consent of the spouse, then it is presumed as the child of the husband in accordance with section 6A of Law 187/91. Section 6A covers cases where a woman is artificially inseminated with the consent of her husband, in which cases the husband is presumed as the father of the child. The presumption is

291. *K.A. v. D.K.*[2005] 1 CLR 527 (in Greek).

rebuttable. There might be some extreme cases where it would not be proper to consider the husband as the father of the child, such as in cases where the husband had initially consented to the treatment, but subsequently, before the artificial insemination took place, the couple separated; in such a case, if the wife proceeded after the separation with the artificial insemination, it might be unreasonable to consider that the separated spouse should still be presumed to be the father because he had consented while the couple was still living together.

*246.* In any event if the husband has not consented to the artificial insemination, then he would not be presumed to be the father of the child; this would also be the position in the unfortunate event that the husband had consented to his wife's eggs being used with his own sperm, but by error another man's sperm was injected into the eggs. In such a case the consent of the husband was given solely for the purpose that his wife is artificially inseminated with his own sperm and not by the sperm of a third party. Thus, the husband shall not be considered as the father of the child.[292] Section 7 of Law 187/91 further provides that if within 302 days from the dissolution or annulment of the marriage a child is born by a woman who has concluded a new marriage, it is presumed that the father of such child is the new husband of the mother. The presumption is rebuttable and may thus be rebutted if paternity is successfully contested, in which case it shall be presumed that the first husband of the mother is the father. If the paternity is successfully contested also with respect to the first husband, then the child shall no longer be born in wedlock.

*247.* Sections 19-22 of the Civil Union Law 184(I)/2015 further provides for analogous presumptions in cases of civil union. If a child was born in civil union or within a period of 302 days from the dissolution or annulment of such civil union, it is presumed that the civil partner of the mother is the father of the child. If the child was conceived in civil union by the sperm of a man other than the civil partner and with his written consent, then it is presumed that the civil partner is the father. Moreover, if within 302 days from the dissolution or annulment of the civil union a child is born by a woman who has concluded a marriage or new civil union, it is presumed that the father of such child is the new husband or civil partner of the mother. The presumption is rebuttable and may thus be rebutted if paternity is successfully contested.

### *B. Contesting Paternity*

*248.* Section 8 of Law 187/91 provides that paternity of a child born in wedlock may be successfully contested before the Family Court, if it is proven that the child had not been conceived by the mother's husband or that during the crucial period of conception (which in accordance with section 9 of Law 187/91 is the period between the one hundred and eighty-first and the three hundred and second (181–302) day before the birth of the child) it was impossible for the child to have

292. *Leeds Hospital v. A&B* [2003] 1 FLR 1091.

been conceived by the husband of the mother. The person contesting paternity carries the burden of proof and normally genetic or blood tests shall be carried out; however, it is not necessary to indicate another person as the child's potential father. The following persons have legal standing to contest paternity: (i) the husband of the mother (who is the presumed father), (ii) the father or mother of the husband if he died before the limitation of his right to contest paternity, (iii) the child, (iv) the mother of the child, or (v) the first husband of the mother in those cases where the presumption of paternity by the second husband of the mother has been successfully contested. The competent Court is the Family Court of the habitual residence of the child in accordance with section 2 of Law 187/91.

*249.* It is striking that the alleged generic father is not included in the list of persons who have legal standing to contest paternity;[293] thus, the generic father may only legitimize his child if another person has successfully contested paternity.[294] Serious reservations might be raised regarding the constitutionality of such provision. Section 11 §1 (e) further provides that the sperm donor in cases of artificial insemination has no legal standing to contest paternity, if the child was conceived in wedlock with the written consent of the spouse in accordance with section 6A of Law 187/91; such provision was unnecessary, since the sperm donor is anyway not included in the list of persons having legal standing to contest paternity by virtue of section 10 of Law 187/91. If the contestation of paternity is successful, the child is no longer considered as a child born in wedlock and it is retroactively considered as a child born out of wedlock in accordance with section 12 of Law 187/91.

*250.* The right to contest paternity is a personal one and thus is not transferable to the heirs or administrators of the estate or executors of the will of a person after his/her death. Furthermore, such right has to be exercised within the limitation periods provided in section 11 of Law 187/91, namely: (i) the husband of the wife may contest paternity within a year from the date that he was informed of the birth and the facts showing that he had not conceived the child, and in any event within five years from the birth of the child, (ii) the father or the mother of the husband may contest paternity within a year since they learned of the death of the latter and of the birth of the child, (iii) the child may contest paternity within a period of one year from the date he/she became an adult (18 years of age), (iv) the mother may contest paternity within one year from the birth or, if there are reasonable grounds for not contesting, within five years from the birth of the child.

*251.* The constitutionality of the limitation periods provided in section 11 of Law 187/91 was challenged in the case of *Giorgalla*.[295] The Supreme Court held that the limitation period of one year for the husband to contest paternity was not inconsistent with Article 15 (right of private and family life) or Article 30 (right of access to courts for the determination of civil rights) of the Constitution, since such limitation period is sufficiently lengthy and the father who is aware of the material

293. *Markitanis v. Moutzouri* [2000] 1 CLR 923 (in Greek).
294. *Re Cleanthous* [1997] 1 CLR 1473 (in Greek).
295. *Yiorgalla v. Hatzichristodoulou* [2000] 1 CLR 2060 (in Greek).

facts may apply before the Court to have his rights determined. However, in the subsequent case of *Polycarpou*[296] the Supreme Court held that the limitation time of five years for the husband to contest paternity, even if he was not aware of the material facts, was inconsistent with Articles 15 and 30 of the Constitution, as well as with Article 8 of the ECHR providing for the right of private and family life.[297]

## §2. Children Born out of Wedlock

### I. Subsequent Marriage of the Parents

*252.* Following the ratification of the Convention for the Legal Status of Children Born out of Wedlock by Law 50/1979 and the abolition of the Children Born out of Wedlock Law, Cap. 278 by Law 187/91, children born out of wedlock may enjoy the same rights as children born in wedlock. Thus, the distinction between the two categories is no longer as important as it once was. Section 13 of Law 187/91 provides that a child born out of wedlock is retroactively considered as a child born in wedlock if his/her parents subsequently conclude marriage and the child is recognized after the conclusion of the marriage or had already been recognized, either voluntarily or judicially, as the child of the husband; such voluntary recognition may be contested in accordance with section 18 of Law 187/91 if the husband is not the biological father of the child. Section 13 might refer either to a minor child or an adult. Section 14 of Law 187/91 further specifies that the death of the child does not prejudice the effect of section 13 on the child's heirs.

### II. Voluntary Recognition

*253.* Maternal affiliation of every child born out of wedlock is based solely on the fact of the birth of the child in accordance with Article 2 of the Convention for the Legal Status of Children Born out of Wedlock. Paternal affiliation, however, may be established only by voluntary recognition or judicial decision; if a child born out of wedlock is either voluntarily or judicially recognized, it is retroactively considered as a child born in wedlock. Section 16 of Law 187/91 provides that the father may voluntarily recognize the child born out of wedlock as his own if the mother consents; a child may be voluntarily recognized either by an affidavit signed before the Registrar of the Court where the child is habitually resident, or by the will of the father by virtue of section 17 §1 of Law 187/91. The consent of the mother may also be provided by an affidavit signed before the Registrar; if the mother is not in Cyprus, then such consent may be provided before the competent consular authorities of the Republic. The mother may refuse to consent to the voluntary recognition only if the person who intends to recognize the child is not his/her generic father (section 17 §3 of Law 187/91 and Article 4 of the Convention for the Legal Status of Children Born out of Wedlock).

296. *Polycarpou v. Polycarpou* [2009] 1 CLR 35 (in Greek).
297. *See also Phinikaridou v. Cyprus*, App. 23890/02, Judgment of 20 Dec. 07.

*254.* If the mother had died or has no legal capacity, then the voluntary recognition by the father is considered as sufficient for the child to be voluntarily recognized. If the father has died or has no legal capacity, then either grandparent hailing from his/her father's side may voluntarily recognize the child on his behalf. The voluntary recognition has effect for the descendants of the child, in case that he/she has died prior to such recognition. There is no specific limitation period for voluntary recognition and accordingly the ten-year general limitation period from the date when the cause of action was completed, provided in section 4 of the Limitation of Actionable Rights Law 66()/2012, may be held to apply. There is no specific provision for the right to revoke such voluntary recognition. The following persons may contest voluntary recognition in accordance with section 18 of Law 187/91: (i) the child, or in case of death, his/her descendants, if the person is not the real father,(ii) the parents of the mother, if she has died or has no legal capacity, (iii) the grandparent hailing from the father's side who has not voluntarily recognized the child, if the parent has died or has no legal capacity, and (iv) the person claiming to be the real father of the child. Voluntary recognition should be contested within six months from the date that the person who contests was informed of such recognition, and in any event within three years from recognition;[298] the child may, however, contest voluntary recognition even within three years from the date he/she became 18 years of age. There is no provision for the right of the person who voluntary recognized the child to subsequently contest such voluntary recognition on the grounds that his consent was given in a defective manner. However, the Supreme Court recently held that Article 4 of the Legal Status of Children Born out of Wedlock Convention, which was ratified in the Republic with Law 50/1979, recognized such a right and that the Convention has superior force to domestic legislation.[299]

## III. Judicial Recognition

*255.* Both the mother and her child have the right to apply before the Family Court against the father (or his heirs),[300] in accordance with sections 20 and 21 of Law 187/91, and seek a judicial decision recognizing the child born out of wedlock; a similar application may be filed by the father or his parents hailing from the father's side, if the mother unreasonably refuses to consent to the voluntary recognition of the child. Such right has to be exercised within the limitation periods provided in section 22 of Law 187/91. If the mother is the applicant the limitation period is five years from birth; however, if the mother was married at the crucial time of birth, the limitation period is within five years from the date of the final judgment rebutting the presumption that the husband of the mother is the father of the child. If the child is the applicant, then the limitation period is three years from

298. For such limitation period, *see Xatzistylli v. Papadema* [2000] 1 CLR 551 (in Greek).

299. *Panayi v. Netsieva*, App. 36/2011, Judgment of 19 Mar. 2014 (in Greek).

300. It is dubious how the application may be filed against the heirs of the father, in view of the fact that in Cypriot law it is the administrator of the estate or the executor of the will of the deceased who represents him/her before the Courts.

the date the child became 18 years of age; if however the material facts become known to the child after the three-year period has elapsed, then such period begins from the date that the child was first informed about the material facts. The child should satisfy the Family Court that he/she has not been able to learn the material facts earlier, despite his/her reasonable efforts.

*256.* Section 22 of Law 187/91 further provides that if the father or his parents are the applicants, the limitation period is three years from the time that the mother refused to consent to the voluntary recognition. While such a limitation period was considered as constitutional by the Supreme Court,[301] the ECtHR subsequently held that such limitation period is inconsistent with Article 8 of the ECHR safeguarding the right to private and family life.[302] The ECtHR has stressed that inflexible limitation periods or other obstacles in applications regarding paternity, which apply irrespective of the father's knowledge of the crucial facts, are not consistent with Article 8 of the ECHR.

*257.* The case of *Chionou Nicolaou* is of particular interest. The petitioner applied before the Family Court in order to be recognized as a child born out of wedlock. The alleged father had died 33 years prior to the petition being filed. The intention of the petitioner was to be recognized as the heir of the brother of the alleged father, who had died two years prior to the submission of the petition and who had left no children and a substantial immovable property with the heirs being first cousins of the deceased brother of the alleged father. The petitioner claimed that she had been informed that she was a child born out of wedlock from the alleged father just prior to the filing of the petition. The petitioner also applied before the District Court for an order of exhumation of the deceased alleged father, pursuant to section 25 of the Cemeteries Law 257(I)/2004, so as to carry out blood and genetic tests. The District Court held that it would not exercise its discretion to order exhumation since there was no conclusive evidence where the alleged father had been buried more than 35 years earlier.[303]

*258.* A subsequent application before the Family Court requesting exhumation was also rejected. The Family Court held that there was an abuse of process and that the competent court to order exhumation was the District Court and not the Family Court. It further held that it had in any event no jurisdiction to order blood and genetic tests on blood or other genetic tissue of a person who could not consent because he was dead.[304] On the substance of the application, the Family Court recognized that the limitation period should be held to commerce from the knowledge of the facts by the applicant and therefore the application was not out of time. However, the only evidence offered to the court by the applicant related to vague

301. *Phinikaridou v. Odysseos* [2001] 1 CLR 1744 (in Greek).
302. *Phinikaridou v. Cyprus*, App. 23890/02, Judgment of 20 Dec. 07.
303. *Nicolaou*, App. 22/2013, Judgment of 4 Mar. 2014 (District Court, in Greek).
304. *Nicolaou v. Pelagias and others*, App. 4/2011, Judgment of 31 Mar. 2016 (Family Court, in Greek).

rumours. There was a clear lack of concrete evidence which could satisfy the Family Court that the deceased was the father of the applicant.[305]

## IV. Blood and Genetic Tests

*259.* Section 24A provides that in any proceedings before the Family Court in accordance with the provisions of Law 187/91, the Court may, following an application of either party, order that blood or genetic tests be carried out in order to establish whether any party is the biological parent of the child or not; section 24A applies not only in cases of children born out of wedlock but also in cases of children born in wedlock. The Court may direct that a sample of blood or other genetic tissue is provided by the child, his/her mother or any party who is allegedly the child's father (either because he so claims, or on the basis of a legal presumption). The person carrying out the blood or genetic test shall report to the Court, after the test is concluded, his/her findings, and particularly, whether the alleged father is the biological father or not and how reliable the test findings are. No blood sample or other genetic tissue may be taken without the consent of the party in question, including the consent of a child over 16 years of age; if the child is under 16 years of age, then the person having his/her parental care should consent, provided that the Court may waive such consent in a proper case. Section 5 of the Convention for the Legal Status of Children Born out of Wedlock further provides that scientific evidence should be accepted in cases of paternal recognition.

*260.* Section 24A §7 of Law 187/91 provides that if a person refuses or fails to take any necessary action for carrying out the orders of the Court regarding blood or genetic tests, then the Court may at its discretion reach any reasonable conclusions with respect to such refusal or failure. Prior to the entry into force of section 24A by law 78(I)/2006, it was held that the refusal of a person to be subject to blood or genetic tests cannot reasonably be considered by the Court as disproving his/her allegations, or as proving the allegations of the other party.[306] However, the Supreme Court has gradually accepted that where the justifications offered by the party for refusing to be subject to blood or genetic tests are not sufficiently convincing, the Family Court may reach its own conclusions on the matter by also taking into account such refusal;[307] such more recent approach is consistent with section 24A §7 of Law 187/91 and balances between the constitutional rights of the person refusing to be subject to blood or generic tests on the one hand and the fundamental right of the child to find out who his/her biological father is on the other.

305. *Nicolaou v. Pelagias and others*, App. 4/2011, Judgment of 31 Jan. 2017 (Family Court, in Greek).
306. *Xenofontos v. Kkeli* [1997] 1 CLR 1307 (in Greek), *Kosiaris v. Nicolaou* [1998] 1 CLR 234 (in Greek).
307. *Thrasyvoulou v. Fikardou* [1999] 1 CLR 1822 (in Greek), *Supatan v. Peristianis* [2006] 1 CLR 1417 (in Greek).

# Chapter 5. Adoption

## §1. Introduction

*261.* Adoption is governed by the Adoption Law 19(I)/95 which abolished the Adoption Law, Cap. 274. However, the Adoption Rules of 1954 continue to be in force in accordance with section 32 of Law 19(I)/95 to the extent that they are not inconsistent with the provisions of Law 19(I)/95. Legal adoption may be effected by an adoption decree issued by the Family Court. If an adoption decree is granted, all rights and obligations of the biological parents towards the minor cease to exist and are vested in the adoptive parents in accordance with section 22 of Law 19(I)/95; the rights and obligations of the parents are not affected retroactively, but only from the time that the adoption order is issued. The effect of the adoption order is far-reaching, affecting not only family law but also succession law. The adopted child shall be considered for all intents and purposes as the child of the adoptive parents, in accordance with section 23 of Law 19(I)/95; the only exception is that the adopted child may not celebrate marriage, not only with his/her adoptive parents or their relatives but also with his/her biological parents or their relatives. Section 23 §3 further provides that the marriage between the adopted person and his/her adoptive parent is prohibited, even if the adopted person is subsequently adopted by another person.

*262.* Section 27 of Law 19(I)/95 expressly provides that the biological parent or guardian of the minor, or the adopted child, may receive no compensation or other remuneration as consideration for the adoption; consequently, any payment or agreement by any person to pay or to provide compensation to the biological parents or guardian of the minor or to the adopted child is illegal. Similarly, no monetary consideration or other compensation may be given with respect to placement of a minor. Any person acting in violation of section 27 is liable to imprisonment for a period not exceeding one year, or to a fine not exceeding EUR 1712.26 (CYP 1,000) or to both imprisonment and a fine. Section 28 of Law 28(I)/95 further provides that any advertisement or publication which implies that: (i) a person wishes to adopt a minor, (ii) a person is willing to proceed to arrangements in order to adopt a minor, or (iii) the parent or guardian of a minor wish for the minor to be adopted, is illegal. Any person causing or publishing such advertisement or other publication is liable to a fine not exceeding EUR 856.13 (CYP 500).

## §2. Requirements for Adoption

*263.* An application for an adoption decree shall be made by originating application in accordance with Rule 3 of the Adoption Rules of 1954; such application shall be supported by an affidavit verifying the several statements therein. The prospective adoptive parents shall be the applicants and should provide full particulars in accordance with Form I of the Adoption Rules of 1954. Section 3 §3 (a) of Law 19(I)/95 provides that an application for adoption may be made by a person or persons, if either of them stays permanently in the Republic, or had his/her residence in the Republic for two years prior to the submission of the application, and so long as the adopted person had his/her residence in the Republic at the date the application was made. The adopted person in such a case shall be considered as having his/her residence in the Republic. In *Ajero* it was held that the adopted person did not have his residence in Cyprus, since he came to Cyprus as an adult for a predetermined period of time; the mere fact that at the date the application was submitted he was in Cyprus as a visitor could not amount to him having his residence in the Republic for the purposes of section 3 §3 (a) of Law 19(I)/95.[308]

*264.* The adopted child should in all cases be a minor, namely a person who has not completed 18 years of age; however, if the adopted child is the biological child of either adoptive parent, he/she may exceptionally be an adult in accordance with section 2 of Law 19(I)/95. It is further provided in section 3 §3 (b) of Law 19(I)/95 that at least one of the adoptive parents should have completed 25 years of age; furthermore, the Court should consider that the adoption decree does not endanger the adopted child and is generally in the best interests of such adopted child. While there is no prescribed age difference between an adoptive parent and an adopted child, it is implied that the adoptive parent should be sufficiently more mature than the adopted child. It has been held that the mere fact that the adoptive parent is a senior citizen is not a substantial ground for rejecting an application for adoption.[309] If the adopted child is the biological child of the spouse of the Applicant, no age difference is required. The age limit is further set at 21 years of age (instead of 25) by virtue of section 3 §3 (c) of Law 19(I)/95, if either of the adoptive parents is a sibling, uncle or aunt of the adopted child, either full blood or half blood and either in blood or in affinity. If the adoptive parent is the biological parent of the adopted child, then no age limits are set.

*265.* An application for adoption is submitted in accordance with section 3 §4 of Law 19(I)/95 by: (i) both spouses for joint adoption, (ii) the biological parent for joint adoption with his/her spouse, and (iii) the spouse of the biological parent. Partners in a civil union may not apply for adoption. Exceptionally, a person may apply for adoption if he/she is unmarried, or without his/her spouse, by virtue of section 7 § 1 of Law 19(I)/95, if the Family Court is satisfied that there are special grounds to do so; such special grounds might include the fact that a person has never married despite reaching a marriageable age, the fact that a person wishes to adopt his/her nephew/niece, but his/her spouse does not wish to jointly adopt, etc. Section 7 §2 of Law 19(I)/95 further provides that an adoption decree may be granted with respect to a person who has already been adopted once, so long as: (a) he/she is a minor who has already been adopted by the spouse of the adoptive parent, (b) the prior adoptive parent has died, or (c) the prior adoption has ceased.

*266.* The Court shall grant a decree of adoption by virtue of section 5 of Law 19(I)/95, if it is satisfied that: (i) any consent required has been given with full knowledge of the nature and effects of adoption, (ii) the decree of adoption shall be

308. *Ajero* [2006] 1 CLR 1165 (in Greek).
309. *Papaioannou v. Palaiologou* [2002] 1 CLR 16 (in Greek).

in the best interests of the adopted child, after taking his/her wishes into accounts, if he/she is of sufficient age and mental capacity, (iii) for at least three months prior to the adoption decree being granted, the minor has resided and continues to reside with the applicant or either of them and is under the applicant's care and supervision, (iv) the applicant has not received, nor agreed to receive and no person has given or agreed to give to the applicant any monetary sum or other remuneration as consideration for the adoption, (v) the report of the Welfare Department states that the applicant is a person suitable for adoption purposes. The Court may further set any conditions it considers necessary and may in particular order that the applicant should ensure the financial well-being of the minor in any way it deems fair. The Court may further grant a temporary decree of adoption for a trial period of up to six months, before granting a final decree of adoption by virtue of section 6 of Law 19(I)/95.

*267.* While an application for an adoption is pending, the biological parents or guardian of the minor who have consented to the adoption may not remove the minor from the direct care and supervision of the applicant, without leave of the Court (section 8 of Law 19(I)/95). Similarly, while an application for adoption is pending, no person may remove a minor who has been under the direct care and supervision of the applicant for a period of at least six months prior to the filing of the application, contrary to the wishes of the applicant or without leave of the Court. Furthermore, without leave of the Court, no person may remove a minor contrary to the wishes of the person having his/her direct care and supervision for a period of at least twelve months, within three months of the date that such person has notified the Welfare Department of his/her intention to apply for adoption. Any person acting contrary to the above is liable to imprisonment for a period not exceeding one year, or to a fine not exceeding EUR 1712.26 (CYP 1,000) or to both imprisonment and a fine in accordance with section 9 of Law 19(I)/95.

## §3. Consent

*268.* Informed consent is a prerequisite for granting a decree of adoption; such consent should be given only so long as the persons consenting have a clear understanding of the nature and effects of a decree of adoption. Section 4 §1 of Law 19(I)/95 provides that no decree of adoption may be granted unless the biological parents or guardian of the minor consent; the consent of the mother of the minor is valid only if it is given at least three months after the child is born, a provision which aims at better safeguarding that the consent of the mother is an informed one. If the adoptive parent is married and his/her spouse is not a joint applicant, the consent of such spouse is also required. It is further provided that the adopted child should also consent, so long as he/she is of sufficient age and mental capacity. Consent is given in accordance with Form 2 of the Adoption Rules of 1954, before a Judge of the Family Court or the consular authorities of the Republic in case that such consent is given abroad (section 4 §2 of Law 19(I)/95). It is expressly provided that the biological parents or guardian of the minor or the spouse of the applicant may consent even if they are unaware of the identity of the applicant; if they subsequently withdraw such consent, the Family Court shall consider that they unreasonably refuse to consent by virtue of section 4 §5 of Law 19(I)/95.

*269.* Consent may be withdrawn at any time prior to the adoption decree being granted, in accordance with section 4 §3 of Law 19(I)/95, if the Court considers that this would be reasonable under the circumstances. While the Court has discretion in the matter, once consent is given it becomes gradually more difficult for the biological parents to show that the withdrawal of their consent should be considered as reasonable.[310] section 4 §4 of Law 19(I)/95 further provides that the Court may waive the need for consent to be given if: (i) the parent or guardian of the minor has deserted or neglects the minor or has systematically mistreated him/her, or has seriously abused him/her, (ii) the parent or guardian of the minor systematically and unreasonably fails to fulfil his/her obligations towards the minor and especially nutrition and maintenance, (iii) the adopted child is not in a position to consent due to the state of his/her mental capacity, (iv) in the case that the consent of the spouse of the applicant is needed, the spouses are separated and such separation is expected to be a final one, or (v) either the spouse of the applicant or the biological parents or guardian of the minor, may not be found or are unable to consent or unreasonably refuse to consent.

## §4. Placement and Return of a Minor

*270.* A minor may be placed under the direct care and supervision of a prospective adoptive parent directly or through the Welfare Department in accordance with section 10 of Law 19(I)/95; no adoption is valid unless it was made in accordance with the provisions of Law 19(I)/95. Section 11 of Law 19(I)/95 provides that for a minor to be placed through the Welfare Department, the biological parents or guardian of the minor should first have authorized the Welfare Department in writing; following such authorization, the Welfare Department may proceed to all necessary arrangements for the placement of the minor under the direct care of a person for adoption purposes, irrespective whether the identity of the prospective adoptive parent is known to the biological parents or guardian of the minor or not. Direct placement of a minor may occur whenever any person directly proceeds to all necessary arrangements for the placement of a minor under the care of a prospective adoptive parent by virtue of section 12 of Law 19(I)/95; such necessary arrangements consist of the conclusion of any agreement or otherwise facilitation of the placement of the minor, or deliberations for the conclusion of such agreement.

*271.* Prospective adoptive parents should notify in writing the welfare officer of their place of residence, in accordance with section 13 of Law 19(I)/95, at least three months in advance of the direct placement of a minor for adoption purposes; such notification should contain the name, sex, date and place of birth of the minor, as well as the name and address of the prospective adoptive parent and the biological

310. *Papaioannou v. Palaiologou* [2002] 1 CLR 16 (in Greek).

parents, if any. After receiving the notification the welfare officer should investigate the suitability of the prospective adoptive parent and should deliver a report within three months which should state whether the prospective adoptive parent is suitable for placement purposes. In order to prepare such report the welfare officer has a duty to visit within a reasonable time the premises where the minor has been placed or is to be placed and inspect such premises and the minor, in accordance with section 17 §1 of Law 19(I)/95; any person refusing to permit such inspection by the welfare officer is liable to imprisonment not exceeding six months or to a fine not exceeding EUR 770.52 (CYP 450) or to both imprisonment and a fine.

*272.* If the prospective adoptive parent or the biological parents disagree with the report of the welfare officer, they may apply before the Family Court.[311] The Court may further direct that the placement should take place prior to the three-month period, if the suitability of the prospective adoptive parent has already been investigated by the welfare officer or if there are special circumstances justifying it. It is noted that in accordance with section 14 of Law 19(I)/95 any person who intends to adopt may request the welfare officer to prepare a report stating whether he/she is a suitable person for adoption purposes, even prior to finding the prospective adopted child and in such cases the welfare officer has to prepare such report within six months. The prospective adoptive parent has to inform the Welfare Department for any change of the residence of the minor fifteen days in advance of such change in accordance with section 15 of Law 19(I)/95; however, if there was a need to immediately change residence due to emergency grounds, the notification to the Welfare Department may be sent within forty-eight hours from the change. If the minor dies while under the direct care of the prospective adoptive parent, the Welfare Department has to be notified in writing within twenty-four hours.

*273.* If the premises where the minor have been placed or is intended to be placed are not suitable for such placement, or if the environment is harmful for the minor, or if the prospective adoptive parent is unsuitable, the Family Court may, following an application by the welfare officer and in accordance with section 16 of Law 19(I)/95, order that the minor be moved to a safe place until other arrangements are made or unless he/she is returned to his/her biological parents or guardian. Furthermore, the minor has to be returned to his/her biological parents or guardian (or to the person who had the direct care and supervision of the minor prior to the placement), in accordance with section 20 of Law 19(I)/95, if the prospective adoptive parent fails to apply for adoption within a period of twelve months from the placement, or informs the Welfare Department that he/she does not intend to proceed with such application for adoption; in such cases the minor has to be returned within seven days from the completion of the twelve-month period, or the date the notification was given. The same provisions apply also if the Family Court refuses to grant the decree of adoption or if the temporary decree of adoption has lapsed without a final decree of adoption being granted.

---

311. *Dorou v. Minister of Labour and Social Securities*, App. 131/05, Judgment of 20 Sep. 2006 (in Greek).

*274.* If the placement had been made through the Welfare Department, then the minor is returned to the Welfare Department, or to the persons directed by the Welfare Department; in the latter case the biological parents or the person who had the direct care and supervision of the minor prior to the placement have to consent. If such consent is not given, the Court may direct accordingly as it deems fair and reasonable under the circumstances by virtue of section 21 of Law 19(I)/95. Any person who fails to return the minor is liable to imprisonment for a period not exceeding six months, or to a fine not exceeding EUR 1712.26 (CYP 1,000) or to both imprisonment and a fine.

## §5. Inter-State Adoptions

*275.* Section 29 of Law 19(I)/95 provides that no person may, without leave of the Court, permit, cause or promote the transfer and assignment of care of a minor outside the Republic in order to arrange for his/her adoption to a person who is not the guardian or relative (grandparent, sibling, uncle, aunt, either full blood, or half blood or in affinity) of the minor; any person who violates the provisions of section 29 is subject to imprisonment not exceeding one year or to a fine not exceeding EUR 1712.26 (CYP 1,000) or to both imprisonment and a fine. The Court may authorize the transfer and assignment of care of the minor to a citizen of the Republic who resides outside the Republic, by virtue of section 30 of Law 19(I)/95, after taking into account the consent of the biological parents or guardian or of the person having the care of the minor, the suitability of the person who is to undertake the care of the minor, as well as the best interests and wishes of the minor.

*276.* The provisions of the Convention on Protection of Children and Cooperation in respect of Intercountry Adoption (Ratification) Law 26(III)/1994 are also relevant. The objects of the Convention are to establish a system of cooperation and recognition of adoptions amongst Contracting States and to establish safeguards so as to ensure that intercountry adoptions take place in the best interests of the child and with respect of his/her fundamental rights. In accordance with Article 2 of the Convention, such Convention shall apply where a child habitually resident in one Contracting State ('the State of origin') has been, is being, or is to be moved to another Contracting State ('the receiving State') either after his/her adoption in the State of origin, or for the purposes of such an adoption in the receiving State or in the State of origin. The Minister of Labour and Social Securities shall be the Applicant; the application should be supported by an affidavit verifying the several statements therein.

*277.* An intercountry adoption within the scope of the Convention shall take place in accordance with Article 4 of the Convention only if the Central Authorities of the State of origin (for Cyprus the Central Authority is the Ministry of Labour and Social Securities of the Republic): (a) have established that the child is adoptable, (b) have determined, after possibilities for placement of the child within the State of origin have been given due consideration, that an intercountry adoption is in the child's best interests, (c) have ensured that the persons, institutions and authorities whose consent is necessary for adoption have been duly informed of the legal effects of their consent and have given their consent freely and in writing in the required legal form and without such consent having been induced by payment or compensation of any kind; provided that the consent of the mother has been given only after the birth of her child and (d) that consideration has been given to the child's wishes and opinions, having regard to his/her age and degree of maturity, and that the child has been duly informed of the legal effects of adoption and consented to such adoption, if required, freely and in writing in the required legal form and without such consent having been induced by payment or compensation of any kind.

*278.* It is further provided that an intercountry adoption shall only take place if the competent authorities of the receiving State have, in accordance with Article 5 of the Convention: (i) determined that the prospective adoptive parents are eligible and suited to adopt, (ii) ensured that the prospective adoptive parents have been counselled as may be necessary; and (iii) determined that the child is or will be authorized to enter and reside permanently in that State. Any decision in the State of origin that a child should be entrusted to prospective adoptive parents may only be made in accordance with Article 17 of the Convention if: (a) the Central Authority of that State has ensured that the prospective adoptive parents agree, (b) the Central Authority of the receiving State has approved such decision, where such approval is required by the law of that State or by the Central Authority of the State of origin, (c) the Central Authorities of both States have agreed that the adoption may proceed; and d) it has been determined, in accordance with Article 5, that the prospective adoptive parents are eligible and suited to adopt and that the child is or will be authorized to enter and reside permanently in the receiving State.

*279.* The Central Authorities of both States shall take all necessary steps, in accordance with Article 18 of the Convention, to obtain permission for the child to leave the State of origin and to enter and reside permanently in the receiving State. An adoption certified by the competent authority of the State of the adoption as having been made in accordance with the Convention shall be recognized by operation of law in the other Contracting States by virtue of Article 23 of the Convention; in accordance with Article 24 of the Convention, the recognition of an adoption may be refused in a Contracting State only if the adoption is manifestly contrary to its public policy, taking into account the best interests of the child. The recognition of an adoption includes, by virtue of Article 26 of the Convention, recognition of: (i) the legal parent–child relationship between the child and his/her adoptive parents, (ii) parental responsibility of the adoptive parents for the child and (iii) the termination of a pre-existing legal relationship between the child and his/her mother and father, if the adoption has this effect in the Contracting State where it was made.

## Chapter 6. Parental Responsibility

### §1. Introduction

*280.* The Relationship between Parents and Children Law 216/90 has abolished the Guardianship of Infants and Prodigals Law, Cap. 277 and currently regulates parental responsibility. Parental responsibility is both a duty and a right of parents and is exercised with respect to all minor children, with the exception of married ones. Such parental responsibility includes, in accordance with section 5 §1 of Law 216/90, the determination of the name of the child, parental care, administration of property and representation of the child in any legal proceedings or legal transaction; parental care includes, *inter alia*, the upbringing of the child, its custody, education and determination of its place of residence (section 9 §1 of Law 216/90). Parental responsibility is exercised by both parents; however, a parent may carry out on his/her own usual acts of parental care or acts of an urgent nature by virtue of section 7 of Law 216/90. If the parents disagree about any issue concerning the exercise of parental responsibility, the Family Court may decide on the matter following an application by either parent by virtue of section 7 of Law 216/90.

*281.* If the child was born out of wedlock the mother has the parental responsibility by virtue of section 16 of Law 216/90; however, once the child is recognized, the father shall also exercise parental responsibility. If the parents have divorced or separated, or their marriage has been annulled, the exercise of parental responsibility shall be assigned by the Court, in accordance with sections 14 and 15 of Law 216/90, unless the parties have themselves agreed on how to exercise such parental responsibility. The Court shall normally assign parental responsibility to one of the parents, although it may assign parental responsibility to both if they so agree. The Court may further allocate the exercise of parental responsibility between the parents or, exceptionally, assign it to a third party. The Court has the power to also issue a temporary order of parental responsibility in such cases.[312] If either parent has died or has been declared as dead *in absentia*, or is absent, parental responsibility is exercised exclusively by the other parent by virtue of section 5 §2 of Law 216/90.[313]

*282.* Section 5 §3 of Law 216/90 further provides that if either parent is unable to exercise parental responsibility for practical reasons, or because of incapability or limited capability, the other parent shall exercise parental responsibility on his/her own; however, the minor parent shall also have custody of the child. If however, either both parents have died or one of the parents has died and the other is unable to exercise parental responsibility, parental responsibility is exercised jointly by the nearest ancestors in accordance with section 5 §4 of Law 216/90;[314] if the nearest ancestors are not in a position to exercise parental responsibility, then parental responsibility is assigned to a Guardian. Parental responsibility may also be

312. *Antoniou* [1999] 1 CLR 1200 (in Greek).
313. *Markitanis v. Moutzouri* [1997] 1 CLR 314 (in Greek).
314. *Kalfopoulou* [1998] 1 CLR 55 (in Greek).

assigned to a Guardian if the parents have been deprived of such parental responsibility by a judgment of the Family Court.

§2. Welfare of the Child

*283.* Section 6 §1 of Law 216/90 expressly provides that any decision of the parents with regard to the exercise of parental care should aim at the welfare (best interests) of the child; parents should bring up the child without discrimination on grounds of sex, in order for the child to develop his/her personality freely, with a social conscience in accordance with section 9 §2 of Law 216/90. The parents should demonstrate the diligence shown in their own affairs during the exercise of parental responsibility in accordance with section 13 of Law 216/90; they are also jointly and personally liable for any damages caused as a result of breach of the obligations of either or both of them. Parents may not make donations from the property of their children (section 11 of Law 216/90); however, they may use the property and income of the child for his/her maintenance, education, and needs with leave of the Court (section 10 of Law 216/90).

*284.* Leave of the Court is also needed in accordance with section 12 of Law 216/90, for carrying out any of the following acts: (i) sell, mortgage, charge, exchange, or in any manner alienate property of the minor, (ii) lease immovable property of the minor for a period exceeding five years, (iii) buy immovable property on behalf of the minor, (iv) invest money of the minor, (v) settle claims or actions of or against the minor. However, the parents may invest the property of the minor in approved investments, even without the leave of the Court; such approved investments are in accordance with section 2 of Law 216/90 the following: (a) securities whose capital or interest has been guaranteed by the Government, (b) bonds, shares or other bills of exchange which have been issued by authorization of a specific law, or in accordance with a loan concluded by the Government, (c) bonds, shares or other bills of exchange of legal persons of public law or authorities of local administration, whose income are under the control of the Government, (d) investments secured by mortgage or other charges of immovable property whose value extends the investment by 1/5, or (e) any other investments characterized as approved by the Minister of Finance.

*285.* Any judgment of the Family Court concerning the attribution of parental responsibility or the manner in which such parental responsibility is exercised, should also aim at the welfare of the child (section 6 §2 of Law 216/90); such judgment should further respect the equality between the parents and not discriminate on grounds of sex,[315] language, religion, conscience, nationality, ethnic or social origin, or property. There is no predetermined definition of the welfare of the child; such welfare should be determined on the basis of the particular characteristics of each given case and after taking into account of all material factors,[316] as well as

315. *Sofocleous v. Tsesmeloglou* [2006] 1 CLR 1153 (in Greek).
316. *Iacovides v. Iacovides* [2000] 1 CLR 1108 (in Greek).

the material, physical, moral, spiritual, mental, as well as any other interests of the child.[317] It has been held that judicial proceedings concerning parental responsibility should not necessarily be adversarial in nature, since their aim is to determine the best interests of the child;[318] parents should therefore not treat their child as a means or weapon for solving their own disputes.[319] It is thus not the aim of the Family Court in applications for parental responsibility to distribute blame or punish the parent who is at fault.[320]

*286.* Determining the welfare of the child is not a simple or straightforward task, especially if the purpose of the judicial proceedings is not to assign parental responsibility, but to decide which of the conflicting views of the parents should be promoted (for instance by choosing whether the child ought to attend a public or private school). If the child is sufficiently mature and is able to understand the nature of the proceedings, the Family Court should request and take into account his/her opinion, before reaching any conclusions concerning parental responsibility in accordance with section 6 §3 of Law 216/90.[321] Giving due account to the opinion of the child is very important, since the child is the interested person in any judicial proceedings regarding parental responsibility.[322] The judge should therefore discuss with the minor in order to determine his/her degree of maturity and understanding.[323] While there are no specific rules governing such discussion, it is mandatory that the judge keeps precise minutes of the substance of the discussion; it is not necessary to record the exact questions and answers.[324] The Court may decide not to hear the opinion of the minor if he/she is very young;[325] furthermore, the Court may decide not to give priority to the opinion of the child, especially if it is at a tender age.

*287.* A Commissioner for the Rights of the Child is appointed by the Council of Ministers for a five-year term in accordance with the Commissioner for the Protection of the Rights of the Child Law 74(I)/2007. Law 74(I)/2007 empowers the Commissioner with the safeguard of the rights of the children and to represent their interests at all level. The Commissioner has the right to submit applications on behalf of children for the appointment of a special representative in judicial cases which affect them, as well as the representation of children and their interests in judicial procedures where she shall be appointed as representative of the child by the Court. The Commissioner shall act independently, taking into account only the legislation, morality and her conscience and is subject to a duty of confidentiality. It has been held, however, that whereas the appearance of the Commissioner in the

317. *Director of the Department of Social Welfare v. Douma* [2001] 1 CLR 1911 (in Greek).
318. *Stylianou v. Stylianou* [1993] 1 CLR 130 (in Greek).
319. *Constantinou v. Constantinou* [2009] 1 CLR 761 (in Greek).
320. *Kkoufou v. Kkoufou* [1997] 1 CLR 1588 (in Greek).
321. S. Liasides, 'Hearing the Minor Child under Family Law', *Family Law Review* 1 (2010): 7–23 (in Greek).
322. *Stylianou v. Stylianou* [1993] 1 CLR 130 (in Greek), *Kalfopoulou* [1998] 1 CLR 55 (in Greek).
323. *Ioannides v. Ioannides* [2002] 1 CLR 1446 (in Greek).
324. *Antoniou v. Harpa* [2001] 1 CLR 194 (in Greek).
325. *Michaelidou v. Markou* [2005] 1 CLR 1020 (in Greek).

procedures before the Family Court is an important tool to enhance the rights of children, her appearance in appellate procedures which involve mainly legal questions is neither needed nor helpful.[326]

## §3. Removal of Parental Responsibility

*288.* Section 18 of Law 216/90 provides that if either parent breach or abuse their duties to parental care or administration of the property of their child, or if they are not in a position to fulfil these tasks, the Family Court may take any appropriate measures following an application by the other parent, or the Director of the Department of Social Welfare; third parties other than the Director of the Department of Social Welfare may not apply before the Family Court under section 18 of Law 216/90.[327] Whenever other measures are deemed to be insufficient to prevent risks of physical, mental or spiritual damage to the child, the Court may order that the exercise of parental responsibility is fully or partly removed from the parent[328] and assign such parental responsibility to the other parent; if parental responsibility is removed from both parents, the Court may partly or fully assign parental responsibility to a Guardian, after considering his/her ethical character, living conditions and general suitability and so long as the Guardian consents. The Guardian is preferably a relative of the child.

*289.* In change of circumstances since parental responsibility was removed, the Court may recall or vary its judgment in accordance with section 20 of Law 216/90, following an application by either parent or the Director of the Department of Social Welfare.[329] Parental responsibility may also be removed by the Court, following an application by the other parent or the Director of the Department of Social Welfare, if the parent has been convicted for an offence against the life, limb or morals of any of his/her children (section 21 of Law 216/90).[330] The Family Court may further order by virtue of section 19 of Law 216/90 that parental responsibility is removed from both parents, if they both request this for a serious cause and they indicate a person who is willing to undertake such parental responsibility. If one of the parents has died or has been declared dead *in absentia*, or if parental responsibility has been removed from him/her, the other parent may apply before the Court requesting that a Guardian be appointed in accordance with section 24 §2 of Law 216/90. Parental responsibility ceases in any event to exist in accordance with section 22 of Law 216/90, for the parent of the child who dies or is declared as dead *in absentia*.

---

326. *Theocharides v. Theocharides*, App. 13/2014, Judgment of 18 Nov. 2015 (in Greek).
327. *Fotiou v. Houvarta* [2004] 1 CLR 366 (in Greek), *Moutzouri* [1999] 1 CLR 1282 (in Greek), *Markitanis* [2001] 1 CLR 1676 (in Greek).
328. *Hjicostanti v. Hjiconstanti* [1998] 1 CLR 1827 (in Greek).
329. *Demetriou v. Demetriou* [1998] 1 CLR 1189 (in Greek).
330. *Charalambous v. Charalambous* [1997] 1 CLR 695 (in Greek).

*290.* The Guardian exercises his/her duties without remuneration; however, the Family Court may, by virtue of section 29 of Law 216/90, determine proper remuneration depending on the circumstances and following an application by the Guardian. The Guardian may further claim any necessary expenses for conducting his/her duties in accordance with section 28 of Law 216/90. In accordance with section 26 of Law 216/90 the Guardian may not exercise the following acts without leave of the Court: (i) sell, mortgage, charge, exchange or in any manner alienate property of the minor, (ii) lease immovable property of the minor for a period exceeding five years, (iii) buy immovable property on behalf of the minor, (iv) invest money of the minor with the exception of approved investments, (v) settle claims or actions of or against the minor; the Family Court shall not grant leave unless it is satisfied that the act is for the welfare of the child. Any disposition of property without leave of the Court may be declared as invalid by the Court. The Guardian may not make donations from the property of the minor (section 27 §2 of Law 216/90).

*291.* The Guardian shall submit to the Family Court accounts for the administration of the property of the minor within twelve months of the date of assignment and subsequently shall submit periodic accounts in accordance with the instructions of the Registrar of the Family Court until the completion of his/her guardianship. When the guardianship is completed, the Guardian is obliged to deliver all property to the child and answer for the administration of such property in accordance with section 30 of Law 216/90. The Registrar shall examine the accounts submitted by the Guardian and request additional information or receipts within a set timeframe. The Court may further appoint a competent person for examining such accounts, if they are complex or bulky. If the Guardian fails to submit proper accounts he/she is subject to a fine not exceeding EUR 1712.26 (CYP 1,000). The accounts are open for inspection by any interested person.

## §4. Blood Transfusion

*292.* Parents who are Jehovah's Witnesses often object to their children receiving blood transfusion, no matter how life threatening their children's condition might be. This situation was considered by the Supreme Court in the case of *Charalambous*.[331] The parents of a young girl, being Jehovah's Witnesses, refused to consent for their child to have blood transfusion, due to their religious beliefs; thus, the child's life was put at risk. The Director of the Department of Social Welfare received the child into his care and undertook the parental rights of the child in order to allow for the necessary blood transfusion to take place, without the parents' consent. The Director based his actions on sections 3 and 4 of the Children Law, Cap. 352. Section 3 of Cap. 352 provides that it shall be lawful for the Director to receive a child under the age of 16 into his care if it appears to him, *inter alia*, that his/her intervention is necessary in the interests of the welfare of the child, while section 4 of Cap. 352 provides that the Director may assume all parental rights

331. *Charalambous v. Director of the Department of Social Welfare* [1994] 1 CLR 396 (in Greek).

over the child in his care, so long as the child's parents are dead and it has no guardian, or if the parent or guardian has abandoned or neglected the child or suffers from some permanent disability rendering the said person incapable of caring for the child, or is of such habits or mode of life as to be unfit to have the care of the child.

*293.* It was argued on behalf of the Director of the Social Welfare Department that the parents' refusal to allow for the necessary blood transfusion to take place meant that they were unfit to have the care of the child. The parents argued that the Director had no power to receive the child, contrary to the wishes of the parents, even on the basis of sections 3 and 4 of Cap. 352. The Court held that since there had been no express objection of the parents, the mere fact that they had not consented to the action of the Director did not signify that the exercise of his rights went beyond the scope of Cap. 352; it was held that since the parents could not consent due to their religious beliefs, it was proper for the Director to assume the parental rights over the child. It was further held that sections 3 and 4 of Cap. 352 do not violate the right to family life of the applicants, as safeguarded by Article 15 of the Constitution, since their aim is to guarantee the life and the welfare of the child, rights which are also enshrined in the Constitution.[332]

*294.* The aforementioned decision of the Supreme Court might be subject to criticism. To begin with, arguing that the Director may exercise his/her powers even without the consent of the parents does not necessarily explain why the parents should be considered to be unfit to have the care of the child. Article 18 §7 of the Constitution expressly stipulates that until a person attains the age of 16, the decision as to the religion to be professed by him/her shall be taken by the person having the lawful guardianship of that person. Thus, receiving blood transfusion is in principle assumed to be contrary, not only to the religious beliefs of the parents, but also to the religious beliefs of the child.[333]

*295.* Section 18 of Law 216/90 stipulates that if the parents fail their duties to care for the child, or administer its property, or if they cannot perform their duties as parents, or if they perform such duties in an abusive manner, the Family Court may remove the parental rights from either, or both parents and provide that a guardian should exercise such parental rights. Removing the parental rights is an extreme measure which may only be ordered, if all other measures have proven to be inadequate in order to prevent bodily or mental harm for the child. While Law 216/90 provides that removing the parental rights is a measure to be exercised with caution, Cap. 352, as interpreted by the Supreme Court in *Charalambous* provides that the powers of the Director of the Social Welfare Department are very wide.

*296.* It might be questioned whether following the enactment of Law 216/90, the Director should still exercise such powers, or whether removing parental rights

---

332. *Charalambous v. Director of the Social Welfare Department* [1994] 1 CLR 396 (in Greek).

333. *See* the discussion in A. Emilianides (ed.), *Welfare of the Child and Beliefs of the Parents* (Nicosia: University of Nicosia Press, 2010), *Glass v. United Kingdom*, Judgment of 9 Mar. 2004; (2004) 39 EHRR 341, *Hoffman v. Austria*, Judgment of 23 Jun. 1993; (1993) 17 EHRR 293.

should be for the Family Courts to decide; there is case law supporting the position that sections 3 and 4 of Cap. 352 providing for the powers of the Director have been implicitly repealed by Law 216/90 to the extent that they are inconsistent with the provisions of the said Law.[334] Cypriot Law thus provides that the Director may undertake the parental rights of the child in order to allow for the necessary blood transfusion to take place, without the parents' consent. However, the case of *Charalambous* does not provide an authority that the Director may also undertake the parental rights of the child in those cases where the parents explicitly object; it is suggested that only the family court may issue a relevant order in the latter case.

## §5. Communication Rights

*297.* The parent not residing with the child in cases of separation or divorce has a right of personal communication with the child in accordance with section 17 of Law 216/90.[335] If the parents disagree with respect to the manner in which such right is to be exercised, the Family Court may order accordingly after taking into account the right of the parent and the welfare of the child; the Court shall usually decide that the parent shall have communication rights, namely spending time alone with the child for certain days and times of the week, as well as certain holidays. The age of the minor, the place of residence of the Applicant, his/her relations with the minor, the child's opinion, as well as other relevant factors may influence the Court's judgment.[336] The Family Court may order that the child is not allowed to travel abroad without the consent of the other parent, if the parent having custody of the child is a foreigner and there is a risk that he/she may leave Cyprus with the child, thus endangering the rights of the other parent.[337] The grandparents of the child also have a right of personal communication with the child and no person may hinder such communication, unless there are serious grounds related to the welfare of the child.[338]

## §6. International Abduction of Children

*298.* The Hague Convention on the Civil Aspects of International Child Abduction (Ratification) Law 11(III)/1994 is of particular importance.[339] Its objects are to secure the prompt return of children wrongfully removed to or retained in any Contracting State and to ensure that rights of custody and of access under the law of

334. *Gerolemou*, Application No. 7/02, decision on habeas corpus application dated 6 Mar. 2002 (in Greek), *Petrou,* Application No. 158/95, decision on habeas corpus application dated 4 Oct. 1995 (in Greek). A different conclusion is supported by *Ioannou,* Application No. 19/95, decision on habeas corpus application dated 8 Mar. 1995.

335. *See also* E. Patera-Dimosthenous, *The Right of Communication in Modern Family Law. An Interdisciplinary Approach* (Athens: Nomiki Vivliothiki, 2017, in Greek).

336. S. Liasides, *Textbook of Family Law* (Nicosia, 2010, in Greek): 107.

337. *Gregory v. Gregory* [2007] 1 CLR 850 (in Greek).

338. *Christofi* [2005] 1 CLR 369 (in Greek).

339. *Savva v. Minister of Justice and Public Order* [2002] 1 CLR 1228 (in Greek).

one Contracting State are effectively respected in the other Contracting States.[340] The Convention refers to the civil aspects of international child abduction and not its criminal aspects; child abduction is also a criminal offence in accordance with section 245A of the Criminal Code, Cap. 154. The aim of the Convention is thus to secure that the abducted children shall return promptly to the country where they habitually reside without undue harm being caused to them.[341] The Convention shall apply to any child who was habitually resident in a Contracting State immediately before any breach of custody or access rights. The Convention shall cease to apply when the child attains the age of 16 years.

*299.* Article 3 of the Convention provides that the removal or the retention of a child is to be considered wrongful where: (i) it is in breach of rights of custody attributed to a person, an institution or any other body, either jointly or alone, under the law of the State in which the child was habitually resident immediately before the removal or retention and (ii) at the time of removal or retention those rights were actually exercised, either jointly or alone, or would have been so exercised but for the removal or retention. The rights of custody may arise in particular by operation of law or by reason of a judicial or administrative decision, or by reason of an agreement having legal effect under the law of that State. Central Authorities (the Minister of Justice and Public Order has been designated as a Central Authority for Cyprus) shall cooperate with each other and promote cooperation amongst the competent authorities in their respective States to secure the prompt return of children and to achieve the other objects of this Convention.

*300.* Any person, institution or other body claiming that a child has been removed or retained in breach of custody rights may apply either to the Central Authority of the child's habitual residence or to the Central Authority of any other Contracting State for assistance in securing the return of the child. The application shall contain information concerning the identity of the applicant, of the child and of the person alleged to have removed or retained the child, where available, the date of birth of the child, the grounds on which the applicant's claim for return of the child is based and all available information relating to the whereabouts of the child and the identity of the person with whom the child is presumed to be. The application may be accompanied or supplemented by an authenticated copy of any relevant decision or agreement, a certificate or an affidavit emanating from a Central Authority, or other competent authority of the State of the child's habitual residence, or from a qualified person, concerning the relevant law of that State and any other relevant document.

*301.* If the Central Authority which receives an application referred to in Article 8 has reason to believe that the child is in another Contracting State, it shall directly

340. *Christofi v. Minister of Justice and Public Order* [2010] 1 CLR 665 (in Greek).

341. *Fasarias v. Minister of Justice and Public Order* [2008] 1 CLR 1024 (in Greek), *Nicolaou v. Minister of Justice and Public Order* [2008] 1 CLR 1311 (in Greek), *Zenonos v. Zisaki* [2009] 1 CLR 661 (in Greek).

and without delay transmit the application to the Central Authority of that Contracting State and inform the requesting Central Authority, or the applicant, as the case may be. The Central Authority of the State where the child is shall take or cause to be taken all appropriate measures in order to obtain the voluntary return of the child. Furthermore, the judicial or administrative authorities of Contracting States shall act expeditiously in proceedings for the return of children. Where a child has been wrongfully removed or retained and, at the date of the commencement of the proceedings before the judicial or administrative authority of the Contracting State where the child is, a period of less than one year has elapsed from the date of the wrongful removal or retention, the authority concerned shall order the return of the child forthwith.

*302.* The judicial or administrative authority, even where the proceedings have been commenced after the expiration of the period of one year shall also order the return of the child, unless it is demonstrated that the child is now settled in its new environment. However, the judicial or administrative authority of the requested State is not bound to order the return of the child if the person, institution or other body which opposes its return establishes that: (a) the person, institution or other body having the care of the person of the child was not actually exercising the custody rights at the time of removal or retention, or had consented to or subsequently acquiesced in the removal or retention; or (b) there is a grave risk that his/her return would expose the child to physical or psychological harm or otherwise place the child in an intolerable situation. The judicial or administrative authority may also refuse to order the return of the child if it finds that the child objects to being returned and has attained an age and degree of maturity at which it is appropriate to take account of its views.

*303.* The judicial or administrative authorities of a Contracting State may, prior to the making of an order for the return of the child, request that the applicant obtains from the authorities of the State of the habitual residence of the child a decision or other determination that the removal or retention was wrongful. The Central Authorities of the Contracting States shall so far as practicable assist applicants to obtain such a decision or determination. The return of the child under the provisions of Article 12 may be refused if this would not be permitted by the fundamental principles of the requested State relating to the protection of human rights and fundamental freedoms. Section 19 of the Convention expressly provides that a decision concerning the return of the child shall not be taken to be a determination on the merits of any custody issue.

# Chapter 7. Maintenance of Children

## §1. Maintenance of Minors

*304.* The obligation to maintain one's minor children is a primary one, taking priority over all other obligations.[342] Such an obligation exists irrespective of whether the parent has parental responsibility or custody of, or enjoys communication with the child, and irrespective of whether the child has been born in wedlock or out of wedlock so long as the child has been recognized either voluntarily or judicially. The obligation, however, does not extend towards persons who are not children of the person in question, but children of the person's spouse from a previous marriage.[343] It should be noted that it is immaterial for the purposes of maintenance of children which spouse was at fault for the breakdown of the marriage of the child's parents.

*305.* Parents have an obligation to jointly maintain their children according to their means by virtue of section 33 §1 of the Relationship between Parents and Children Law 216/90; such means might in principle include not only the actual income of the spouses but also their total earning capacity.[344] In order to determine the amount due by each parent towards the maintenance of their child the Court shall multiply the sum of the income of the parent in question with the sum of the total needs of the child and subsequently divide the product with the sum of the income of both parents[345] in the following way:

$$\frac{\text{Income of the Parent X Needs of the child}}{\text{Income of both Parents}}$$

*306.* Both parents have to contribute equally to the maintenance of the child in accordance with their capabilities; in order for such capabilities to be determined the Court has to consider the income of each spouse. Income earned by a parent while abroad should properly be considered as part of their income, as should any public assistance or pension.[346] It has been held that contribution should in principle refer only to monetary contribution and that the various 'services' offered by a parent to a child as part of the essential functions of the parental role, may not be taken into account while determining the amount of contribution of each parent.[347] The amount of the maintenance due may be such so as to cover the needs of the child regarding maintenance, well-being, and education, on the basis of his/her personal conditions on the one hand and the financial capabilities of the parents on the other. Admittedly, the measure of maintenance cannot be predetermined in absolute

342. *Zacharia v. Zacharia* [1969] 1 CLR 307.
343. *Menelaou v. Menelaou* [1993] 1 CLR 381 (in Greek).
344. *Demetriou v. Demetriou* [2005] 1 CLR 1418 (in Greek).
345. *Kyprianides v. Kyprianides* [2010] 1 CLR 382 (in Greek).
346. *Palazi v. Palazi* [2007] 1 CLR 381 (in Greek).
347. *Charalambous v. Charalambous* [2010] 1 CLR 951 (in Greek). *See*, however, the different approach in *Palazi v. Palazi* [2007] 1 CLR 381 (in Greek).

numbers; common sense and experience should always guide the Court for determining the proper amount of maintenance to be awarded so that the children would be in as similar a situation as if the parents lived together.[348]

*307.* An application for maintenance is in practice filed by the parent who has the parental care or custody of the child. The pleadings should contain all relevant facts which shall enable the Court to determine the proper amount to be awarded for maintenance. Both spouses in child maintenance applications have an obligation to truthfully reveal their respective income and expenses before the Family Court.[349] Whenever a person fails to truthfully reveal their respective income, the Family Court may take into account the nature of his/her profession and compare it with other employees or professionals of the same field in order to determine his/her true income. However, the Family Court may not consider that if the person liable to pay maintenance fails to testify before it, this should imply that the maintenance requested is reasonable. The Court has an obligation to determine that the maintenance requested is a reasonable one.[350] The Family Court may further grant an interim maintenance decree, pursuant to an application by the beneficiary, until such time as the main application is adjudicated by the Court.

*308.* In view of the mandatory character of maintenance of minor children by their parents, a child shall have a right to be maintained by his/her parents, even if he/she has sufficient income or property in accordance with section 33 §3 of Law 216/90. Furthermore, a parent may not refuse to pay maintenance or argue that the amount of maintenance due should be restricted because he/she pays or intends to pay ad hoc sums of money in order to cover specific needs of the child. Maintenance is normally paid periodically at the beginning of every month; however, the Family Court has the power to further order, if it is necessary, for a specific sum to be awarded once, for instance if it relates to medical expenses.[351] The Family Court may further order for the maintenance decree to include a thirteenth or fourteenth monthly payment, if the debtor receives a thirteenth or fourteenth bonus salary. No decree for maintenance may be granted with respect to a period prior to the submission of the application for maintenance; the Family Court has discretion, however, to decide whether maintenance should be paid retroactively from the date that the application for maintenance was filed before it, or whether it should be paid from the date the judgment was delivered, or from any other date.[352]

*309.* It should be noted that payments made as maintenance at a time when there was no maintenance decree in force may not subsequently be taken into account and

348. *Panayiotou v. Sfiktou* [2001] 1 CLR 625 (in Greek), *Markoullides v. Markoullides* [1998] 1 CLR 1386 (in Greek), *Korellides v. Korellides* [2012] 1 CLR 1975 (in Greek), *LL v IS*, App. 37/2015, Judgment of 4 Sep. 2018 (in Greek).

349. *Markoullides v. Markoullides* [1998] 1 CLR 1386 (in Greek).

350. *Efthymiou v. Efthymiou and another*, App. 30/2012, Judgment of 27 Jun. 2014 (in Greek).

351. *Cleovoulou v. Christodoulou* [2009] 1 CLR 886 (in Greek).

352. *Palazi v. Palazi* [2007] 1 CLR 381 (in Greek), *Cleovoulou v. Christodoulou* [2009] 1 CLR 886 (in Greek).

retracted from the amount due if eventually the maintenance decree does not provide for maintenance to be paid retroactively from the date that the maintenance application was filed.[353] The amount due under a maintenance decree, either interim or final, may be collected as a monetary debt in accordance with the provisions of the Civil Procedure Law, Cap. 6 (section 40 of Law 216/90). It may further be ordered that the maintenance due is paid directly from the debtor's monthly salary by virtue of section 38A of Law 216/90. A maintenance decree shall cease in all cases, in accordance with section 39 of Law 216/90, whenever the beneficiary or the debtor dies, since the right is personal and non-transferable, unless the decree refers to the time prior to the death of the beneficiary or the debtor or to payments which were due at the time of death. The Convention on the Recovery Abroad of Maintenance (Ratification) Law 50/1978 also applies with respect to the maintenance of children.

## §2. Variation of Maintenance Orders

*310.* In addition to the above, the obligation to pay maintenance ceases, or the amount paid may increase or decrease, whenever the circumstances have changed and it is to the interests of justice to vary the order, in accordance with section 38 of Law 216/90. The needs of the children are by no means static[354] and usually older children have more needs than younger ones; similarly, the financial means of either parent may have increased or decreased, a fact which should be taken into account while amending a maintenance decree.[355] If the debtor has in the meantime established a new family, or have children, this should also be taken into account by the Family Court; however, the obligation to maintain children from a previous marriage is not invalidated by the fact that the debtor now has an obligation to maintain also others. In any event the Court may only vary an order by taking into account facts which are subsequent to the date when the decree was granted, since otherwise the Family Court would be called upon to retrial the case contrary to the principles governing res judicata.[356]

*311.* Section 3(b) of Law 68(I)/2008 has recently amended section 38 §2 of Law 216/90. The amended section 38 §2 provides that the amount of the maintenance awarded shall automatically be increased by 10% every twenty-four months; the Court has the power to declare that such automatic increase shall not take force or be restricted, following an application by the debtor. The aim of providing for such automatic increase of the amount of maintenance every two years is to enable the beneficiary to receive an increased amount without the need to continuously resort to the Family Court in accordance with the principle that the needs of the children increase as they get older. The Supreme Court held by a majority of 8-4 that the law

353. *Kyprianides v. Kyprianides* [2010] 1 CLR 382 (in Greek).
354. *Zacharoudiou v. Ioannou* [2000] 1 CLR 1614 (in Greek).
355. *Aristidou v. Chrysanthou* [1994] 1 CLR 711 (in Greek).
356. *Christodoulou v. Christodoulou* [1993] 1 CLR 195 (in Greek), *Zeniou v. Zeniou* [1998] 1 CLR 796 (in Greek).

did not violate Article 30 § 2 of the Constitution safeguarding the right to due process, nor the principle of separation of powers.[357]

*312.* However, as the dissenting judgment correctly noted by providing for the automatic increase of an amount specified in a judicial order, without any action by the Court itself, the amended section 38 §2 unconstitutionally interferes in the judicial decision. It has repeatedly been held that the Constitution of Cyprus is based upon a strict separation of powers and that any intervention of the legislative organs in the exercise of judicial powers is strictly forbidden.[358] While it is true that the Court might have the opportunity to consider whether such automatic increase ought to be restricted, this does not change the fact that such automatic increase constitutes an interference with a judicial decree and amends, by a legislative provision, the content of such judicial decree. The legislator could provide that the Court itself may order for such an automatic increase of the amount of maintenance every two years. However, it is not consistent with the principle of separation of powers to provide that a judicial decree may be automatically amended, without any action by the Court itself.

## §3. Maintenance of Adults

*313.* The obligation to pay maintenance to one's children may continue even after a child becomes 18 years of age. An adult child may apply himself/herself before the Family Court and request that a decree of maintenance should be granted, by virtue of section 33 §2 of Law 216/90, so long as there are specific circumstances which justify such a decree being granted;[359] such specific circumstances include studies in academic institutions or professional schools, service at the National Guard of the Republic, or incapacity or incapability of the child. A maintenance decree concerning an adult child shall be issued only if the parent has sufficient means to support such child[360] and only so long as the circumstances of the case justify such a decree being granted;[361] the adult children should make all efforts to restrict their own expenses and any substantial income they might have shall be taken into account by the Court while determining whether (and for which amount) a maintenance decree ought to be granted.[362]

*314.* In addition to the above, children may also have an obligation to maintain their parents, in accordance with section 34 of Law 216/90, if the parents may no longer maintain themselves from their own income, property or employment, after considering all relevant considerations; the child may, by virtue of section 35 of Law 216/90, have an obligation to maintain their parents in such cases, also by the income of property which the parents had themselves donated to the child.

357. *Loizou-Christoforou v. Christoforou*, Legal Question 373, Judgment of 2 May 2017.
358. *See* in detail A. Emilianides, *Constitutional Law in Cyprus* (The Hague: Kluwer, 2013).
359. *Titsinides v. Titsinides* [1994] 1 CLR 385 (in Greek).
360. *Christou v. Christou* [2000] 1 CLR 1891 (in Greek).
361. *Vounou v. Vounou* [1998] 1 CLR 490 (in Greek).
362. *Kyprianides v. Kyprianides* [2010] 1 CLR 382 (in Greek).

## Chapter 8. Kinship and Relationships of Affinity

*315.* Section 3 of the Children (Kinship and Legal Substance) Law 187/1991 provides that two persons are blood relatives in a direct line if they are direct ascendants or descendants of each other, while they are blood relatives not in a direct line if they both have the same ascendant. The degree of kindred between any two persons is ascertained in accordance with section 4 of Law 187/91, which provides that when the two persons are in the direct line of descent, each generation (birth) from either of them to the other shall constitute a degree; where the persons are not in the direct line of descent, each generation from either of them up to their common ancestor and from the common ancestor downwards to the other of them shall constitute a degree. Thus, degrees are determined by the number of births. Children and parents are related in the first degree in the direct line of descent, while grandchildren and grandparents are related in the second degree in the direct line of descent. The most common relatives not in the direct line of descent are siblings (second degree), uncles, aunts, nephews and nieces (third degree), first cousins, children of nephew or niece, great uncles or aunts (fourth degree). Section 5 of Law 187/91 further provides that the kin of one of the spouses is related by affinity to the other spouse in the same lines and degrees; by virtue of section 5 §2 the kinship in affinity is maintained even after the dissolution or annulment of a marriage.

# Part III. Matrimonial Property Law

## Chapter 1. Rights and Obligations of Spouses

### §1. General Principles

*316.* So long as the spouses live together in harmony, it was considered by the legislator that there was no need for the law to regulate in detail their rights and obligations. There are therefore no provisions in the legislation which create legal rights and obligations of the spouses during the period they are married, other than providing in section 3 of Law 232/1991 that the spouses have, proportionally to their means, a mutual obligation for maintenance. The same obligation exists for civil partners pursuant to section 23 of Law 184(I)/2015. There are, however, detailed legal provisions which stipulate the rights and obligations of spouses once the marital relation breaks down. The Matrimonial Property of the Spouses Law 232/1991 provides for the maintenance and matrimonial property of the spouses in cases of separation or divorce, while the Family Courts Law 23/90 provides for the occupation of the former matrimonial home. The aim of such provisions concerning maintenance or matrimonial property is not to punish any of the spouses or former spouses;[363] rather the aim of the legislator and the courts should be to find just and equitable solutions for the settlement of the property relationship of the former spouses. The Family Courts normally enjoy some discretion, within the limits of the Law, when dealing with the rights and obligations of spouses after separation or divorce; this is unavoidable, since all the varying circumstances of each case have to be considered.

*317.* It should be observed that commencement of divorce proceedings is not a prerequisite for the settling of the matrimonial property or for issuing maintenance decrees or granting occupancy of the matrimonial home. So long as the parties have separated, the Family Courts shall have jurisdiction to adjudicate disputes concerning maintenance or matrimonial property. Petitions concerning matrimonial property, maintenance or requesting occupancy of the former matrimonial home are separately filed and adjudicated and are further filed and adjudicated separately than the divorce petition; such petitions are anyway adjudicated by a single judge of the Family Court, while divorce petitions are adjudicated by three judges of the Family Court. It has been held that ending cohabitation is not necessarily a prerequisite of

363. *Reckendorfer v. Reckendorfer* [2004] 1 CLR 1132 (in Greek).

the notion of 'separation' or 'interruption of marital life; there are cases where a married couple cohabitates, but does not live together, because the spouses have no psychological or physical relationship.[364]

## §2. Maintenance

### I. Maintenance after Separation

*318.* Maintenance of the other spouse is governed by sections 3-12 of the Matrimonial Property of the Spouses Law 232/91. Identical provisions apply to the civil partners pursuant to sections 23-32 of the Civil Union Law 184(I)/2015. The spouses have a mutual obligation to maintain each other in accordance with section 3 of Law 232/91. Each spouse is bound to contribute according to his/her means; such means include not only the actual income of the spouses but also their total income potential.[365] If the spouses separate, but their marriage has not been dissolved, either spouse may file a petition for maintenance before the Family Court and the Family Court has the power to order the other spouse to grant periodical payments to the petitioner as maintenance.

*319.* The amount of the maintenance due may be such so as to cover either all the needs of the other spouse, if he/she has no income, or part of the needs of the other spouse, depending on the circumstances of the case and the interests of justice; the Family Court shall take into account the needs of the beneficiary as such arise from the lifestyle he/she enjoyed prior to the separation in accordance with section 7 of Law 232/91; the fact that either spouse (the debtor or the beneficiary depending on the case) might be faced with additional expenses after the separation due to the duplication of homes should always be taken into account. The Family Courts should always use their common sense and experiences for determining the proper amount of maintenance to be ordered.

*320.* Maintenance is paid periodically at the beginning of every month in accordance with section 9 §1 of Law 232/91. No decree, however, for maintenance may be granted with respect to a period prior to the submission of the application for maintenance. Section 9 §1 of Law 232/91 effectively provides that the Family Court has the power to order for the payment of maintenance only from the date that the application is filed before the Court;[366] however, if the defendant was out of the jurisdiction of the Family Court, or was of unknown residence, the period covered by the decree for maintenance may be extended up to six months prior to the date that the petition was filed. Section 8 of Law 232/91 further provides that the Family Court may grant an interim maintenance decree, pursuant to an application by the beneficiary, until such time as the main application is adjudicated by the Court. The

364. *Pichides v. Pichides* [1997] 1 CLR 1612 (in Greek).
365. *Menelaou v. Menelaou* [1993] 1 CLR 381 (in Greek).
366. *Philippou v. Philippou* [2000] 1 CLR 751 (in Greek). *See also Stylianou v. Stylianou* [1993] 1 CLR 839 (in Greek).

amount due under a maintenance decree, either interim or final, may be collected as a monetary debt in accordance with the provisions of the Civil Procedure Law, Cap. 6 (section 12 of Law 232/91); it may thus be ordered that the maintenance due is paid directly from the debtor's monthly salary.

## II. Maintenance after Divorce

*321.* A former spouse may, under some circumstances, have an obligation to pay maintenance to the other former spouse, even after a decree of divorce is granted. Such post-marital maintenance might be due, in accordance with section 5 of Law 232/91, if either of the former spouses' income or property does not suffice to maintain himself/herself and additionally if: (i) at the time when the divorce decree was issued he/she is not young enough, or healthy enough to commence or continue the exercise of an appropriate profession so as to maintain himself/herself, (ii) if he/she has the care or custody of a minor or adult child or other dependent persons who due to bodily or mental incapability are incapable of maintaining themselves, and because of that reason he/she are not in a position to exercise an appropriate profession,[367] (iii) if he/she cannot find an appropriate stable profession or if he/she needs professional education, in both cases up to three years from the date divorce was granted, or (iv) in any other case where providing maintenance is justified on grounds of equity. The criteria for determining the amount of the maintenance are the same as in the case of separation.

## III. Variation of Maintenance Orders

*322.* The obligation to pay maintenance ceases, or the amount paid may increase or decrease, whenever the financial means of the spouses or the needs of the beneficiary spouse change and it is to the interests of justice to vary the order, in accordance with section 10 of Law 232/91. In cases where the maintenance decree was granted after the separation of the spouses, the obligation to pay maintenance ceases if the spouses are no longer separated. The spouse or former spouse who wishes for the maintenance decree to be modified may file a by summons application before the Family Court; any application for modification of the maintenance decree should be based upon facts subsequent to the date the maintenance decree was issued, since otherwise the Family Court would be called upon to retry the case contrary to the principles governing res judicata.[368] The Family Court may, at its discretion, order that the modification of the maintenance decree has a retroactive effect.[369]

*323.* The Family Court has discretion to restrict the ambit of a maintenance decree, or decide not to grant a maintenance decree, in accordance with section 6 of

367. *Aristidou v. Chrysanthou* [1994] 1 CLR 711 (in Greek).
368. *Zeniou v. Zeniou* [1998] 1 CLR 796 (in Greek).
369. *Charalambous v. Zacharia* [2002] 1 CLR 1439 (in Greek).

Law 232/91, if this is justified by important grounds, as if the marriage had a very brief duration, or if the beneficiary was seriously at fault for the dissolution of the marriage, or if he/she willingly caused his/her own poverty. However, it has been held that the fact that the beneficiary spouse was spending money wastefully is not by itself a ground for not granting a maintenance decree, so long as the beneficiary was not seriously at fault for the interruption of marital life.[370] A maintenance decree shall in any event cease, in accordance with section 11 of Law 232/91, whenever: (i) the beneficiary spouse or former spouse remarries or permanently lives with another person in a free union; in such a case the maintenance decree shall cease and may not be modified[371] (ii) the beneficiary or the debtor die, since the right is personal and non-transferable, unless the decree refers to the time prior to the death of the beneficiary or the debtor or to payments which were due at the time of death or (iii) if it was terminated by the Court. It should be noted that the rules governing maintenance are mandatory and thus, the obligation to pay maintenance may not be excluded by the conclusion of a premarital agreement to this effect.

## IV. Recovery of Maintenance Abroad

*324.* The Convention on the Recovery Abroad of Maintenance (Ratification) Law 50/1978 is also relevant.[372] The purpose of the Convention is to facilitate the recovery of maintenance to which a person who is in the territory of one of the Contracting Parties (Claimant), claims to be entitled from another person who is subject to the jurisdiction of another Contracting Party (Respondent). Article 3 of the Convention provides that where a Claimant is in the territory of one Contracting Party (the State of the claimant) and the Respondent is subject to the jurisdiction of another Contracting Party, (the State of the Respondent), the Claimant may make application to a Transmitting Agency in the State of the Claimant for the recovery of maintenance from the Respondent. The application shall be accompanied by all relevant documents, including, where necessary, a power of attorney authorizing the Receiving Agency to act, or to appoint some other person to act, on behalf of the claimant. It shall also be accompanied by a photograph of the Claimant and, where available, a photograph of the Respondent.

*325.* The Transmitting and Receiving Agency for Cyprus is the Minister of Justice and Public Order which shall act as the Applicant on behalf of the Claimant. The Transmitting Agency shall take all reasonable steps to ensure that the requirements of the law of the State of the Receiving Agency are complied with. Furthermore, the Transmitting Agency shall, in accordance with Article 5 of the Convention and at the request of the Claimant, transmit any order, final or provisional, and any other judicial act, obtained by the Claimant for the payment of maintenance in a competent tribunal of any of the Contracting Parties, and, where necessary and possible, the record of the proceedings in which such order was made. The Receiving

370. *Kyriacos Ioannou v. Androulla Ioannou* [1993] 1 CLR 900 (in Greek).
371. *Charalambous v. Zacharia* [2002] 1 CLR 1439 (in Greek).
372. *Minister of Justice and Public Order v. Karapataki* [2007] 1 CLR 503 (in Greek).

Agency shall, subject always to the authority given by the Claimant, take, on behalf of the Claimant, all appropriate steps for the recovery of maintenance, including the settlement of the claim and, where necessary, the institution and prosecution of an action for maintenance and the execution of any order or other judicial act for the payment of maintenance.

## §3. The Matrimonial Home

*326.* Section 17 §1 of the Family Courts Law 23/90[373] provides that if the marital life is interrupted or if notification is sent to the bishop in accordance with section 3 of the Attempt of Reconciliation and Spiritual Dissolution of the Marriage Law 22/90, or if a petition for divorce has been filed, the Family Court has discretion, at the application of either spouse, to grant to one of the spouses the exclusive or partial use of the matrimonial home. The powers of the Family Court under section 17 §1 of Law 23/90 may be exercised only if the marriage has not been dissolved;[374] the Family Court has no jurisdiction to grant exclusive or partial use of the former matrimonial home after the dissolution of the marriage.[375] While Law 23/90 does not define the term 'matrimonial home', it is generally accepted that such matrimonial home is the immovable property where the spouses had been permanently residing prior to the interruption of marital life. Any immovable property, either house, or apartment, or other immovable property, may be considered as the matrimonial home, so long as such was the main home of the family prior to the interruption of marital life; secondary residences may not be considered as the matrimonial home.

*327.* Such order of the Family Court may be granted so long as there are grounds of equity dictating it and after taking into account the specific circumstances of each spouse and the interests of the children, if any; the aim of section 17 §1 is to safeguard the best interests of the weakest members of the family. As held in *Katsourides* the aim of section 17 §1 of Law 23/90 is not to punish either party, but rather to restrict any further deterioration of the marital relation or avoid any negative consequences to either spouse.[376] Exclusive or partial use of the former matrimonial home may be granted, irrespective of who has ownership of the home or who has the right to tenancy or use of the home; however, if the right to use the former matrimonial home stems from an employment contract between either of the spouses and a third party, then granting exclusive or partial use of the home to other spouse is only possible if the third party consents. The petitioner should be able to prove that the other party is at fault for the interruption of the marital life of the spouses;

373. Section 17 s. 1 was held to be both in force (*Christou v. Argyri* [1994] 1 CLR 753, in Greek) and constitutional (*Michalias v. Michalias* [2007] 1 CLR 675, in Greek).
374. *Christodoulou v. Christodoulou* [1996] 1 CLR 260 (in Greek).
375. *Constantinou v. Constantinou* [2004] 1 CLR 1192 (in Greek).
376. *Katsourides v. Katsourides* [1997] 1 CLR 415 (in Greek).

it would be contrary to the rules of equity if the person who is at fault for the interruption of the marital life also claims that he/she should be granted exclusive or partial use of the matrimonial home on grounds of equity.[377]

*328.* The difficulty of either spouse to find another home, the fact that either spouse uses the matrimonial home for professional reasons, the financial situation of the spouses, the health of the spouses, are all grounds to be considered by the Family Court when granting a decree of exclusive or partial use of the matrimonial home. The interests of the children are always an important parameter; such interests might include the continuation of attending a specific educational establishment, residing at the same neighbourhood or home as before, the relationship with the parents, the effect of the separation of their parents to their mental health, as well as other factors.[378] The decision of the Family Court is subject to amendment, whenever the circumstances have changed; the effect of the order anyway ends when the marriage is dissolved.[379] It is observed that the Family Court has the power to grant an interim order of exclusive or partial use of the matrimonial home, pursuant to an application by the beneficiary, until such time as the main petition is adjudicated by the Court.

### §4. Distribution of Movables

*329.* Section 17 §2 of the Family Courts Law 23/90 provides that if the marital life is interrupted or if notification is sent to the bishop in accordance with section 3 of the Attempt of Reconciliation and Spiritual Dissolution of the Marriage Law 22/90, or if a petition for divorce has been filed, either spouse may receive the movables belonging to him/her, even if they are used by both of the spouses or only the other spouse. However, he/she is obliged to grant to the other spouse the use of such household objects which are absolutely necessary for his/her separate residence, so long as there are grounds of equity dictating it. Movables may include any property which is not immovable, including electrical apparatus, furniture, cars, but excluding money, bonds or shares; household objects are objects such as plates, cutlery or utensils.

*330.* In view of the fact that the spouses shall no longer live together in the matrimonial home, it is thus provided that each should receive the movables belonging to him/her, with the exception of such movables which are necessary for the other spouse in order to live separately following the separation. Section 17 §3 of Law 23/90 provides that the movables which belong to both of the spouses are distributed in accordance with their personal needs; if the spouses disagree, then the Family Court may distribute the movables of the parties and, if necessary, order either spouse to pay fair compensation for the use it grants to either spouse. It should be observed that the purpose of sections 17 §2 and 17 §3 of Law 23/90 is not to finally

377. *Ibid.*
378. *See also* S. Liasides, *Textbook of Family Law* (Nicosia, 2010, in Greek): 67–68.
379. *Savva v. Savva* [2003] 1 CLR 1025 (in Greek).

decide who is the owner of the movables owned by the parties; this shall be decided at the adjudication by the Family Court of the petition for the settlement of the matrimonial property of the spouses. The purpose of sections 17 §2 and 17 §3 of Law 23/90 is rather to provide for the distribution of the movables of the spouses, until such time as a divorce decree is granted or the matrimonial property is settled. Thus, the Family Court has no jurisdiction to entertain petitions for determining the ownership in cases of disputed movable property on the basis of section 17 of Law 23/90.[380]

380. *Vasiliades v. Vasiliades* [1995] 1 CLR 328 (in Greek).

## Chapter 2. The Marriage Settlement

*331.* Section 2 of the Contract Law, Cap. 149 provided that dower is the property given from one of the spouses or future spouses, or from a third party, to the other spouse or future spouse, in consideration for the performance of the marriage.[381] Following, however, the enactment of section 3 of Law 22(I)/1995 any contracts for dower performed after Law 22(I)/1995 was enacted, are null and void. Marriage settlements in the sense of prenuptial agreements between the spouses are not valid, or at least not binding under Cypriot law; the same is true with respect to any agreements for the future settlement of the matrimonial property which were concluded between the spouses after the marriage was celebrated, but prior to separation. It is only after the spouses have separated that the claim for contribution to the increase of the matrimonial property provided in section 14 of Law 232/91 may be enforced and thus, any marriage settlements or agreements for the distribution of the matrimonial property which were concluded prior to the separation of the spouses, is not binding upon the parties and shall be disregarded by the Family Court. This is because the provisions of Law 232/91 are of a mandatory character and cannot be undermined by private agreements signed between the parties (presumably under duress) which either restrict or exclude the right safeguarded under section 14 of Law 232/91. Consequently, marriage settlements may only be concluded after the parties have separated and not before.[382]

381. *Oikonomou v. Ttofini* [1993] 1 CLR 436 (in Greek).

382. G. Serghides, 'Matrimonial Property of the Spouses according to Cypriot Law', in *Id.* (ed), *Matrimonial Property of the Spouses and Partners and Various Legal Issues* (Nicosia, 2010 in Greek), 15.

# Chapter 3. The Legal Matrimonial Regime

## §1. Introduction

*332.* Section 13 of Law 232/91 provides that marriage does not affect the proprietary independence of the spouses; each spouse retains and acquires his/her own property even after the marriage is celebrated. The spouses may acquire joint property; however, each spouse shall in such a case have an undivided share in such property. If the marriage is annulled, or dissolved, or if the parties have been separated, then either party may claim his/her contribution to the increase of the property of the other spouse. In particular section 14 of Law 232/91 provides that if the property of either spouse has increased during the duration of the marriage and the other spouse has contributed to such increase, then the other spouse may file a matrimonial property petition before the Court and claim the part of the property which has been increased due to his/her contribution.[383] Such contribution is rebuttably presumed at one-third of the increase, unless it is proven to be greater or smaller. If the spouses have acquired property from donations, inheritance, legacies or other *ex gratia* cause, this is not taken into account when calculating whether there has been increase of the property of the spouses. Section 14 of Law 232/91 shall be analysed in greater detail in the subsequent paragraphs. It is noted that its provisions as well as the other relevant provisions of Law 232/91 relating to contribution are replicated in sections 34-42 of the Civil Union Law 184(I)/2015 with regards to civil partners.

## §2. Ambit

*333.* Section 14 of Law 232/91 applies only with respect to persons who were spouses and have either divorced, or separated, or their marriage has been annulled. Section 14 does not apply to persons who were engaged, or were living in a free union, or otherwise never married.[384] The Family Court has exclusive jurisdiction regarding claims between the spouses for property acquired by them during the duration of their marriage.[385] The Family Court, however, has no jurisdiction to adjudicate proprietary disputes between former spouses which arose after the dissolution or annulment of the marriage, which accordingly do not fall within the ambit of section 14.[386] It should be noted that if the spouses have settled their matrimonial property by an agreement which was concluded after separation, then the

383. S. Karatsis, *The Claim for Contribution to Property* (Limassol: Limassol Bar Association, 2007, in Greek).

384. *Savva v. Georghiou* [2006] 1 CLR 658 (in Greek), *Clerides v. Stavrides* [1998] 1 CLR 521 (in Greek).

385. *Leftis v. Georghiou* [2010] 1 CLR 211 (in Greek), *Logginos v. Logginos* [2000] 1 CLR 1347 (in Greek).

386. *Savva v. Savva* [2003] 1 CLR 1022 (in Greek), *Constantinou v. Constantinou* [2004] 1 CLR 1192 (in Greek).

Family Court no longer has jurisdiction to adjudicate the matrimonial property dispute; this is because the claim under section 14 of Law 232/91 for which the Family Court has exclusive jurisdiction,[387] would have been substituted by an agreement of the parties, the interpretation of which falls under the jurisdiction of the District Court.[388] It is immaterial whether the agreement is a written or oral one.[389] It has further been held that the District Court, and not the Family Court, shall have jurisdiction regarding an agreement between the former spouses in accordance to which a house has been sold from one spouse to the other; such dispute is contractual and not related to family law.[390]

*334.* Section 15 (a) stipulates that the claim for contribution is further subject to a three-year limitation period; thus, any petition has to be filed within three years from the dissolution or annulment of the marriage;[391] The limitation period does not begin at the time when the Family Court has jurisdiction, but at the time when the marriage was dissolved or annulled.[392] Any counterclaim is considered as having been filed at the same time as the main petition. The right of a spouse to claim contribution is personal and non-transferable.[393] In the case of death of the other spouse, the surviving spouse may still claim his/her contribution in accordance with section 14; the amount of such contribution shall not be part of the estate of the deceased. In *Hadjikypri* the spouse of the Appellant had died while a claim for contribution in accordance with section 14 was pending; the Court allowed the petition to proceed against the Administrators of the estate of the deceased.[394] If, however, the spouse claiming contribution has died, then his/her heirs, or administrators or executors of the estate, may not claim such contribution, unless a relevant petition has been served while the spouse was alive, or unless the claim has been contractually recognized by the other spouse (section 15 (b) and (c) of Law 232/91).[395] In any event Law 232/91 does not have retroactive effect and thus, if the marriage was dissolved prior to the entry into force of Law 232/91, a spouse may not claim his/her contribution in accordance with section 14 of Law 232/91.[396]

*335.* The claim pursuant to section 14 is in principle a contractual right and not a right in rem.[397] Consequently, the beneficiary spouse may claim and be awarded

387. *Michael v. Yiangou* [1999] 1 CLR 1348 (in Greek).
388. *Kozaki v. Kozaki* [2003] 1 CLR 1047 (in Greek). *See also Fotsiou v. Irodotou* [2010] 1 CLR 1172 (in Greek), *Petraki v. Fotiou* [2012] 1 CLR 625 (in Greek).
389. *See also Orfanou v. Onisiforou*, App. 27/2013, Judgment of 21 Feb. 2017 (in Greek).
390. *Masouras v. Papamarcou* [2005] 1 CLR 385 (in Greek).
391. Held to be constitutional in *Karatzias v. Papakyriacou* [2001] 1 CLR 2113 (in Greek), *Demetriou v. Demetriou*, Legal Question 371, Judgment of 14 Sep. 2016 (in Greek). *See also Nicolaou v. Nicolaou* [1998] 1 CLR 1030 (in Greek).
392. *Demetriou v. Demetriou* [2012] 1 CLR 834 (in Greek).
393. *Gregoriou v. Gregoriou* [2001] 1 CLR 1461 (in Greek).
394. *Hadjikypri v. Giorgalli* [2007] 1 CLR 1239 (in Greek).
395. *See* the concurring judgment of Economou J. in *Nicolas v. Antoniou*, Civil App. 458/2011, Judgment of 19 Jul. 2017 (in Greek).
396. *Nicolaou v. Nicolaou* [1998] 1 CLR 1030 (in Greek).
397. *Papaioannou v. Papaioannou* [2000] 1 CLR 656 (in Greek), *Andreou v. Andreou* [2002] 1 CLR 896 (in Greek), *Hadjikypri v. Giorgalli* [2007] 1 CLR 1239 (in Greek).

monetary compensation for his/her contribution to the increase of the property of the other spouse, irrespective of whether such property is movable or immovable; however, by virtue of section 14E of Law 232/91 the Family Court may order the transfer of any property of the defendant to the claimants' compensation. Transfer of property in accordance with such order of the Family Court is not subject to any duties or charges. It has been suggested that the existence of such powers of the Family Court might indicate that the claims pursuant to section 14 might, in certain cases be rights in rem, since that the petitioner might consequently seek the transfer of specific property of the other spouse to him/her as a remedy.[398] It is in our view more accurate to state that the right remains a contractual right, despite the powers of the Family Court to order the transfer of specific property, since the trial is concerned with the increase of the property of the other spouse and the contribution to which the petitioner is entitled to; it is not concerned with the specific property, irrespective of the relief which might be sought or granted.[399] The Court has further the discretionary power to order the payment of interest on the amount awarded by virtue of section 32 §2 of the Courts of Justice Law 14/60.[400]

## §3. Determining the Contribution

*336.* In order to determine whether the property of the other spouse has increased or not the crucial time is the time of separation of the spouses; it is therefore essential that the Court decides on the basis of the evidence presented before it, when the spouses have separated as a matter of fact.[401] It is the increase of property and not the property by itself that is the subject of a matrimonial property petition in accordance with section 14 of Law 232/91.[402] Determining the precise time when the spouses were separated is thus of extreme significance in order to determine the contribution.[403] The Court should compare the property that either spouse had at the time when the marriage was celebrated with the property that either spouse had at the time of separation, in order to determine whether such property has increased during the marriage of the parties. If there is no increase, or if the property of a spouse has decreased, then section 14 does not apply and the other spouse can claim nothing.[404] Consequently, it is not sufficient for the petitioner to present evidence that the defendant has property at the time of separation. The petitioner should further prove that the property of the defendant has increased during the marriage of the parties. Thus, sufficient evidence has to be presented about the property that the defendant owed at the time when the marriage was celebrated.[405] Furthermore, sufficient evidence, including expert testimony, should be provided with respect to the

398. S. Liasides, *Textbook of Family Law* (Nicosia, 2010, in Greek), 229.
399. *See also Orphanides v. Orphanides* [1998] 1 CLR 179 (in Greek).
400. *Moustaka v. Ioannou* [2010] 1 CLR 173 (in Greek).
401. *Mylonas v. Mavronicola* [2005] 1 CLR 1267 (in Greek).
402. *Orphanides v. Orphanides* [1998] 1 CLR 179 (in Greek), *Papaioannou v. Papaioannou* [2000] 1 CLR 656 (in Greek).
403. *Tsounta v. Demetriades*, App.29/2010, Judgment of 20 Feb. 2014 (in Greek).
404. *Papaioannou v. Papaioannou* [2000] 1 CLR 656 (in Greek).
405. *Orphanides v. Orphanides* [1998] 1 CLR 179 (in Greek).

value of the property and especially of immovable property; expert witnesses should provide sufficient data enabling the Court to review the accuracy of their findings.[406]

*337.* When determining the value of the property, the Court should take into account only the net value of such property, after the payment of obligations or debts.[407] If the defendant had property prior to the marriage and the value of such property has increased simply due to inflation, this should not normally be considered as 'increase' of the property in the sense of section 14 of Law 232/91. Thus, property which the defendant had prior to the marriage should be evaluated taking into account inflation, so that there is no fictional increase to which the claimant had not contributed.[408] Furthermore, property donated by either spouse to the other during the marriage shall be taken into account by the Family Court, in accordance with section 16 of Law 232/91, in order to determine the amount that should be awarded for contribution to the increase of the property of the other spouse.

*338.* It is accepted that contribution is not only of a monetary nature; a spouse taking care of the minor children of the family and the household of the spouses and providing moral support to this/her working spouse, might well be considered to have contributed to the increase of the other spouse's property. Section 2 defines contribution as the contribution by the spouses in any form, to the acquisition of property and it includes taking care of the matrimonial home and the family members.[409] Monetary or other contribution of the relatives of the petitioner to the other spouse, contribution of the petitioner to the business of the other spouse, work of the petitioner in the matrimonial home, the amount each spouse was contributing towards the monthly expenses of the household, social activities, or even attendance to social events promoting the professional life of the other spouse, assistance received by the State due to the fact that the petitioner was a displaced person, and any other kind of contribution, might be taken into account by the Court in order to determine the extent of the contribution of the petitioner to the increase of the property of the other spouse.

*339.* The presumption in accordance to which the contribution is presumed at one-third of the increase is a rebuttable one; accordingly, if the claimant proves that his/her contribution was greater or smaller than one-third, he/she may be awarded a greater amount as compensation by the Family Court. The introduction of the presumption is an acknowledgment by the legislator of the difficulties the petitioner might face in proving his/her contribution, often after many years of marriage.[410] If

406. *Malaos v. Malaos* [2005] 1 CLR 1191 (in Greek), *Sofocleous v. Kyriacou* [2010] 1 CLR 665 (in Greek).
407. *Sofocleous v. Sofocleous* [2005] 1 CLR 1030 (in Greek).
408. G. Serghides, 'Matrimonial Property of the Spouses according to Cypriot Law', in *Id.* (ed), *Matrimonial Property of the Spouses and Partners and Various Legal Issues* (Nicosia, 2010), 10 (in Greek).
409. *Ibid.*, 17 (in Greek).
410. *Malaos v. Christou* [2005] 1 CLR 1191 (in Greek).

the evidence before the Court is not conclusive regarding the extent of the contribution of the petitioner to the increase of the property of the other spouse, then the Family Court might order that the petitioner is awarded one-third of the increase in accordance with the presumption.[411] If the petitioner seeks to be awarded an amount exceeding one-third of the increase, then he/she shall have to provide sufficient evidence proving that his/her contribution exceeded one-third.[412]

*340.* As already stated, if the spouses have acquired property from donations, inheritance, legacies or other *ex gratia* cause, this is not taken into account when calculating whether there has been increase of the property of the spouses. Property acquired as a result from the disposal of such donations, inheritance, legacies or other *ex gratia* cause, is also excluded. The exclusion of such property from the calculation of the increase of the property of the other spouse is reasonable, since in those cases the contribution of the other spouse is non-existent. Section 17 of Law 232/91 further provides that the Family Court has discretion not to award any amount as contribution to the petitioner, or to reduce the amount the petitioner is entitled to, if he/she has been convicted for murder or homicide of the other spouse or one of the children of the other spouse, or if he/she has been convicted for wilfully causing grievous bodily harm to the other spouse or one of his/her children, or if he/she behaved towards the other spouse or one of his/her children immorally or cruelly.

## §4. Powers of the Court

*341.* In addition to its powers to award compensation for the petitioner's contribution to the increase of the property of the other spouse, the Family Court has the power to grant an interim order prohibiting the alienation or encumbrance of the property in question by virtue of Article 14C of Law 232/91. The Court may further exercise its powers to grant interim orders by virtue of section 32 of the Courts of Justice Law 14/60 and section 9 of the Civil Procedure Law, Cap. 6; the three-stage test that a petitioner has to satisfy for interim protection to be granted are the following: (i) the existence of a serious issue to be tried (in matrimonial property cases this is self-evident), (ii) the possibility that the petitioner shall be entitled to the remedies he/she seeks, namely that he/she has a good cause of action and (iii) that it would be impossible or difficult for justice to be achieved at any subsequent stage, unless the interim order is issued.[413] The Court should further consider whether it would be on the balance of convenience fair and just to grant the interim order.[414]

411. *Orphanides v. Orphanides* [1998] 1 CLR 179 (in Greek), *Theori v. Chrysostomou* [2003] 1 CLR 386 (in Greek).
412. *Sfiktou v. Panayiotou* [2007] 1 CLR 28 (in Greek).
413. *Odysseos v. Pieris Estates* [1982] 1 CLR 557.
414. *Kokkinou v. Kokkinou*, App. 29/2014, Judgment of 3 Nov. 2016 (in Greek).

*342.* The aim of interim protection is to ensure that nothing occurs pending the trial, such as alienation or encumbrance of immovable property, which will prejudice the rights of the petitioner. At the stage of interim protection the Court shall not try to resolve conflicts of evidence as to the material facts, or to decide difficult questions of law which call for detailed argument.[415] The main criterion in matrimonial property cases is whether there are prima facie good chances for the petition to succeed at its substance.[416] The fact that the claim of the petitioner is not to the amount of the estimated property of the property that is the subject of the interim order is not an obstacle to granting such interim order.[417] The Court may further annul any transfer, disposal or encumbrance of property or part of it, which aimed at circumventing the provisions of Article 14 or an order issued by the Court.

*343.* Section 14A of Law 232/91 provides that the Family Court may, following an application by either party, order that the other party should submit to the Court an affidavit, describing fully and in a detailed and precise manner his/her property at the time of separation or any other date that the Court might consider as appropriate. If the spouse revealing such property no longer has an interest in or ownership of such property at the time of trial or at any other time, the Family Court may, following an application by either party, request that the spouse in question provides particular and convincing evidence of the alienation or disposal of the property in question with a complementary affidavit. The Court may further order the spouse in question to instruct any banking or financial institution to transfer or restore such property. The affiant may be examined as to the content of his/her affidavit or complementary affidavit.

*344.* The aim of section 14A is for the spouses to reveal their property so as to avoid fraudulent transfers and concealment of property. It has been held that the provisions of section 14A do not violate any provisions of the ECHR;[418] Section 14A does not deprive the property of either spouse but rather fulfils the legitimate aim of safeguarding the rights of both spouses without discrimination. Any person who provides false, inaccurate or incomplete information is subject to imprisonment for up to two years or to a fine not exceeding EUR 3418,79 (CYP 2,000) or both imprisonment and a fine in accordance with section 14B of Law 232/91. Any person who fails or delays to comply with an order of the Court issued pursuant to section 14A is guilty of contempt in accordance to section 14B and section 44 of the Courts of Justice Law 14/60. If such person is a petitioner in divorce proceedings, the Family Court may suspend any further proceedings until full compliance is effected.

415. *Douglas v. Douglas* [2004] 1 CLR 629 (in Greek), Y. Constantinides, 'The Powers of the Courts to Issue Interim Orders in Cyprus', in *Corpus de Jure Cyprii* (Nicosia: Legal Studies Council, 1987, in Greek), 211.
416. *Reckendorfer v. Reckendorfer* [2004] 1 CLR 1132 (in Greek).
417. *Aristotelous v. Benfleet* [2006] 1 CLR 280 (in Greek).
418. *Kolarides v. Cyprus*, No. 64039/00, Admissibility Decision of 11 Apr. 2001.

### §5. Equity and Matrimonial Property

*345.* Prior to the enactment of Law 232/91, where property exclusively belonged to one of the spouses, the Court had no right to intervene; the Court could only intervene in cases where it was held that a trust had been created in which case the law of equity applied.[419] In *Pentafkas* the Supreme Court held that for a constructive trust to be created in favour of the spouse, the requirements were either: (i) an express agreement that the property be shared beneficially and detriment suffered by the partner who is not the legal owner, or (ii) inferred common intention that the property be shared beneficially in light of financial contributions to the purchase price or mortgage payments.[420] In *Constantinou* it was held that where the contribution of a spouse to the acquisition of immovable property is minimal, it cannot be stated that a trust has been created in his/her favour.[421]

*346.* The question whether equity could apply even after the enactment of section 14 remains a controversial issue. In *Orphanides* it was held that section 14 of Law 232/91 is not encoding the principles of equity; its rules exclusively govern the distribution of property and provide for the contribution in cases of increase of the property of either party, in such a way that the complementary application of the principles of English law on equity is not possible.[422] In the subsequent case of *Christophorou*, the Supreme Court held that the principles of equity may apply in Cyprus by virtue of section 29 §1 (c) of the Courts of Justice Law 14/60, unless there is a contrary provision in any law, such as in section 14 of Law 232/91; the judgment in *Orphanides* was cited with approval.[423]

*347.* Contrary to the aforementioned case law on the matter, the subsequent case law of the Supreme Court held that the Family Court may apply the principles of equity also in matrimonial property disputes. In *Logginos* it was held that the Family Courts have the power to grant any remedies which a party might be entitled to in accordance with the principles of equity;[424] such approach was reiterated in *Michael*[425] and the majority of the Appellate Family Court in *Philippou.*[426] It is apparent that recent case law clearly holds that the doctrine of equity can still be applied alongside section 14 of Law 232/91. It is submitted that this approach is highly problematic. Section 14 of Law 232/91 is a mandatory rule and the rules of

---

419. *Pentafkas v. Pentafka* [1991] 1 CLR 547 (in Greek). *See also* S. Loizidou, 'The Witch's Brew: Cohabitation And its Property Implications on Relationship Breakdown in Cyprus', in *Matrimonial Property of the Spouses and Partners and Various Legal Issues*, ed. G. Serghides (Nicosia, 2010), 37ff.
420. *Pentafkas v. Pentafka* [1991] 1 CLR 547 (in Greek).
421. *Constantinou v. Demosthenous* [1992] 1 CLR 621 (in Greek). *See also Reckendorfer v. Reckendorfer* [2004] 1 CLR 1132 (in Greek).
422. *Orphanides v. Orphanides* [1998] 1 CLR 179 (in Greek).
423. *Christoforou v. Christoforou* [1998] 1 CLR 1551 (in Greek). Also *Papaioannou v. Papaioannou* [2000] 1 CLR 656 (in Greek).
424. *Logginos v. Logginou* [2000] 1 CLR 1347 (in Greek).
425. *Michael v. Yiangou* [2001] 1 CLR 1643 (in Greek).
426. *Philippou v. Philippou* [2003] 1 CLR 1343 (in Greek).

equity should never be contrary to legal provisions, much less provisions of a mandatory character. As correctly noted, equity prevents a multiplicity of suits or double compensation and these are additional grounds why the rules of equity should be considered as no longer applying in matrimonial property disputes following the enactment of Law 232/91.[427]

*348.* Despite such criticism in the recent case of *Pericleous* the Appellate Family Court emphatically stated once again that the principles of equity apply in matrimonial property disputes.[428] Even more so, it was held that the Family Court has jurisdiction even in cases where the alleged constructive trust refers to the property of a third person. In *Pericleous* the Appellant had separated from his wife. Prior to the marriage the Second Respondent, a limited company owned by the Respondent's parents had bought immovable property in which the matrimonial home was subsequently built. The Appellant argued that he had contributed to the increase of the Respondent's property and claimed half of the immovable property referred to above. The Appellate Family Court held that the mere fact that the property was registered in the name of a third person could not change the nature of the claim as one of contribution to the increase of the property of the other spouse for which the Family Court has jurisdiction.

*349.* It was thus held that whenever the property is allegedly owned either by the spouse as a beneficiary owner of a trust or a third person with the intention to defraud, the Family Court has jurisdiction. In view of the fact that the Second Respondent company had bought the immovable property before the marriage and had consented to the use of such property as the matrimonial home, the Family Court had jurisdiction to hear the case irrespective of the fact that the said immovable property was still registered in the name of the Second Respondent and not one of the spouses. Thus, the Appellant had the right to sue not only his/her spouse, but also the Second Respondent. It emerges that the jurisdiction of the Family Courts is continuously extended,[429] in order to include not only cases where the alleged trusts have been created between the spouses, but also to cases where the property is owned by a third person. Where, however, the claim does not relate to contribution to the matrimonial property, but the spouse claims that her spouse has stolen her own property, or has acted with the intention to defraud, it is the District Court and not the Family Court that has jurisdiction to determine the claim.[430]

---

427. *See* the analysis of G. Serghides, 'Matrimonial Property of the Spouses according to Cypriot Law', in *Id.* (ed), *Matrimonial Property of the Spouses and Partners and Various Legal Issues* (Nicosia, 2010), 11ff (in Greek).

428. *Pericleous v. Egglezou and Another* [2011] 1 CLR 1015 (in Greek). *See also Varnava v. Kallitsionis*, App. 4/2013, Judgment of 27 Jun. 2014 (in Greek), *Kourou v. Konou*, Civil App. 325/2009, Judgment of 10 Oct. 2014 (in Greek).

429. *Leftis v. Georghiou* [2010] 1 CLR 211 (in Greek).

430. *Tsiklauri v. Isakov and others*, Civil App. E8/2010, Judgment of 25 Jan. 2016 (in Greek). *See also Kokkinou v. Discovery Advertising Ltd*, App. 23/2015, Judgment of 26 Sep. 2018 (in Greek).

# Part IV. Succession Law

## Introduction

*350.* Succession may occur, in accordance with section 4 of the Wills and Succession Law, Cap. 195, in the following three ways:[431]

(1) By will: Deceased persons have in principle the right to choose their heirs by making a will before their death. However, such right is a limited one; whenever the testator has died leaving close relatives (children, grandchildren, parents or spouse) a statutory portion is reserved for the statutory heirs, as opposed to testamentary heirs. The aim of the legislator for introducing such restrictions to the right of the testator to choose his/her own heirs is to safeguard that the spouse and next-of-kin of the deceased will inherit a fair portion of the deceased's estate.
(2) By law: A deceased may die intestate, without making a valid will. In such a case, the provisions of the Wills and Succession Law, Cap. 195 govern the distribution of the deceased's estate.
(3) By both will and the Law: As already mentioned under (1) above, the testamentary right is not absolute. Thus, there are cases where the estate of the deceased, despite the deceased's intentions, will be governed partly by the contents of the will (insofar as the disposable portion is concerned) and partly by the provisions of Cap. 195 (insofar as the statutory portion is concerned). Such a case may also occur whenever the testator has not provided in the will for the distribution of the entire estate, but only for part of the estate in which case there is undisposed portion of the estate.

*351.* The provisions of the Wills and Succession Law, Cap. 195 govern the succession of natural persons (since legal persons may not anyway be the subject of succession and inheritance). With regards to the succession of persons who died until 16 August 2015, Cap. 195 shall apply only if such persons had immovable property located in the Republic, or were domiciled in the Republic of Cyprus at the time of their death. If the deceased was domiciled in Cyprus at the time of death, then Cypriot law governs the succession to the movable property of the deceased, both in Cyprus and abroad, as well as the succession to the immovable property of the deceased which was situated in Cyprus; immovable property of the deceased

431. *See* in detail A. Emilianides, *Cypriot Succesion Law* 3rd edn (Nicosia: Hippasus, 2015, in Greek).

which was situated outside Cyprus is not governed by Cypriot law, but is governed by the *lex situs* (the law of the land where such property is situated).[432]

*352.* If on the contrary the deceased was domiciled outside Cyprus, then Cypriot law governs only the succession to the immovable property of such person situated in Cyprus; the immovable property of such person situated outside Cyprus is governed by the *lex situs*. Insofar as the movable property of such a person is concerned, a distinction has to be made on the basis of the place where the deceased actually died. If the deceased died in Cyprus, then section 12 of Cap. 195 provides that the movable property of such a person is to be governed by the law of the deceased's domicile at the time of death. If the deceased died outside Cyprus and did not have Cypriot domicile, then the relevant rules of Private International Law shall apply.[433]

*353.* If Cypriot law applies in accordance with the above, then Cap. 195 will determine both the formal and substantial validity of a will and succession in cases of intestacy and Cypriot courts will enjoy jurisdiction with respect to movable property situated both in Cyprus and abroad, as well as with respect to immovable property situated in Cyprus.[434] Immovable property situated outside Cyprus is not to be taken into consideration for the determination of the shares of the heirs or the disposable portion, even if the deceased was domiciled in Cyprus.

*354.* With regards to the succession of persons who died after 17 August 2015, The rules of Cypriot private international law are harmonized with Regulation 650/2012 of the European Parliament and of the Council of 4 July 2012 on jurisdiction, applicable law, recognition and enforcement of decisions and acceptance and enforcement of authentic instruments in matters of succession and on the creation of a European Certificate of Succession. Regulation 650/12 provides for a system of unity of succession, whereby a single law, mainly the law where the deceased had his habitual residence, shall govern the succession to the whole of the estate of the deceased, irrespective of whether such refers to movables or immovable property; this is undeniably a major development for the Cypriot legal system.[435]

*355.* Thus, the notion of habitual residence has replaced the notion of domicile as far as movable property is concerned, and the *lex situs* as far as immovable property is concerned; a single law, that of the habitual residence of the deceased at the time of death, shall govern the entire estate of the deceased, either movable or immovable, either in Cyprus or outside of Cyprus. An escape clause stipulates that where by way of exception it is clear from all the circumstances of the case that at

432. *Kochino v. Irfan* [1976] 1 CLR 240, A. Emilianides, 'Private International Law', in *Symposium on Cypriot Juridical Issues* (Thessaloniki, 1974), 90 (in Greek).
433. For an extensive analysis *see* A. Emilianides et al, *Private International Law in Cyprus* (The Hague: Kluwer, 2015), *Idem, Cypriot Succession Law* 3rd edn (Nicosia: Hippasus, 2015, in Greek).
434. *See also Academy of Athens v. Panayiotou* [1994] 1 CLR 472 (in Greek).
435. *See* in detail A. Emilianides et al, *Private International Law in Cyprus* (The Hague: Kluwer, 2015), *Idem, Cypriot Succession Law* 3rd edn (Nicosia: Hippasus, 2015, in Greek).

the time of death, the deceased was manifestly more closely connected with a State other than the State of the habitual residence, the law applicable to the succession shall be the law of that other State. Regulation 650/2012 further enables the deceased to organize his succession in advance and choose the *lex successionis*, by providing that a person may choose the law of the State whose nationality he possesses at the time of making the choice or at the time of death, as the law to govern his succession as a whole. A person possessing multiple nationalities may choose the law of any of the States whose nationality he possesses at the time of making the choice or at the time of death. Such right of the deceased person to choose the applicable law is a novel one, since the existing Cypriot legislation does not provide for such a possibility.

# Chapter 1. Intestate Succession

## §1. The Opening of the Succession

### I. Death

*356.* Death may be proven before a court by any evidentiary means. Section 20 of the Population Registry Law 141(I)/2002 provides that the death of any person who dies in Cyprus is registered by the Registrar of the District where the death occurred. If there is no information with respect to the place and time of death, then it is registered by the Registrar of the District in which the corpse was found. For a death to be registered, medical certification of the death has to be provided in accordance with sections 23, 25 and 26 of Law 141(I)/02. However, if there are reasonable suspicions that the deceased died violently or abnormally or from unknown causes, then an inquest is carried out in accordance with the provisions of the Coroners Law, Cap. 153; the coroners are to send to the Registrar a certificate containing their findings in relation to the causes of death of the deceased person.

*357.* The General Registrar, namely the Permanent Secretary of the Ministry of Interior, maintains a General Register of all deaths which were registered in any District of Cyprus in accordance with section 35 of Law 141(I)/02. In addition, the General Registrar maintains in accordance with section 57 of Law 141(I)/02 a special Registry in which the deaths of citizens of the Republic which occur outside Cyprus are registered. Persons with legal interest, such as the heirs of the deceased, may be granted an authenticated death certificate from the Registrar in accordance with the provisions of sections 48 and 48 of Law 141(I)/02. In legal proceedings, the person claiming hereditary rights by alleging that the deceased died on a given date, other has the burden of proof that the deceased died on a specific date.[436]

### II. Missing Persons and Absentees

*358.* It is often the case that there is not sufficient evidence whether a person had died or not, or when the corpse may not be found; this is the case of missing persons and absentees. Section 14 of Cap. 195 provides exhaustively about the circumstances under which missing persons and absentees may be declared dead, either because no news has been heard of them for a very long time, or because they have been missing following a serious danger to their lives.[437] An order for the declaration of death may be declared, in accordance with section 14 §9 of Cap. 195 by the District Court in the jurisdiction of which, the missing person last resided in the

436. *Constantinou and others v. Director of Land Registry* [2012] 1 CLR 1990 (in Greek).

437. C. Tornaritis, 'The Institution of Death in Absentia in the Cypriot Legal System', *Cyprus Law Review* 24 (1988): 3709, 3715 (in Greek) suggests that the common law presumption that a person is dead if no news has been heard of him/her for seven years applies in parallel to the provisions of s. 14 of Cap. 195. It is suggested, however, that since the legislator has exhaustively provided for the presumption of declaration of death *in absentia*, the parallel application of common law presumptions should not be legally permissible.

Republic. The order may be requested by either a person who deduces rights from the declaration of death of the person concerned, or by the Attorney-General of the Republic. Persons who are considered to deduce rights in the declaration of death are the prima facie heirs and legatees of the deceased; relatives of the missing person who are not heirs or legatees are not considered as such. It would seem that the creditors of the missing person should not properly be considered as persons who deduce rights in the declaration of death either; this is due to the fact that the declaration of death *in absentia* aims to promote the best interests of the absentee and not to protect the missing person's creditors.

*359.* Death may be declared in accordance with section 14 §2 of Cap. 195 if no news has been heard that the missing person is still alive for a period of ten consecutive years.[438] Information that the person is still alive may originate either from the missing person himself/herself, or from third persons and may be either written or oral. However, a person may not be declared dead before the end of the year in which such person would have reached 28 years of age had he/she continued to be alive. If a person is declared dead in accordance with the general rule of section 14 §2, then the death is presumed – unless there is sufficient evidence to the contrary – to have occurred from the lapse of the period of ten or five years, or of the conclusion of twenty years of age, depending on the case. In accordance with the provisions of Interpretation Law, Cap. 1, the periods of ten and five years respectively begin to count from the last day of the calendar year (31 December) during which there had been news that the missing person was still alive. It should be further noted that if the missing person would have completed 70 years of age had he/she continued to be alive until the date the application for declaration of death was filed, then death may be declared if no news has been heard that the missing person is still alive for a period of five consecutive years prior to the filing of the application.

*360.* In addition to the general rule of section 14 §2 of Cap. 195, section 14 further provides for three special cases:

(a) Section 14 §3 provides that if a person had taken part in a war as a member of an armed force, either as an official, employee, volunteer or muleteer, and disappeared during the war and has not been heard since, then such person may be declared dead after three years from the conclusion of peace or from the end of the war. It would seem that section 14 §3 applies only with respect to traditional wars, and not with regard to terrorist attacks.
(b) Section 14 §4 further provides that if a person was a passenger on a ship or an aircraft which has disappeared during a sea or air passage respectively, then such person may be declared dead after one year from the loss of the ship or aircraft. Such loss will be presumed if the ship or aircraft has not arrived at its place of destination within three years; if there is no fixed place of destination, then the ship or aircraft is presumed lost if it has not returned within three years from the beginning of the ship or air passage respectively.

438. According to the prevailing opinion, the ten-year period must have been completed before the application for declaration of death is filed.

(c) Finally, section 14 §5 provides that if a person has disappeared under life-threatening circumstances other than those referred to in sections 14 §3 or 14 §4, then such person may be declared dead if there has been no news that such person is still alive for a period of three years since the occurrence of the life-threatening event. Section 14 §5 may apply, *inter alia*, in cases of terrorist attacks, earthquakes, tsunami or other similar cases.

If a person is declared dead in accordance with the special cases of section 14 §3, 14 §4, or 14 §5, then the death is presumed – unless there is sufficient evidence to the contrary – to have occurred from (i) the conclusion of peace or the end of the war, (ii) the loss of the ship or aircraft, or (iii) the date on which the life-threatening situation occurred, respectively.

*361.* A judicial order for declaration of death is granted whenever sufficient evidence is presented before the District Court, on the balance of probabilities, that the legal requirements are fulfilled. However, the application is rejected, if during the trial the missing person appears, or there is credible news that the missing person is still alive, or the missing person is proven dead. The order for declaration of death is a presumption which may be rebutted in accordance with section 14 §6 of Cap. 195 if following the declaration of death, the missing person appears. Any person who has a legal interest may apply before the District Court, at any given time, for an order annulling the declaration of death, of the missing person; in such a case the persons who had unjustly enriched from the declaration of death, either heirs or legatees, are liable to return the product of such unjust enrichment.

*362.* There are specific provisions governing the case of the missing persons of the Turkish Invasion of 1974. The Certain Issues related to the Estate of the Missing Persons Law 178(I)/2003 refers to citizens of the Republic who became missing persons due to the 1974 Turkish Invasion, and there is still no evidence whether they are dead or alive. Section 3 of Law 178(I)/03 provides that irrespective of the provisions of section 14 of Cap. 195, the citizens of the Republic who have disappeared as a result of the Turkish Invasion, may be declared *in absentia* by Order of the District Court of the district where they had their last known residence in the Republic; if their last known residence was not in the Republic of Cyprus, then the District Court of Nicosia has jurisdiction.

*363.* Declaration *in absentia* may occur if there have been no news that the missing person is still alive for five years. The Attorney-General of the Republic, or any person who has a legal interest in the Estate of the missing person may apply before the Court for a judicial declaration *in absentia*.[439] A person is considered to have legal interest, in accordance with section 2 of Law 178(I)/03, if he/she would have become the heir of the missing person, had the missing person died following the lapse of the five-year period since the disappearance; a fiancé who gave birth to the child of the missing person and remains unmarried until the date that the judicial

439. If the Attorney-General of the Republic is not the petitioner, then the petition has to be served to him/her.

order becomes final, is also considered to have legal interest. The petition is rejected, if the missing person appears, or there is credible news that he/she is still alive, or he/she is proved dead (section 4 of Law 178(I)/03). Otherwise, the order is declared; section 3 §3 of Law 178(I)/03 provides that a certificate signed by the Attorney-General of the Republic and the Head of the Missing Persons Service, which states the last date news about the missing person were heard, constitutes sufficient and complete proof of the facts referred to it.

*364.* A judicial Order *in absentia* does not constitute declaration of death, contrary to section 14 of Cap. 195; the missing person is legally presumed to be alive, a position which is consistent with the official policy of the Republic that the missing persons of the Turkish Invasion are to be presumed as alive, until their remains are found. The order is rebutted wherever the missing person is proven either alive or dead. In accordance with section 5 of Law 178(I)/03, when the order *in absentia* is declared, the court appoints administrators of the Estate of the missing person who have the same powers as the administrators of the Estate of a deceased person. The heirs of the missing person are those who would legally be heirs in accordance with the provisions of Cap. 195; the sole exception is that the fiancé who has given birth to the child of the missing person receives the share of a legal spouse; such share of the fiancé is retained even if subsequently the missing person is declared dead.

## §2. The Heir

### I. Capacity to Succeed

*365.* The general rule is that every person is capable of inheriting, except in those cases where the potential heir has been declared unworthy on the basis of the provisions of section 17 of Cap. 195. Section 17 provides exhaustively for the circumstances under which a person may be declared as unworthy. No person shall be incapable of succeeding to an estate on grounds that he/she is of a different nationality, religion, race, sex or domicile of the deceased. In the case of *Christophi*, which was decided prior to the enactment of Cap. 195, an Orthodox Christian woman had performed a marriage with a Muslim and had renamed into Ayshe, a Turkish name. The Supreme Court held that the grounds for unworthiness were exhaustively provided for in the Wills and Succession Law 20/1895 and the change of religion was not a ground of unworthiness.[440]

*366.* A posthumous child born alive shall have, in accordance with section 15 of Cap. 195, the same right of succession as if he/she had been born before the death of the deceased. The legal presumption introduced by section 15 of Cap. 195 will not apply if the child who was *en ventre sa mere* is not born alive; if the child is born alive, it is irrelevant for the application of the presumption whether he/she subsequently dies. For the presumption to apply, it has to be proven that the child had

440. *Christophi v. Christophi* (1910) 9 CLR 65.

already been conceived before the death of the person to be succeeded. The born alive child will become the heir of not only his/her father but also of other relatives in cases of intestacy.

## II. Commorientes

*367.* If more than one person died in the same accident, or during the same danger, it is often difficult to determine who died first. If there is no sufficient evidence, on the balance of probabilities, so as to enable a court to make a declaration of the order of death, there is a rebuttable presumption that all persons died at the same time (section 14 §7 of Cap. 195). Furthermore, section 14 §8 provides that in cases where the order of death of more than one person is disputed, the person alleging that one of them died first, has the burden to present evidence proving such allegation. If no such evidence is produced, then there is a presumption that the deceased persons died at the same time.[441]

## III. Unworthiness to Succeed

*368.* Section 17 of Cap. 195 provides exhaustively for the circumstances under which a person may be declared as unworthy to succeed. The justification for declaring a person as unworthy is that nobody should prosper from illegal acts. The provisions concerning unworthiness apply to all heirs, either legal or testamentary. Both natural and legal persons may be declared unworthy; the latter when they are liable for the illegal acts of their representatives. It should be further stressed that a person is declared unworthy to succeed only with respect to a specific inheritance; there is no general declaration of unworthiness, but only specific grounds of unworthiness which relate to a given inheritance. Thus, a person may be unworthy to succeed a specific deceased person, but worthy to succeed another deceased person.

*369.* Section 17 provides for seven specific grounds on the basis of which a person may be declared as unworthy to succeed. The common characteristic of all grounds is the existence of an illegal or unjust action of the unworthy heir. The grounds may be further split into three major categories, namely (a) causing or attempting to cause death of the deceased, or a child, parent or spouse of the deceased, (b) illegally causing the deceased to make a will or illegally preventing the deceased from making or revoking a will and (c) altering or destroying a will, or submitting a suppositious will. Such grounds of unworthiness will be analysed in turn in the subsequent paragraphs. Aiding or abetting any person in the commission of any of the acts specified in section 17 of Cap. 195 constitute a separate ground of unworthiness.[442]

441. *See also* C. Tornaritis, *The Legal Effect of Death, Especially in Accordance with Cypriot Law* (Nicosia, 1973, in Greek), 14.

442. For an extensive analysis *see* A. Emilianides, *Cypriot Succession Law* 3rd edn (Nicosia: Hippasus, 2015, in Greek).

*370.* A person shall be declared as unworthy if he/she wilfully and unlawfully caused or attempted to cause the death of the deceased. The cause of death of the deceased may have occurred either with an act or an omission and presupposes the conviction of the unworthy heir from the Assize Court, either for murder in accordance with section 203 of the Criminal Code, Cap. 154, or for homicide in accordance with sections 205 and 208 of Cap. 154. A person shall also be declared unworthy if he/she attempts to cause the death of the deceased in accordance with section 214 of Cap. 154. However, causing the death of the deceased because of negligence in accordance with section 210 of Cap. 154, or causing bodily harm to the deceased without causing the deceased's death, are not considered as grounds for unworthiness. The heir may further be declared unworthy if either before or after the death of the deceased, he/she has been convicted for deliberately causing, or attempting to cause the death of a child, parent or spouse of the deceased.

*371.* Another ground for declaring a person as unworthy to succeed is if he/she caused the person to whose estate he/she would otherwise have succeeded to make a will by coercion, fraud or undue influence. The will made has to be a valid one; however, it is not required that such will is the one on the basis of which the unworthy is the heir of the deceased. Consequently, the person would still be declared as unworthy, even if the will was subsequently revoked by the deceased. A person will further be declared as unworthy if he/she deliberately and illegally prevents, through act or omission, the deceased from making a new will or revoking an existing one. Such behaviour of the unworthy could aim at either his/her own benefit or the benefit of a third person. A person will thus be declared unworthy if he/she tricked the deceased into making a void will, instead of a valid one, so that the unworthy would succeed through the application of the rules of intestacy.

*372.* Finally, a person shall be declared as unworthy if he/she illegally altered or destroyed a valid will; this includes any addition, removal or alteration of the contents of the will, as well as the acts of stealing or hiding a will in violation of sections 263 and 274 of the Criminal Code, Cap. 154 respectively. The person shall be declared as unworthy even if subsequently the will is found, or its true content is determined, or if a new will is made; what is important is the illegal behaviour of the unworthy, rather than the actual destruction or alteration of the will. Submitting a suppositious will to the deceased, as well as forging a will in violation of section 336 of Cap. 154, are actions which would also lead to a declaration that the perpetrator is unworthy to succeed to the estate of the deceased. Such actions may take place either before, or after the death of the deceased.

*373.* Section 18 of Cap. 195 provides that the deceased may voluntarily and expressly pardon the otherwise unworthy person, either by a provision made in his/her will or by a signed declaration before the District Commissioner. The pardon may be provided only by the deceased and only in the manner mentioned above; pardon provided for with a letter, or by oral statements is not considered as sufficient. For the pardon to take effect, the deceased ought to have knowledge of the illegal act of the unworthy; thus, the deceased cannot pardon in advance, or in general terms, the unworthy for any future illegal acts, since such a pardon would unduly restrict the free will of the deceased. Any court action alleging unworthiness has to be commenced before the lapse of three years from the death of the deceased, in accordance with section 20 of Cap. 195. Any person having a legal hereditary interest from the declaration of unworthiness may be the petitioner.

*374.* If a person is declared as unworthy, then such person is no longer entitled to succeed the deceased. If the unworthy would have become an heir according to a provision in the will of the deceased, then such provision of the will shall not be implemented. If on the contrary, the unworthy would have become an heir on the basis of the law, then his/her portion shall be claimed by his/her direct descendants as if the unworthy had died in the lifetime of the deceased; the incapacitated person upon whose descendants the estate devolves shall be debarred from any subsequent right of enjoyment thereof, in accordance with section 19 of Cap. 195. If the unworthy has no direct descendants, then the intestate succession will take place as if the unworthy had died in the lifetime of the deceased.

## §3. The System of Descent

### I. Introduction

*375.* Whenever a person dies intestate, or to the extent that the deceased's right to dispose by will is restricted because of the existence of statutory heirs, the estate shall be distributed to the heirs in accordance with the provisions of Cap. 195. If there is a surviving spouse, then the share of the surviving spouse shall first be distributed and the remaining part of the estate shall be distributed to the persons of kin of the deceased. There are four classes of kinship, set out in the First Schedule of Cap. 195; persons of one class shall exclude persons of a subsequent class from succeeding to the estate of the deceased person. The heirs are always determined at the time of death.[443] The degree of kindred between any two persons is ascertained in accordance with section 48 of Cap. 195. Section 48 provides that when the two persons are in the direct line of descent the one from the other, each generation from either of them to the other shall constitute a degree; where the persons are not in the direct line of descent, each generation from either of them up to their common ancestor and from the common ancestor downwards to the other of them shall constitute a degree. The degrees of kindred down to the sixth degree are shown in a table set out in the Second Schedule of Cap. 195. If there is no person of kin to the sixth degree, the undisposed portion of the estate becomes the property of the Republic of Cyprus.

443. *Remzi v. Sencer* [1972] 1 CLR 52.

## A. *The Classes of Heirs*

### 1. Surviving Spouse

#### a. Determining the Surviving Spouse

*376.* Where a person died leaving a wife or husband, such surviving spouse shall be entitled to a share in the statutory portion and in the undisposed portion of the estate. The existence of a valid marriage is the only requirement; thus, the duration of marriage is immaterial. Persons who were married to the deceased, albeit such marriage had been dissolved or annulled prior to the deceased's death, are not entitled to receive any shares in the statutory portion of the estate; however, the surviving spouse shall be entitled to his/her statutory share, even if divorce proceedings were pending, so long as no divorce decree has been issued prior to the death of the deceased person. Persons who were not married to the deceased, but were cohabitating with the deceased are not entitled to a share in the statutory portion of the estate. However, the provisions of Cap. 195 apply, *mutatis mutandis*, to partners of a registered civil union, pursuant to section 44 of the Civil Union Law 184(I)/ 2015.

*377.* With respect to marriages which have been annulled after the deceased's death, the situation is rather complicated. Section 21 of the pre-existing Marriage Law 21/1990 provided that the effects of a marriage are retroactively lifted whenever a judicial declaration of annulment of the marriage is pronounced. Furthermore, section 23 of Law 21/90 provided that if the surviving spouse was unaware that the marriage was void and he/she had acted in good faith, then the marriage would be void only from the time the decree was issued, without any retroactive effect; consequently, the bona fide spouse would be entitled to a share in the statutory portion, while in all other cases where the marriage was annulled following the death of the deceased, the surviving spouse would not be entitled to a statutory portion of the estate. Section 24 of the Marriage Law 104(I)/2003 which replaced Law 21/90 provides, however, that the effects of void marriages are no longer retroactive, but the marriage is void only from the time the decree is issued.

*378.* In view of the above the surviving spouse shall be entitled to a share in the statutory portion in the estate in all cases where the marriage was declared void following the death of the deceased (including cases where the surviving spouse was bona fide in accordance with section 26 of Law 104(I)/03, regarding a marriage which was declared null and void *ab initio*); this includes marriages performed under the provisions of both Law 104(I)/03 and the pre-existing Law 21/90 for which the provisions of Law 104(I)/03 apply. What cannot be explained, however, is the following: if void marriages do not have retroactive effect, then why are persons 'whose right to inherit are affected by the existence of the marriage' entitled to file an action in order to seek the annulment of the marriage in accordance with section 22 §4 of Law 104(I)/2003? If the right of the surviving spouse to receive a share in the statutory portion is not affected by the subsequent declaration that the marriage is void, then why should the legislator expressly provide for the right of other heirs or legatees to seek the annulment of the marriage? It is submitted that the relevant provisions of Law 104(I)/2003 are highly problematic.[444] In any event, it is noted that the competent court to declare whether a marriage is void is the Family Court in accordance with section 21 of Law 104(I)/2003 and this cannot be incidentally decided by the District Court while adjudicating a succession law dispute.[445]

*379.* In any event, if the parties had not married in accordance with Law 104(I)/03, or in accordance with Law 21/90, but had married in accordance with the Charter of the Orthodox Church, or the doctrines and rites of the three religious groups of the Republic, then the effects of declaring a marriage as void continue to be retroactive. Consequently, whenever a judicial declaration of annulment of the marriage is pronounced following the death of the deceased, the surviving spouse shall not be entitled to a share in the statutory portion of the estate. Similarly, whenever the marriage was performed in accordance with Cap. 279 prior to the entry into force of Law 104(I)/03, or the marriage was performed in the Church of the Old Calendar Church in accordance with Law 60(I)/1994, or was performed abroad, the surviving spouse shall not be entitled to a share in the statutory portion of the estate if the marriage is declared as void following the death of the deceased; this is due to the fact that the validity of the marriage in such cases is governed by the English Marriage Act, 1959 and common law as it applied prior to 1960.

b. The Share of the Surviving Spouse

*380.* The surviving spouse is always entitled to a share in the statutory portion and in the undisposed portion of the estate; thus, the surviving spouse is entitled to a share irrespective of whether the deceased had made a valid will or not. The share of the surviving spouse is determined on the basis of the existence of other heirs, and in accordance with section 44 of Cap. 195, as follows:

(a) If the deceased had left besides the spouse, any child, or descendant thereof, then the portion of the spouse is equal to the portion of each child. Thus, if the deceased left a spouse and two children, the portion of the spouse shall be equal to 1/3. If a child of the deceased had died in the lifetime of the deceased, then its children (namely the grand children of the deceased) shall be entitled to receive the share that their parent would have received if he/she was alive.
(b) If the deceased had left besides the spouse, no child nor descendant thereof, but any ancestor or descendant thereof within the third degree of kindred to the deceased, such share shall be the one-half of the statutory portion and of the undisposed portion. According to one view I the term 'ancestor or descendant thereof' should include also kindred not in the direct line, since otherwise any reference to descendants would be meaningless; any descendants in the direct line would be covered by (i) cited above. Thus, if the deceased had left parents, or grandparents, or siblings, or uncles, or aunts, or nephews or nieces, the share

444. A. Emilianides, *Cypriot Succession Law* 3rd edn (Nicosia: Hippasus, 2015, in Greek).
445. *Kofteros v. Jimerson* [2010] 1 CLR 435 (in Greek).

of the surviving spouse shall amount to ½. However, it should be noted that in *Valdaseridou* the Supreme Court held for the purposes of a different provision of Cap. 195 that the term 'ancestor' only refers to ancestors in the direct line.[446] If such an interpretation is also to be adopted for the purposes of the portion of the surviving spouse, then the only relatives to be covered would be parents and grandparents. It is immaterial whether the deceased left one or several ancestors or descendants thereof within the third degree of kindred; the existence of only one is sufficient for the share of the surviving spouse to be restricted to ½.

(c) If the deceased had left besides the spouse, no child nor descendant thereof, nor any ancestor or descendant thereof within the third degree of kindred, but left any ancestor or descendant thereof of the fourth degree of kindred to the deceased, such share shall be the ¾ of the statutory portion and of the undisposed portion. Thus, if the deceased died leaving cousins, or siblings of grandparents, or grandchildren of a sibling, the statutory share of the spouse shall be restricted to ¾. If it is considered that 'ancestors' would refer to ancestors in the direct line only, then this provision becomes rather pointless.

(d) If the deceased had left besides the spouse, no child nor descendant thereof, nor any ancestor or descendant thereof within the fourth degree of kindred to the deceased, the share of the spouse shall be the whole statutory and the whole undisposed portion of the estate.

*381.* Section 44 further provides that where the deceased has left more than one lawful wife, the share given to the wife shall be divided equally between such wives. Such provision indirectly legalizes polygamy for the purposes of the law of succession, if the deceased had performed polygamy in legal systems which recognize polygamy. Section 44 applies despite the fact that in other areas of law polygamy is considered as being contrary to the public order of the Cypriot legal system. In *Nesreen*, the Supreme Court of Cyprus held, within the context of a recourse against an administrative decision rejecting a permit of temporary stay, that while the religious beliefs of each person should be respected, the laws of Cyprus recognize only monogamous marriages and rights may be accrued only from such monogamous marriages.[447] It would therefore seem that polygamous marriages may be recognized for the purposes of succession law, despite the fact that they might be considered as contrary to public policy for the purposes of family law.

*382.* It is submitted that *de lege ferenda* it is rather incomprehensible why, in a modern nuclear family, the surviving spouse should have to share the statutory or the undisposed portion of the estate with ancestors or descendants of the third or fourth degree of kindred, whenever there are no children or descendants thereof. In any event, the deceased has the power to dispose by will his/her entire estate to his/her spouse if he/she left no children or descendants of children, or parents at the time of death. It is further noted that, in accordance with section 45 of Cap. 195, a spouse who becomes entitled to a share in the statutory portion or in the undisposed

446. *Valdaseridou v. Lada* [2005] 1 CLR 1011 (in Greek).
447. *Nesreen v. Republic*, App. 1182/2005, judgment of 20 Jun. 2007 (in Greek).

portion shall not bring into account in reckoning such share any movable or immovable property received from the deceased by virtue of a marriage contract.

*383.* A question which has not yet been settled is whether the surviving spouse has, in addition to his/her share pursuant to Cap. 195, a right to receive his/her contribution for the increase of the property of his/her deceased spouse pursuant to section 14 of Law 232/1991. Section 14 may be activated whenever the marriage has been dissolved and section 27 § 5 of the Marriage Law 104(I)/2003 explicitly provides that a marriage may be dissolved either by divorce or by the death of the other spouse. Whereas section 15 of Law 232/1991 provides that the heirs of the other spouse have no right to claim contribution, there is no exclusion of the right to the surviving spouse himself/herself to apply. If the right of the surviving spouse to apply also for contribution was to be recognized, then this would imply that the contribution would be exempted from the estate of the deceased and then the surviving spouse could claim, in addition to his/her contribution pursuant to section 14 of Law 232/1991, his/her share as a heir pursuant to the provisions of Cap. 195.

## 2. Kindred

### a. First Class

*384.* There are four classes of kinship, set out in the First Schedule of Cap. 195; persons of one class shall exclude persons of a subsequent class from succeeding to the estate of the deceased person. The first class of kinship includes the legitimate children of the deceased living at his/her death and descendants, living at the death of the deceased, of any of the deceased's legitimate children who died in his/her lifetime. While the First Schedule refers to legitimate children, children born out of wedlock have the same rights as legitimate children. The Children Born out of Wedlock Law, Cap. 278 provided that the right of succession of children born out of wedlock would be restricted to the relatives of their mother; however, Article 9 of the Convention on the Legal Status of Children Born out of Wedlock (Ratification) Law 50/1979 provides that a child born out of wedlock shall have the same rights to succession as a legitimate child. In the case of *Malachtou* the Supreme Court held that any provisions of Cap. 195 or Cap. 278 which are inconsistent with the Convention are invalid, since the Convention has superior force by virtue of Article 169 §3 of the Constitution.[448]

*385.* It is submitted that whenever a child is legalized, either voluntarily or judicially, or because the child's parent subsequently performed a valid marriage, such child has exactly the same rights as a legitimate one with respect to succession. Similarly, an adopted child shall have exactly the same rights to succeed as a legitimate child, in accordance with the provisions of section 23 of the Adoption Law 19(I)/1995 which provides that the adopted child shall be considered as a legitimate and natural child of the adoptive parents; the adopted child shall have the right to

448. *Malachtou v. Armefti* [1987] 1 CLR 207.

succeed his/her adoptive parents, as well as their relatives,[449] but shall not have the right to succeed his/her natural parents or their relatives, since after adoption there is no longer any kinship between the child and his/her natural parents.

*386.* Children of the deceased are entitled to equal shares in the statutory portion and the undisposed portion; thus, if the deceased had three children, each child shall receive 1/3 of the statutory and undisposed portion. The descendants of the deceased's children are entitled to an equal share per stirpes in the statutory and the undisposed portion of the estate. The term per stirpes is defined in section 49 of Cap. 195 where it is provided that 'the child of any person of the defined class who shall have died in the lifetime of the deceased and who, if he had survived the deceased, would have become entitled on the death of the deceased to a share in the statutory portion, and the undisposed portion if any, shall become entitled only to the share which the parent would have taken if he has survived the deceased'. In other words the descendants of a child of the deceased that died in the lifetime of the deceased would be entitled to the share that their parent (the child of the deceased) would have received had the deceased died before him/her.

*387.* Consequently, if the deceased died leaving two children and he/she had a third child who had died during his/her lifetime, leaving three children (grandchildren of the deceased), each of the two children of the deceased shall receive 1/3 of the statutory and of the undisposed portion, while the three children of his/her third child shall split the remaining 1/3 of the statutory and undisposed portion. A grandchild of the deceased shall not be entitled to a share in the statutory or the undisposed portion, if his/her parent has not died in the lifetime of the deceased; thus, if the child of the deceased died after the deceased, it shall be the child who shall be entitled to a share and not the grandchild.[450]

b. Second Class

*388.* The second class of kinship includes a) the parents of the deceased living in his/her death (or if not living at his/her death, the nearest ancestor living at his/her death) and brothers and sisters of the full and half blood of the deceased living at his/her death and b) descendants living at the death of the deceased of any of the deceased's brothers or sisters who died in his/her lifetime. If the parents or siblings of the deceased are alive, they all receive equal shares in the statutory and undisposed portion of the estate. In *Kamilari* the Supreme Court held that since the deceased died leaving his mother and four brothers, the share of the mother and each of the brothers amounted to 1/5 of the statutory and undisposed portion of the estate.[451] If, however, the siblings of the deceased are half blood, they receive half the share of a brother or sister of the full blood.

449. *Nicolaides v. Yerolemi* [1982] 1 CLR 656.
450. *Cacoyiannis v. The Republic* [1988] 3 CLR 1860.
451. *Kamilari v. Minister of Finance*, App. 839/99, Judgment of 18 Jul. 2002 (in Greek).

*389.* The notion of parents includes parents of children born out of wedlock who subsequently recognized their children, either voluntarily or judicially, as well as adoptive parents (but not the natural parents of an adopted child). Similarly, children born out of wedlock or adopted children are included in the notion of siblings. Descendants living at the death of the deceased of any of the deceased's brothers or sisters who died in his/her lifetime are entitled to equal shares per stirpes; they are thus, entitled to the share their parent – sibling of the deceased – would otherwise receive if he/she had outlived the deceased; if their parent has anyway outlived the deceased, then he/she is entitled to a share and his/her descendants are not entitled to receive any share of the statutory or the undisposed portion of the estate.[452]

*390.* If neither parent of the deceased is alive at the time of his/her death, then it is provided that the nearest ancestor living at the deceased's death is entitled to a share in the statutory and undisposed portion of the estate. In *Valdaserides* the Supreme Court examined the question whether the term 'ancestor' includes only ancestors in the direct line of descent (such as grandparents and great-grandparents), or also ancestors not in the direct line of descent, such as uncles or aunts.[453] The Supreme Court held that for the purposes of the First Schedule of Cap. 195, the term 'ancestor' has to be defined as including only ancestors in the direct line of descent[454] and noted:

> *We consider that the aforementioned interpretation of the term «ancestor» is consistent also with common sense, since if such term included also persons of kin who are not in the direct line of descent of former generations of a given deceased, the first cousins of the parents or the grandparents of the deceased would inherit the deceased, since they would belong in the third class of the First Schedule, by excluding the deceased's first cousins, irrespective of the fact that the deceased's first cousins are persons of kin of a nearer degree of kindred when compared to the cousins of the deceased's parents or grandparents.*

*391.* Consequently, the ancestors of the deceased for the purpose of the second class of the First Schedule of Cap. 195 are only ancestors in the direct line of descent, namely the grandparents and great-grandparents of the deceased; such ancestors shall receive equal share to the siblings of the deceased, so long as the parents of the deceased have died in the lifetime of the deceased. It would seem, however, that the ancestors of the deceased may only fall within the second class if there are also siblings of the deceased or descendants of the siblings of the deceased. In any event, it is observed that the drafting of the relevant provision is unnecessarily complicated and in addition might lead to curious results; if for instance the deceased died leaving four grandparents and a brother, each shall receive 1/5 of the

452. *Cacoyiannis v. The Republic* [1988] 3 CLR 1860.
453. *Valdaserides v. Lada* [2005] 1 CLR 1011 (in Greek).
454. *See also Knowles v. Attorney-General* [1951] 54.

statutory and undisposed portion of the estate, while if the parents of the deceased were alive, the brother would have received 1/3 of the statutory and undisposed portion of the estate.

### c. Third Class

*392.* The third class of kinship includes the ancestors of the deceased nearest in the degree of kindred living at his/her death. If there are ancestors of equal degree of kindred on both the father's side and on the mother's side, the ancestors on each side shall take half of the statutory portion, and of the undisposed portion, and if there are more than one of them on either side, in equal shares. As held by the Supreme Court in *Valdaserides* the term 'ancestors' includes only ancestors in the direct line of descent, namely grandparents and great-grandparents of the deceased.[455]

### d. Fourth Class

*393.* The fourth and final class of the First Schedule of Cap. 195 includes the nearest kin of the deceased living at the time of death within the sixth degree of kindred, the nearer degree excluding those more remote; kin of the same degree inherit in equal shares. The third degree of kindred includes uncles, aunts, nephews and nieces, the fourth degree of kindred includes first cousins, great uncles or aunts and the grandchildren of siblings, the fifth degree of kindred includes great great uncles or aunts, children of great uncles' or aunts', or children of first cousins, while the sixth degree of kindred includes second cousins, grandchildren of first cousins and children of great great uncles or aunts. Since the nearer degree excludes the more remote,[456] there is no question of inheriting per stirpes, as in the case of the first two classes.[457]

## 3. Rights of Religious Organizations

*394.* In the 2007 case of the *Monastery of Mahairas*, the Supreme Court examined the issue of the hereditary succession of monks in Cyprus.[458] The deceased had been a monk of the Monastery of Mahairas from 1949 until 2000, when he passed away. According to the Charter of the Orthodox Church of Cyprus and the internal regulation of the Monastery, the property of all monks belongs to the monastery and

---

455. *Valdaserides v. Lada* [2005] 1 CLR 1011 (in Greek).
456. *Michael v. Antoniou* [1969] 1 CLR 547.
457. In *Kotzapasis and others v. Hatziyianni and others*, Action 378/2010, Judgment of 9 Feb. 2015 (District Court, in Greek) it was held that such provisions are not inconsistent with the Constitution.
458. *Holy Monastery of Mahairas v. Papasavva* [2007] 1 CLR 436 (in Greek). *See* A. Emilianides *Law and Religion in Cyprus* 2nd edn (The Hague: Kluwer, 2014): 112ff.

not personally to them. The relatives of the deceased monk argued that such property should belong to them and not to the monastery and that all contrary Articles of the Charter of the Orthodox Church violated Article 23 of the Constitution safeguarding the right of property.

*395.* The Supreme Court acknowledged that according to Article 110 §1 of the Constitution, the Autocephalous Greek Orthodox Church of Cyprus shall continue to have the exclusive right of regulating and administering its own internal affairs and property in accordance with the Holy Canons and its Charter in force for the time being. However, it did not accept that the exclusive right of the Orthodox Church to regulate and administer its property extends also to the property of its monks, or that the property of its monks could be considered to be the property of the Church. In view of the above, it was held that each monk continues to have a right to his own property, as safeguarded by the Constitution and that the monastery does not have any right to such property. Thus, the relatives of the deceased monk were considered to be the heirs of the deceased monk. A similar interpretation might in the future be followed also with respect to members of the clergy.

*396.* The case of the Monastery of Mahairas could be criticized, due to the fact that it failed to examine the application of Article 18 with respect to religious freedom. The monk had exercised his religious freedom by acquiring the capacity of the monk and by accepting the provisions of canon law and the internal regulation of the monastery, where he had been a monk for fifty years. The right to individual property cannot be examined in isolation and without examining whether in the circumstances of the particular case the monk had exercised his religious freedom which is also safeguarded by the Constitution.[459] In any event, however, it is correct that hereditary succession does not fall within the ambit of the Charter of the Orthodox Church, since it is the House of Representatives and not the Greek Communal Chamber which has competences with regard to laws relating to hereditary succession; Article 110 may not safeguard the competence of the Orthodox Church concerning matters which would not fall within the exclusive competences of the Greek Communal Chamber.

*397.* Nevertheless, the Court failed to examine the application of section 53 of the Succession Law, Cap. 195, which stipulates, that the recognized rights of religious organizations should be safeguarded.[460] The notion of a religious organization undoubtedly includes the Orthodox Church of Cyprus. Furthermore, the right of the Orthodox Church to acquire the property of a monk was safeguarded by the Charter of 1914, as well as by the Charter of 1980 and was therefore an established and well-recognized right of a religious organization at the time of entry into force

459. *See* A. Emilianides, 'The Constitutional Position of the Charter of the Orthodox Church of Cyprus', *Nomokanonika* 1 (2005): 41–54 (in Greek).

460. *See* A. Emilianides, 'Hereditary Succession of Monks in Cyprus: New Developments', *Cyprus and European Law Review* 5 (2007): 368–378 (in Greek).

of the Succession Law, Cap. 195.[461] The property of a monk might not become the subject of hereditary succession within the meaning of Cap. 195, precisely due to the fact that a monk does not own any property which could legally become the subject of hereditary succession and this is the reason for including the specific exception of section 53 of Cap. 195. There was therefore no incompatibility between Cap. 195 and the Charter of the Orthodox Church that needed to be resolved, since section 53 of Cap. 195 explicitly safeguarded all recognized rights of religious organizations which were based on their canon law.[462]

*398.* Section 55 of Cap. 195 further provides that the provisions of Cap. 195 do not apply to vakf. The Vakf had a specific meaning at the time of the coming into operation of the Constitution. It denoted the tying up of a property and the imposition of an interdiction on its transfer, in such a manner that its benefit is given to men, on the condition that the property is to be regarded as the property of God. A Vakf was thus, the equivalent of a 'dedication'. A Vakf further denotes the object of the dedication and not only the act.[463] This is consistent with Article 110 of the Constitution which provides that all matters relating to, or in any way affecting the institution or foundation of Vakf, or the vakfs, or any vakf properties, including properties belonging to Mosques and any other Muslim religious institution, shall be governed solely by, and under the Laws and Principles of Vakfs (ahkamul evkaf) and the Laws and Regulations enacted or made by the Turkish Communal Chamber.[464]

### *B. Representation (Hotchpot)*

*399.* In accordance with section 51 of Cap. 195, any child or other descendant of the deceased who becomes entitled to succeed to the statutory portion and to the undisposed portion of the estate shall in reckoning his/her share, bring into account all movable and immovable property that he/she has at any time received from the deceased, (a) by way of advancement, (b) under a marriage contract, (c) as dower, or (d) by way of gift made in contemplation of death. The aim of this contribution, called hotchpot, is to ensure that the distribution of the property of the deceased shall be as fair as possible.[465] Section 2 of the Contract Law, Cap. 149 provides that dower is the property given from one of the spouses or future spouses, or from a

461. *See* C. Tornaritis, 'The Property of Monks and whether it is subject to Estate Duty Tax', *Cyprus Law Review* 1 (1983): 177.
462. A. Emilianides, 'Hereditary Succession of Monks in Cyprus: New Developments', *Cyprus and European Law Review* 5 (2007): 368–378 (in Greek).
463. O. Effendi, *The Laws of Evqaf*, 2nd edn (Nicosia: 1922); K. Dizdar, 'The Origin and Administration of the Cyprus Evkaf', in *Proceedings of the First International Cyprological Conference*, vol. II (Nicosia: Society for Cypriot Studies, 1973), 63–78.
464. *See* A. Emilianides, *Annotated Legal Documents on Islam in Cyprus* (Leiden: Brill, 2014).
465. C. Emilianides, 'The Law of Succession in Cyprus', *Corpus de Jure Cyprii* 2 (1988): 466 (in Greek).

third party, to the other spouse or future spouse, in consideration for the performance of the marriage.[466] In accordance with section 3 of Law 22(I)/1995 any contracts for dower performed after Law 22(I)/1995 was enacted, are null and void. Donations given to the spouses by the parent after the marriage because of natural love and affection are not considered as received either as dower or under a marriage contract.

*400.* Advancements are provided by the parent to the child in order to assist the child in a more permanent way; not every donation of property is considered an advancement for the purposes of section 51.[467] An advancement is an important donation from the parent, such as a donation given in order to enable the child to set up a permanent employment, or the donation of immovable property; the donation of jewellery or other everyday donations shall not be considered as advancements. In order to distinguish between advancements and other donations, the Court shall consider the age of the child, the amount of the donation, the purpose of the donation and other related factors.[468]

*401.* If the child or descendant has received such movable or immovable property during the lifetime of the deceased, it should be brought into account in order to determine the shares of each child in the statutory and undisposed portion. It has now been settled that such property shall be evaluated on the basis of its value on the date of death of the deceased.[469] If, for instance, the net value of the estate is EUR 100,000 and the deceased died leaving two children and one of the children had received an advancement of EUR 20,000, then the value of the estate shall be estimated at EUR 120,000, namely the actual value of the estate and the hypothetical value of the advancement; thus, the first child shall receive EUR 60,000 and the second child shall receive EUR 40,000 (EUR 60,000-the advancement of EUR 20,000). If the advancement was not taken into account, then each child would have received EUR 50,000. If the advancement received by a child is more than the actual value of the estate, the child is by no means under an obligation to return the surplus, but he/she simply will not receive any additional shares to the statutory and undisposed portion of the estate.

*402.* It is noted that no movable or immovable property shall be brought into account if the deceased had left a will and has made specific provision that such property shall not be brought into account. Furthermore, it is observed that such contribution only takes place between direct descendants of the deceased and not between the deceased's descendants and other heirs, or the surviving spouse. In *Ismail* the Privy Council examined whether in reckoning the share of the children of a predeceased son the property given to their father by way of advancement by the deceased should be brought into account; the Court held that in estimating the

466. *Oikonomou v. Ttofini* [1993] 1 CLR 436 (in Greek).
467. *Taylor v. Taylor* (1875) Lr 20 Eq 155, *Hatfield v. Minet* (1878) 8 Ch D 136, *Hardy v. Shaw* [1976] Ch 82. *See also Enver v. Kasim* (1976) 7 JSC 1186, District Court.
468. *Re Hayward* [1957] Ch 528.
469. *Kyriakides v. Dikigoropoulou* [2012] 1 CLR 1164 (in Greek), *Azina* v. *Azina and others*, Civil App. 7/2012, Judgment of 10 Sep. 2018 (in Greek).

share of the grandchildren, the property received from the deceased by their predeceased father by way of advancement should be brought into account.[470] It is further noted that Cypriot law does not contain any clawback provisions pursuant to which an heir may seek to return to the estate assets which had been donated to third parties during the life of the deceased. A person has the right to alienate in any way he/she wishes any property assets while he/she is alive, even his/her entire property.

## §4. The Rights of the State on the Bona Vacantia

*403.* If there is no person of kin to the deceased within the sixth degree of kindred living at his/her death, then the deceased is considered to have died without heirs and any undisposed portion of the estate becomes the property of the Republic of Cyprus.

470. *Suing v. Ismail* (1959) 24 CLR 15.

# Chapter 2. Testamentary Succession

## §1. The Capacity to Make a Will

*404.* Any person, who is over 18 years of age and is of sound mind, has the capacity to make a valid will, in accordance with section 22 of Cap. 195; consequently minors or persons of unsound mind may not make a valid will. A will is defined in section 2 of Cap. 195 as the legal declaration in writing of the intentions of a testator with respect to the disposal of his/her movable or immovable property after his/her death and includes codicil; codicil is defined as an instrument in writing made in relation to a will explaining, adding to, altering or revoking in whole or in part its disposition and it shall be considered as forming an amendment or additional part of the will.

*405.* In *Moumdjis* the Supreme Court of Cyprus held that the crucial time for determining whether a person is of sound mind is the time he/she made the will in question; it is therefore irrelevant whether the testator was of unsound mind at any time prior to, or after making the will.[471] Defining a person of unsound mind for the purposes of Cap. 195 necessitates certain additional distinctions. To begin with, section 2 of Cap. 195 provides that a mental patient is a person who has been adjudged as a mental patient under the provisions of the Mental Patients Law, Cap. 252. However, Cap. 252 is no longer in force and has been substituted by the Psychiatric Hospitalization Law 77(I)/1997. Persons who have been adjudged as psychiatrically ill in accordance with the provisions of Law 77(I)/97 may be considered as persons of sound mind. Furthermore, a person who has been declared as incapable in accordance with the provisions of the Administration of the Estate of Incapable Persons Law 23(I)/1996, should be considered as a person of unsound mind.

*406.* In addition a person may be considered as of one of unsound mind, even without the existence of a prior court judgment to this effect, so long as the person has no free will, because he/she is incapable to appreciate the consequences of his/her actions due to old age, or disease.[472] While section 2 of Cap. 195 defines an incapable person as a person who is certified as incapable by two duly qualified medical practitioners, it is suggested that such definition does not preclude proving that a person is incapable by any other convincing means. Persons who made a will under the influence of intoxication should also be considered as persons of unsound mind and incapable of making a valid will; thus, unsoundness of mind may refer also to a limited period of time.

*407.* There is a rebuttable presumption that the testator was of a sound mind; therefore, the person claiming that the testator was of an unsound mind has the burden to prove such allegations.[473] If, however, there is evidence that the testator suffered from mental illness, or disorder or alcoholism, or intoxication or other mental

471. *Moumdjis v. Michaelidou* [1974] 1 CLR 226.
472. *Re Fuld* [1968] 675, *Waring v. Waring* (1848) 6 Moo PC 530.
473. *Antoniades v. Solomonidou* [1980] 1 CLR 441.

injury, the burden of proof is reversed and it has to be proven that the will was the result of the exercise of the free will of the testator.[474] The Court shall give appropriate weight to contemporary medical evidence that the testator was of sound mind;[475] however, the Court might disregard the medical opinion of doctors who did not have the opportunity to medically examine the testator at the crucial time, if there is other conflicting and credible evidence with respect to the true condition of the soundness of mind of the testator at the crucial time.[476]

*408.* Section 29 of Cap. 195 further provides that a will, or any part of a will, the making of which has been caused by coercion, fraud, or by the exercise of undue influence upon the testator, shall be null and void. Coercion, fraud and undue influence cannot be presumed;[477] they have to be proven positively and by adducing convincing evidence on the basis of the balance of probabilities.[478] Undue influence is defined in section 2 of Cap. 195 as 'the exercise by a person of influence to dominate the will of another person where the relations subsisting between them are such that one of them is in a position to dominate the will of the other and used that position to obtain an unfair advantage over the other'.[479] In *Wingrove* it was held that:

> *to be undue influence in the eye of the law there must be – to sum it up in one word – coercion. It must not be a case in which a person has been induced, by means such as I have suggested to you, to come to a conclusion that he will make a will in a particular person's favour, because if the testator has only been persuaded or induced by considerations which you may condemn, really and truly to intend to give his property to another, though you may disapprove of the act, yet it is strictly legitimate in the sense of its being legal. It is only when the will of the person who becomes a testator is coerced into doing that which he does not desire to do, that it is undue influence.*[480]

*409.* Coercion is defined in section 2 of Cap. 195 as the committing or threatening to commit any act (or omission) forbidden by the Criminal Code or the unlawful detaining or threatening to detain any property, to the prejudice of any person whatever with the intention of causing any person to do any act against his/her will, and it is immaterial whether the Criminal Code is or is not in force in the place where the coercion is employed. Fraud is defined in section 2 of Cap. 195 as the suggestion as to a fact, of that which is not true by one who does not believe it to be true, or the active concealment of a fact by one having knowledge or belief of

474. *Banks v. Goodfellow* (1870) LR 5 QB 549.
475. *Antoniades v. Solomonidou* [1980] 1 CLR 441.
476. *Karaolis v. The estate of the deceased Christodoulos Karaolis* [1965] 1 CLR. 24, *Moumdjis v. Michaelidou* [1974] 1 CLR 226, *Hoppi v. Panayi* [1992] 1 CLR 534 (in Greek), *Aitken and another v. McMeckan* [1895] AC 310.
477. *Baker v. Batt* (1838) 2 Moo PC 317. *Boyse v. Rossborough* (1857) 6 HLC 2.
478. *Hoppi v. Panayi* [1992] 1 CLR 534 (in Greek), *Kakopieros v. Kalama* [2009] 1 CLR 413 (in Greek), *Mosaikos v. Eren* (1958) 23 CLR 286, District Court.
479. *Christopoulou v. Christopoulou* [1971] 1 CLR 437, *Georghourou v. Anastasiades* [1973] 3 JSC 337.
480. *Wingrove v. Wingrove* (1885) 11 PD 81.

the fact, or a promise made without any intention of performing it, or any other act fitted to deceive, if 'committed by a person or with his connivance or by his agent, with intent to deceive another person or his agent or to induce him' to do any of the above acts.

## §2. Different Types of Wills

### I. The Requirements for Making a Valid Will

*410.* In accordance with section 23 of Cap. 195, no will shall be valid unless it is in writing and executed in a specific manner provided for in section 23. Oral wills are thus not permitted in Cyprus. However, there are no restrictions with respect to the material or the language used in order to write the will; the will may be handwritten, typed and may be written in Greek or any other language.[481] It is further necessary to write upon the will that it is such.[482] Section 23 introduces four requirements for making a valid will; such requirements are mandatory and consequently any will not conforming to such requirements shall be invalid.[483] However, as will be explained below, Law 96(I)/2015 has amended Cap. 195 so as to provide for the discretion of the court in some cases to waive any of the four requirements for making a valid will.

*411.* The first requirement is that the will shall be signed at the foot or end thereof by the testator or by some other person on his/her behalf, in his/her presence and by his/her direction. If the testator is illiterate, he/she may, in accordance with section 2 of Cap. 195, sign by using his/her mark or seal; signature by the initials of the testator,[484] a well-recognized nickname,[485] by the use of the words 'your dear Mother',[486] or even by the use of the testator's thumb,[487] might be considered, depending on the circumstances, as sufficient. It has further been held that a testator who is incapable to sign due to medical reasons which restrict the use of his/her hands or fingers may also use his/her thumb.[488] If the testator has no hands, or is incapable of signing due to medical reasons, or is blind, then a third person may sign on the testator's behalf in the presence of the testator and by the testator's direction. Such person may also act as a witness;[489] such third person may further guide the hand of the testator so as to enable him/her to sign the will.[490] If the testator was

481. *Whiting v. Turner* (1903) 89 LT 71.
482. *Re Mundy* (1860) 2 Sw & T 119, *Towers v. Hogan* (1889) 23 LR 53.
483. *Charalambous v. Demetriou* [1961] CLR 30.
484. *Re Savory* (1851) 15 Jur 1042.
485. *Re Redding* (1850) 2 Rob 339, *Re Glover* (1847) 11 Jur 1022.
486. *In the Estate of Cook* [1960] 1 WLR 353.
487. *Vassili Ricca v. Haji Towli Haji Vassili* (1922) 11 CLR 16.
488. *Papadopoulos and others v. Sergi and another*, Civil App. 294/2011, Judgment of 15 Feb. 2017 (in Greek).
489. *Re Bailey* (1838) 1 Curt 914, *Smith v. Harris* (1845) 1 Rob 262.
490. *Ricca v. Haji Vassili* (1922) 11 CLR 57.

blind or illiterate, then the will ought to have been read to him/her prior to execution in accordance with Regulation 16 of the Administration of Estates Regulations of 1955; a form of attestation that the will has been so read to the testator in such cases would be highly suggested.

*412.* The second requirement is that the testator's signature shall be made or acknowledged by the testator in the presence of two or more witnesses who are present at the same time. Witnesses should have the opportunity either to see the testator signing the will, or seeing the signature of the testator and having the testator acknowledging that this is his/her signature;[491] it is not, however, sufficient if the testator has assured the witnesses that he/she has signed, but they did not have the opportunity to see his/her signature.[492] If the testator signs the will in the presence of only one witness and subsequently the testator acknowledges his/her signature in the presence of the second witness, the will shall still be invalid, since the testator will not have signed or acknowledged the will in the *simultaneous* presence of two witnesses.

*413.* The third requirement is that the two or more witnesses shall attest and subscribe the will in the presence of the testator and each other. The attestation of the witnesses necessarily follows the signing of the will by the testator. The witnesses are not supposed to attest and subscribe the content of the will, which they might as well be unaware of; they need not even know that they are subscribing a will.[493] What is expected is that the witnesses attest that the testator has signed (or acknowledged his/her signature) before them a paper which he/she has also asked them to subscribe.[494] Attestation does not imply certification; there is thus no obligation to add the word witness to the will, but only to sign the will.[495] Contrary to what happens in the case of the signature of the testator, the signature of the witnesses may be placed anywhere in the will so long as it is clear that they attest and subscribe it.[496] No form of attestation is necessary;[497] however, lawyers typically adopt a specific form of attestation so as to prove that the requirements of section 23 of Cap. 195 have been fulfilled.[498]

*414.* The fourth requirement is that if the will consists of more than one sheet of paper, then each sheet has to be signed or initialled[499] by or on behalf of the testator and the witnesses. In *Charalambous* the Supreme Court held that if the witnesses fail to sign or initial each sheet of paper, then the will is invalid; the fact that the

491. *Parisinou v. Charalambides* [1998] 1 CLR 781 (in Greek), *Daintree v. Butcher* (1888) 13 PD 102.
492. *Re Gunstan* (1882) 7 PD 102, *Hudson v. Parker* (1844) 1 Robb Eccl. 14.
493. *In the Estate of Benjamin* [1934] All ER 359.
494. *Koumi* [1975] 1 CLR 239.
495. *Pavlides v. Potamiti* (1910) 9 CLR 119, *Parisinou v. Charalambides* [1998] 1 CLR 781 (in Greek).
496. *Re Braddock* (1876) 1 PD 433.
497. *Parisinou v. Charalambides* [1998] 1 CLR 781 (in Greek).
498. '*Signed by the said A.B. in the sight and presence of us, all present at the same time, who, in his sight and presence, at his request, and in the presence of each other, subscribe our names as attesting witnesses*'.
499. *Christopoulou v. Christopoulou* [1971] 1 CLR 437, District Court.

will was handwritten or that the sheets of paper were connected by a paper clip, could not save the validity of the will.[500] However, if the will consists of more than one pages of the same sheet of paper, it is sufficient if it is signed at its foot or the end of the sheet of paper.[501] In *Koumi* the will consisted of more than one sheet of paper which were connected by a paper clip; the testator and the witnesses had signed at the end of the second sheet. Each sheet contained a corrigendum in accordance to which a word of the will ought to be substituted with another; the corrigendum was initialled by both the testator and the witnesses. The first instance Court held that, while the corrigendum was made simultaneously with the will, the testator and the witnesses had initialled only with respect to the corrigendum and not the will and thus, it could not be claimed that they had signed or initialled each sheet of paper. The Supreme Court reversed the first instance judgment and held that so long as each sheet of paper was initialled, this was sufficient and thus the will should be considered as valid.[502]

*415.* A will which is formally defective shall be void, irrespective of whether its content corresponds to the genuine intentions of the testator. However, it has been held that if there are multiple originals of the same will, then formal defects would not affect the validity of the will if at least one of the originals has been properly executed.[503] Furthermore, section 23A of Cap. 195, which was added by amending Law 96(I)/2015, provides that the court may correct an error or omission which is inconsistent with the four mandatory requirements, or any numerical error in the content of the will. Any interested party may apply before the court for a declaration that the error or omission should be corrected accordingly and that the will should be considered as a valid one as corrected and the court may order accordingly if it is convinced that it would be fair and just to do so. The powers of the court pursuant to section 23A of Cap. 195 may be exercised even if the will had been executed prior to the enactment of the amending Law 96(I)/2015, so far as the will has not been declared as void by a final judicial decision. The powers of the court introduced with Law 96(I)/2015 are of significance, since they grant the court the right to waive any of the mandatory requirements and hold that a will is a valid one, despite the existence of formal defects.

*416.* The character of the witness, the length of time which has elapsed since the will was signed, the nature of the facts deposed to and all other circumstances of the case, may be examined by the Court in order to declare whether a will has been properly executed.[504] If a form of attestation has been included, then there is a rebuttable presumption that the requirements set out in section 23 of Cap. 195 have been fulfilled in accordance with the legal maxim *omnia praesumuntur rite esse acta.*[505]

500. *Charalambous v. Demetriou* [1961] CLR 30.
501. *Georgiades v. Pittakas* [1980] 2 JSC 320, District Court.
502. *Koumi* [1975] 1 CLR 239.
503. *Lambi v. Palaiomylitou*, Action 9945/2007 and others, Judgment of 31 May 2013 (District Court, in Greek).
504. *Thomson v. Hall* (1852) 2 Rob Eccl 426.
505. *Vinnicombe v. Butler* (1864) 3 Sw & Tr 580, *Harris v. Knight* (1890) 15 PD 170, *Georgiades v. Pittakas* [1980] 2 JSC 320 District Court.

The mere fact that the witnesses no longer remember having attested the will,[506] or that the witnesses are dead,[507] or that there is no form of attestation[508] should not imply that the will has not been properly executed. Regulation 13 of the Administration of Estates Regulations of 1955 further provides that if there is no form of attestation, then the Registrar should request for an affidavit by one of the witnesses, or if they have died, by other persons who were present in the execution of the will. If there are no witnesses alive, then other evidentiary means, including a graphologist, ought to be provided.

*417.* For a person to act as a witness to a will he/she should, in accordance with section 24 of Cap. 195, have completed the age of 18 years, be of sound mind and be able to sign his/her name. Thus, it is not possible for a third person to sign on behalf of a witness, as in the case of the testator. Section 25 further provides that if any person attests as a witness the execution of any will giving to him/her or to his/her spouse or child, any beneficial legacy, then such legacy shall be utterly null and void. Section 25 aims at avoiding conflict of interests between witnesses and beneficial legatees; the will remains valid and the witness may prove the execution or validity of the will, but the beneficial legacy to him/her, or to his/her spouse or child is invalidated. It is suggested that whenever the witnesses are more than the legally required (in other words more than two), then the additional attestation by the beneficial legatee could simply be ignored, rather than invalidating the beneficial legacy.[509]

*418.* Section 25 clarifies that the beneficial legacy is not invalidated if it refers to existing charges or to directions for the payment of any debt towards the witness, or his/her spouse or child. Such clarification was probably superfluous, since legacy is defined in section 2 of Cap. 195 as a gift by will of movable or immovable property and if the provision refers to a debt of the testator, then there could be no reference to a gift. It is further provided in section 26 of Cap. 195 that any creditor of the Estate or his/her spouse or child shall be admitted as a witness to prove the execution or validity of the will of the testator. The person named as an executor of the will is also competent to be admitted as a witness in order to prove the execution or validity of the will in accordance with section 27 of Cap. 195.

## II. Members of the Armed Force Exception

*419.* Section 43 of Cap. 195 provides that any declaration made by any person with respect to the disposal of his/her property after his/her death, which would have been valid and effective under either section 11 of the English Wills Act, 1837, or

506. *Re Gunstan* (1882) 7 PD 102, *Wright v. Sanderson* [1884] 9 PD 149, *Papavasiliou v. Papafedia* [1975] 1 JSC 96, District Court.
507. *Re Phibbs* [1917] 93.
508. *Re Peverett* [1902] 205, *Re Denning* [1958] 2 All ER 1.
509. A. Emilianides, *Cypriot Succession Law* 3rd edn (Nicosia: Hippasus, 2015, in Greek).

the English Wills (Soldiers and Sailors) Act, 1918, shall be valid and effective, notwithstanding any other provisions of Cap. 195. Section 11 of the Wills Act, 1837 and Wills (Soldiers and Sailors) Act, 1918 provide that any soldier or sailor being in actual military service or any mariner or seaman being at sea, may dispose of their estate even with an oral will, or a written will which does not fulfil the requirements of Cap. 195 and even if they are minors; the exception should be extended so as to further include members of the military air force. A will made by such persons may be revoked as informally as it was made.[510] It has been decided that such exception covers members of the armed forces at any rank, and even military doctors, priests or nurses;[511] however, the will must have been made during actual military service and therefore military operations must be ongoing.[512]

## III. International Treaties

*420.* Article 30 of the bilateral Convention for Legal Cooperation between the Republic of Cyprus and the Republic of Greece in matters of Civil, Family, Commercial and Criminal Law, which was ratified by Law 55/1984, provides for dual recognition of wills in certain cases. However, the provisions of Article 30 of the Convention should be considered as no longer being in force, since Regulation 650/2012 has superior force and excludes bilateral conventions to the contrary between Member States of the EU. Other bilateral conventions, however, which have been concluded with third countries and which, *inter alia*, provide for dual recognition of wills remain in force; these are the Conventions with Russia,[513] Belarus,[514] Georgia,[515] Ukraine,[516] and Libya.[517] The Republic of Cyprus has ratified the Washington Convention of 26 October 1973 providing for a Uniform Law on the Form of an International Will, by Law 22/1980. Thus, international wills are applicable in Cyprus. Furthermore, the Republic has ratified the Basel Convention of 16 May 1972 on the Establishment of a Scheme of Registration on Wills, by Law 64/1974. It has not, however, ratified the Hague Convention of 5 October 1961 on the Conflict of Laws relating to the Form of Testamentary Dispositions.

## §3. The Joint Will

*421.* A joint will is a single document executed by more than one person, typically husband and wife, which has effect in relation to each signatory's property

510. *Wood v. Gossage* [1921] 194.
511. *Andrews v. Wingham* [1949] 187.
512. *Ibid.*
513. Ratified by Laws 172/1986 and 34(III)/2001.
514. Ratified by Law 172/1986 and the Exchange of Notes between the Republic of Cyprus and the Republic of Belarus, Minsk 1/11/1996 and Nicosia 2/11/1996.
515. Ratified by Law 172/1986 and the Exchange of Notes between the Republic of Cyprus and the Republic of Georgia, Tbilisi 6/7/2000 and Nicosia 7/7/2000.
516. Ratified by Law 8(III)/2005.
517. Ratified by Law 32(III)/2005.

upon his/her death. It has been held that joint wills, while rare, are lawful.[518] A mutual will is an agreement as to the disposition of property upon death, which may be concluded by a joint will and which does not allow for its revocation without the agreement of the other party. Until recently it was unclear whether the Cypriot legal system allowed for the making of mutual wills. However, the Supreme Court emphatically held that in *Lesseps* that mutual wills between spouses are valid in Cyprus by virtue of the common law and the principles of equity which form part of Cypriot law pursuant to s. 29 § 1 (c) of Law 14/60. A mutual agreement is essentially an agreement between the spouses and accordingly it is not possible for a spouse to recall her mutual will after the death of her spouse, despite the fact that the mutual will precluded such a possibility. It was thus held that the agreement included in the mutual will remained binding for the spouse who had signed it, even after the death of her spouse and accordingly she could not unilaterally revoke it or change its content.[519]

## §4. Deposit and Discovery of Wills

*422.* Any person may, in accordance with section 9 section 1 of the Administration of Estates Law, Cap. 189, deposit his/her will to the Registry of a District Court; the will should be delivered personally by the testator in a closed envelope which is sealed by the Registrar in accordance with Regulation 3 of the Administration of Estates Regulations of 1955. If the testator is not personally known to the Registrar, then his/her identity should be confirmed by the affidavit of a person who is known to the Registrar, such as an advocate. If the testator is unable to attend to the Registry, due to illness or other reasons, the President of the District Court may order that the Registrar visits the testator in order for the will to be deposited, in accordance with Regulation 7 of the Administration of Estate Regulations of 1955; in such a case the testator has to pay the travel expenses of the Registrar.

*423.* In accordance with Regulation 4 of the 1955 Regulations, the testator has to sign the envelope in the presence of the Registrar. The Registrar then files the deposited will and informs accordingly the Chief Registrar of the Supreme Court who is also the Chief Registrar with respect to deposited wills in accordance with section 9 section 4 of Cap. 189. Following the death of the testator, the will may be unsealed by the executor of the will or other authorized person in the presence of the Registrar, in accordance with Regulation 8 of the 1955 Regulations. Approximately 1500 wills are deposited yearly with the cost of deposit being merely symbolic; however, the Register is not kept electronically. If a testator who has deposited a will during his/her lifetime in the Registry has died and no steps have been taken, or seem likely to be taken for the opening of such will, the Court may take action in order to bring the existence of the will to the notice of any person likely to be interested; in practice the Court is unlikely to take such action.

518. *Kouti*, App. 236/2011, Judgment of 15 Dec. 2011 (in Greek).

519. *Lesseps and another v. Theophanous and others*, Civil App. 239/2010, Judgment of 18 Feb. 2016 (in Greek).

*424.* It is also possible to keep a will at home or hand it over to an advocate for safekeeping. Any person having in his/her possession or under his/her control any will of a deceased person, should, in accordance with section 11 of Cap. 189, deliver it to the probate registrar of the Court within fourteen days from the time he/she became aware of the death of the testator; otherwise, he/she shall be liable to a fine. The Court has the power to order any person possessing a will to bring it into Court; the Court may further order that any person is examined before the Court if it appears that there are reasonable grounds for believing that he/she has knowledge of a will.

## §5. Revocation of a Will

*425.* There are three ways of revoking a will; these are provided exhaustively in section 37 of Cap. 195.[520] The first is by a subsequent will expressly revoking the former one, for instance by writing on the subsequent will: '*I hereby revoke all testamentary dispositions heretobefore made by me and declare this to be my last will.*' Such subsequent will should be a valid one; however, it is not necessary that it provides for the disposal of the estate of the testator, since it might simply provide for the revocation of the former will.[521] The burden upon a plaintiff who argues that despite the revocatory clause, the testator did not intend to revoke a specific bequest in the former will – if this is at all possible under Cypriot law is extremely high.[522]

*426.* A will may further be revoked by a subsequent will which is inconsistent with the provisions of the former one, but only insofar as the provisions of the two wills are inconsistent. It is noted that there is no presumption that the subsequent will revokes the former one, nor may such an intention be presumed by the mere fact that the subsequent will is called as the 'last will';[523] there has to be express revocation.[524] Otherwise, the two wills shall be read together in order to determine to which extent they are inconsistent.[525] The subsequent will may revoke either completely or partly the former will.[526] If it is impossible to determine which will is subsequent, then if the two wills may coexist they shall both be executed;[527] if, however, the two wills are inconsistent with each other, then none will be executed under the proviso that if they contain a revocation clause previous wills shall be deemed to have been revoked.[528]

520. *Kathitzioti v. Mavronicolas* [1995] 1 CLR 447 (in Greek).
521. *Re Howard* [1944] 39.
522. *Lowthorpe-Lutwidge v. Lowthorpe-Lutwidge* [1935] 151.
523. *Simpson v. Foxon* [1907] 54, *Re Hawksley* [1934] Ch 384.
524. *Stoddart v. Grant* (1852) 1 Macq HL 163.
525. *Cadell v. Wilcocks* [1898] 21, *Re Petchell* (1874) LR 3 P & D 153.
526. *Dempsey v. Lawson* (1877) 2 PD 98, *Thorn v. Dickins* [1906] WN 54.
527. *Townsend v. Moore* [1905] 66.
528. *Re Howard* [1944] 39.

*427.* The third way of revoking a will is by burning, tearing or otherwise destroying it with the intention of revoking it; for the revocation to take effect the will has to be burned, torn or otherwise destroyed by the testator or by some person in the testator's presence and by his/her direction. If the intention is to revoke a specific part of the will, then only this part will be revoked.[529] Deleting words with a pen is not considered to amount to a revocation of the will;[530] nor is a symbolical destruction of the will sufficient.[531] If, however, the signature of the testator or the witnesses is destroyed, with an intention to revoke the will, then the will shall be considered as revoked in its entirety.[532] If the testator has destroyed only one of several copies of the will, the will shall be considered to have been revoked only if it is proved that the testator had the intention to revoke it.[533] The person alleging revocation shall bear the burden of proof[534] unless the will was under the control of the testator and was found destroyed, in which case it is rebuttably presumed that it was revoked.[535]

*428.* The rule which provides for the destruction of the will by the testator or in the testator's presence and by his/her direction implies that the destruction of a will by a third person after the death of the testator, even by his/her direction shall not amount to revocation;[536] similarly, the destruction of a will by a third person which is subsequently approved by the testator does not amount to revocation.[537] In the case of *Kathitzioti* the testator had deposited the will to the Registrar for safe keeping.[538] The Appellant, a third person, provided to the Registrar a special proxy signed by the testator, on the basis of which she was authorized by the testator to destroy the will in order to revoke it. The testator herself sent a letter to the Registrar confirming such wishes. However, the Registrar refused to comply, maintaining that such an action would be contrary to section 37 of Cap. 195. The Supreme Court held that the intention of the testator to revoke a will is not sufficient, unless the will is destroyed in the physical presence of the testator; the fact that the lawyer or proxy of the testator would be present in the destruction of the will could not be considered as sufficient for the will to be revoked. Similarly, if the testator himself/herself destroys a will, this will not amount to a revocation of the will, unless the

---

529. *Clarke v. Stripps* (1852) 2 Rob Eccl 563.
530. *Iracleous v. Avraamides* [2010] 1 CLR 807 (in Greek).
531. *Cheese v. Lovejoy* (1877) 2 PD 251.
532. *Hobbs v. Knight* (1838) 1 Curt 769.
533. *Pemberton v. Pemberton* (1807) 13 Ves 290.
534. *Benson v. Benson* (1870) LR 2 P & D 172.
535. *Bell v. Fothergill* (1870) LR 2 P & D 148, *Drake v. Sykes* (1907) 23 TLR 747. Στην *Welch v. Phillips* (1836) 1 Moo PC 299 it was mentioned that: '*The presumption is founded on good sense; for it is highly reasonable to suppose that an instrument of so much importance would be carefully preserved by a person of ordinary caution in some place of safety, and would not be lost or stolen; and if on the death of the maker, it is not found in his usual repositories, or else where he resides, it is in a high degree probable that the deceased himself has purposely destroyed it.*'
536. *Stockwell v. Ritherdon* (1848) 1 Rob 661.
537. *Gill v. Gill* [1909] 157.
538. *Kathitzioti v. Mavronicolas* [1995] 1 CLR 447 (in Greek).

testator intended for the will to be revoked; if the testator was intoxicated or mentally ill, or drunk, the will shall not be revoked.[539]

*429.* Furthermore, a will shall be deemed to be revoked, in accordance with section 38 of Cap. 195, if after the execution of the will, the testator is married or has children for the first time. The aim of section 38 is to safeguard the interests of a testator who made a will at a point when he/she did not have children or had not married and who would not have made such a will if he/she was aware of the subsequent developments in his/her life. For a marriage to revoke the will, it has to be a valid one.[540] It is, however, in our view immaterial whether the children were born within the marriage, adopted, or recognized by the testator, so long as the testator did not have any children before. Such marriage or birth shall not be deemed to revoke the will, if from the content of the will it appears that it was made in contemplation of such marriage or birth.[541]

*430.* It is accepted that a will may be conditionally revoked. In *Georgiades* the testator had torn the original of the former will and had executed a subsequent will which expressly revoked the former one. However, the subsequent will was considered to be formally defective and thus, invalid. The Court held that the intention of the testator was to revoke the former will, only if the subsequent will was valid; thus, since the condition had not been fulfilled, the former will had never been revoked.[542] This view has been confirmed by the Supreme Court in *Iracleous*.[543] However, a testator might intend for the former will to have been revoked, even if the subsequent will is held to be invalid.[544] The Court has to establish the true intentions of the testator. The test was set out in *Re Jones* as follows:

> *If he had an intention of revoking the will, was his intention absolute or qualified, so as to be contingent or conditional? If it was absolute, that is the end of the investigation, for the act takes effect as revocation ... If the testator's intention is found to have been a qualified one, subject to some condition or contingency, the final question arises: has that condition or contingent been satisfied or occurred? If the condition or contingency to which the intention to revoke was subject has not been satisfied or occurred, the revocation is ineffective; if it has been satisfied or occurred, the revocation is effective.*

*431.* A revoked will might be revived, in accordance with section 39 of Cap. 195, by its re-execution on the basis of the provisions of section 23 of Cap. 195 and so long as there is an intention to revive the will. A revoked will may further be revived with a codicil which explicitly refers that the revoked will is revived. In practice it might be simpler to execute a new will, rather than revive a revoked one, since in both cases the requirements of section 23 have to be fulfilled.

---

539. *Brunt v. Brunt* (1873) LR 3 P & D 37, *Re Brassington* (1902) 1.
540. *De Reneville v. De Reneville* [1948] 100.
541. *Re Langston* [1953] 100, *Pilot v. Gainfort* [1931] 103.
542. *Georgiades v. Pittakas* [1980] 2 JSC 320, District Court.
543. *Iracleous v. Avraamides* [2010] 1 CLR 807 (in Greek).
544. *Dixon v. Treasury Solicitor* [1905] 42.

## §6. Provisions in a Will

### I. Validity of Legacies

*432.* A legacy is any gift of movable or immovable property by will. Section 31 (a) of Cap. 195 provides that a legacy shall not be valid if it is made to a person who was not in existence at the time of the death of the testator;[545] such clause is mandatory and therefore the testator may not provide in his/her will that he/she wishes to make a legacy to a person he/she knows shall not be existent at the time of his/her death.[546] There are, however two exceptions. The first exception is that a legacy to a posthumous child of the testator shall be valid; however, a legacy to other posthumous children, such as children of relatives of the testator shall not be valid. The second exception provides that where the testator has left a legacy to any child or other issue who dies in the lifetime of the testator, such legacy shall not lapse so long as the child or issue of the testator has left issue who outlived the testator; in such a case the legacy shall take effect as if the death of the child or issue of the testator happened immediately after the death of the testator, unless a contrary intention appears in the will. It is suggested that the second exception should apply even if the legatee, child or issue of the testator, had left a posthumous child, since in such a case the general rule of section 15 of Cap. 195 would apply and the posthumous child ought to have rights to the legacy of his/her ascendants.

*433.* There was a question as to whether section 31 (a) of Cap. 195 also applies with respect to legal persons and whether legacies made to legal persons which were not in existence at the time of death of the testator are also invalid. In *Christopoulou* the District Court of Nicosia had held that the term 'person' in section 31 (a) refers only to natural persons and not to legal persons.[547] Such interpretation was eventually reversed by the Supreme Court in the case of *Stivadorou.*[548] The deceased in the case of *Stivadorou* had bequeathed his estate to a foundation named Greek Institute of Cypriot Studies, which had not yet been founded until his death. The Supreme Court held that section 2 of the Interpretation Law, Cap. 1 provides that whenever a legislation refers to 'persons', this also includes legal persons, unless the law otherwise provides or unless such interpretation is not consistent with the purpose of the relevant legal provisions; it was thus held that section 31 (a) of Cap. 195 refers to both natural and legal persons. Consequently, the legacy was invalid, since it was given to a person who was not in existence at the time of the death of the testator.

*434.* The judgment of the Supreme Court in *Stivadorou* may be criticized for failing to refer to the then in force section 28 of the Associations and Foundations Law 57/1972 which provided that a foundation may be founded either during the lifetime of the founder, or with a testamentary provision. If it was to be accepted

545. *Demetriades and another v. Ioannides*, Civil App. 35/2012, Judgment of 2 Jun. 2017 (in Greek).
546. *Re Ladd* [1932] 2 Ch 219.
547. *Christopoulou v. Christopoulou* [1971] 1 CLR 437, District Court.
548. *Stivadorou v. Hatzikosta* [2002] 1 CLR 497 (in Greek).

that it is not possible to bequeath any legacy to a legal person who was not existent at the time of death of the testator, then what would be the purpose of section 28 of Law 57/72 providing that a foundation (namely a donation of property) may be founded by a testamentary provision. 27 § 1 of the new Associations and Foundations Law 104(I)/2017 has corrected the anomaly by providing that the restrictions of section 31 (a) of Cap. 195 do not apply in foundations which have been founded by a testamentary provision. Thus, legacies to foundations which are legally founded subsequently to the death of the testator are valid. All other legacies to legal persons, either associations, partnerships, limited companies, shall be invalid if such persons were not in existence at the time of the death of the testator, either because they had not yet been founded or established or because they had in the meantime been dissolved.[549] The legacy will of course be valid, if the legal person simply changed its name.[550]

*435.* Section 31 (b) of Cap. 195 further provides that no legacy shall be valid if it does not express a definite intention; such intention may refer to the testator's will for a specific person to become his/her legatee, or for benevolent causes.[551] A legacy shall not be declared invalid merely because the executor may choose from a wide range of persons for whose benefit the legacy was made,[552] nor because the category of persons benefiting from the legacy is many and varied, such as in the case of an established foundation.[553] Thus, a legacy in accordance to which the executor of the will is directed to choose one of various named foundations or associations shall be valid.

## II. Specific Provisions on Legacies

*436.* Section 30 of Cap. 195 provides that a testator may make provision in his/her will for the substitution of any legatee for any other legatee mentioned therein; such substitution may occur whenever the original legatee has died, or a legal person has dissolved, in the lifetime of the testator, or whenever the original legatee has become unworthy in accordance with section 17 of Cap. 195. A legacy may further be dependent upon the fulfilment of specific conditions; however, if such conditions are impossible, illegal or immoral, the legacy shall be valid, but the condition shall be void.[554] A condition that the legatee has to remain widowed, or single, or according to which the legatee has to change religion or political affiliation, or profession, are instances of conditions which might be considered as immoral. Illegal conditions are those according to which the legatee has to commit a criminal offence, while an example of an impossible condition is the condition that the legatee has to determine whether there is a God or not.

549. *Re Rymer* [1895] 1 Ch 19.
550. *Re Dawson's Will Trusts* [1957] 1 WLR 391.
551. *Christopoulou v. Christopoulou* [1971] 1 CLR 437, District Court.
552. *Weir v. Crum-Brown* [1908] AC 162.
553. *Re Brown* [1888] 1 Ir R 423.
554. *See also Terzis v. Petoufa* [2011] 1 CLR 336 (in Greek).

*437.* It is further provided in section 33 of Cap. 195 that no legacy may be bequeathed to any religious corporation by a person having any relationship within the third degree of kindred, unless his/her will was executed at least three months before his/her death; if the testator has no relatives within the third degree of kindred, then the legacy shall be valid even if his/her will was executed at the day of his/her death. A religious corporation may include, in accordance with section 2 of Cap. 195, any religious establishment or religious institution belonging to any denomination and any Throne, Church, Chapel, Monastery, Mosque, Tekye, Shrine, or Synagogue of any known religion, namely any religion whose doctrines and rites are not secret in accordance with Article 18 of the Constitution. If the testator is a Muslim, a legacy shall be deemed to be valid irrespective of when the will was executed.

*438.* Section 34 of Cap. 195 provides that a father or mother may appoint a guardian for their child by will during the time that such child is a person under disability or an incapable person; the Court may for good reason and at its discretion remove such guardian and appoint another guardian in his/her stead. In view of the enactment of the Relation between Parents and Children Law 216/1990, it is highly questionable whether there is still a possibility to appoint a guardian by will contrary to the provisions of such Law, or for an adult person, even if such person is under disability or incapable.

## §7. Restrictions

### I. The Legitim

*439.* The right of a person to dispose of his/her property by will is not absolute. In accordance with section 41 of Cap. 195 such right is qualified to the disposal of the disposable portion of the estate, namely the portion of the estate that a person is legally allowed to dispose by will. Thc disposable portion is determined at the time of death of the testator and not at the time of making the will; thus, a person cannot precisely know at the time of making his/her will what shall be the disposable portion at the time of his/her death. The disposable portion of the estate refers to the net value of the estate, namely the value of the estate after all obligations, debts, and taxes have been paid; immovable property situated out of Cyprus is not taken into consideration for the determination of the disposable portion, even if the testator is domiciled in Cyprus.[555]

*440.* Section 41 of Cap. 195 provides for three distinct cases for determining the disposable portion:

(a) If the testator died leaving a spouse and a child, or a spouse and a descendant of a child, or no spouse but a child or a descendant, the disposable portion shall

555. *Kochino v. Irfan* [1976] 1 CLR 240.

not exceed ¼ of the net value of the estate; thus, if the testator died leaving descendants, he/she may only dispose by will only ¼ of his/her estate.

(b) If the testator died leaving a spouse or a father or a mother, but no child, nor descendant thereof, the disposable portion shall not exceed ½ of the net value of the estate; thus, if the testator died leaving spouse or parent, he/she may dispose by will only ½ of his/her estate.

(c) If the testator died leaving neither spouse, nor child, nor descendant, nor a father, nor a mother, the disposable portion shall be the whole of the estate. Thus, if the testator died leaving brothers, sisters, uncles, aunts, nephews, nieces, cousins or other relatives, this does not affect his/her right to dispose of his/her estate by will; in such a case the right to dispose of his/her estate by will shall be absolute. In Efthymiou it was held that although the testator died leaving a parent, since the parent had opted to renounce the inheritance, the siblings of the deceased had no right to contest the terms of the will regarding the disposable portion.[556]

*441.* If the testator had purported to dispose by will of a part of his/her estate in excess of the disposable portion, such disposition shall be reduced proportionally so as to be limited to the disposable portion; thus, a will on the basis of which the testator disposed more than he/she was legally allowed is by no means invalid, but the various legacies shall be reduced proportionally in order to conform to the legal stipulation about the disposable portion.[557] It is, however, provided that if the testator died leaving spouse, but neither descendants, nor parents, then such person may dispose the whole of the estate to the surviving spouse; this was the case of *Antoniades* where the testator died leaving only a spouse and a sister and his intention was for the spouse to become his only heir.[558] It is further noted that the testator may opt to dispose by will additional shares to persons who would anyway be entitled to a statutory portion of the estate; thus, if the testator died leaving two children, he/she may opt to dispose by will to one of the children the disposable portion of the estate, namely an additional ¼ of his/her estate.

*442.* The portion of the estate which is not disposable by will forms the statutory portion of the estate, namely the part of the estate which shall be distributed in accordance with the provisions of the law, irrespective of the wishes of the deceased. The descendants, spouse, and parents of the deceased are considered as statutory heirs, because if one of these persons is alive at the time of death of the deceased, his/her right to freely dispose of his/her estate by will is restricted. The statutory portion if the deceased died leaving a descendant amounts to ¾ of the estate, and if the deceased died leaving a spouse or a parent it amounts to ½ of the estate.

556. *Panayides v. Efthymiou*, Action 6705/2008, Judgment of 18 Feb. 2014 (in Greek).
557. *Papavasiliou v. Papafedia* [1975] 1 JSC 96, District Court.
558. *Antoniades v. Solomonidou* [1980] 1 CLR 441, *Ioannou v. Marcou* [1981] 1 CLR 349.

*443*. Section 42 of Cap. 195 restricted the ambit of the application of the rules on disposable portion, since it provided that section 41 does not apply in the following cases:

(a) With regard to the disposal of any movable or immovable property of a person born in the United Kingdom or whose father was born in the United Kingdom, or any of the Member States of the Commonwealth, irrespective whether such a person is domiciled in Cyprus or not.
(b) With regard to the disposal of any movable property of a foreigner irrespective of whether he/she has is domiciled in Cyprus or not.

Section 42 of Cap. 195 has been repealed by the amending Law 96(I)/2015 and accordingly does not apply to the succession of persons who died after 3 July 2015.

§8. Interpretation of a Will

## I. Principles of Interpretation

*444*. Section 36 of Cap. 195 provides that every will shall be construed with reference to the estate comprised in it, to speak and take effect as if it had been executed immediately before the death of the testator, unless a contrary intention shall appear by the will. In view of the fact that a will may only become effective after the testator has died, the applicable law in relation to a will is the law in force at the death of the testator.[559] In addition, section 35 of Cap. 195 provides that no will shall be held to have become invalid nor shall the construction thereof be altered by reason of any subsequent change of domicile of the person making the same. Unavoidably, the interpretation of legal terms included in the will should take into account the legal system that the testator had in mind while making the will, irrespective of the law otherwise applicable to the will; thus, if the testator had made the will in Greece with the help of a Greek lawyer and using Greek terminology, this should be taken into account while interpreting the will, even if the applicable law is Cypriot due to the fact that the testator had his/her domicile in Cyprus at the time of death.

*445*. The golden rule of interpretation of a will is that the Court should attempt to determine the true intention of the testator by construing the words on the basis of their natural legal meaning.[560] The question is not of course what the testator theoretically intended to do, but what he/she actually meant by using the written words he/she chose in the specific will, namely what is the expressed intention of the testator.[561] The Court should respect the expressed intention of the testator even if it considers such intention as capricious, eccentric, or arbitrary.[562] Whenever the

559. *Antoniades v. Solomonidou* [1980] 1 CLR 441, *Ioannou v. Marcou* [1981] 1 CLR 349.
560. *Winter v. Perratt* (1832) 6 Man & G 314.
561. *Perrin v. Morgan* [1943] 1 All ER 187.
562. *Bird v. Luckie* (1850) 8 Hare 301.

letter of the will is sufficiently clear, extrinsic evidence ought to be avoided; extrinsic evidence will, however, be admitted in order to clarify vague elements of the will or in order to prove that certain terms ought to be interpreted in a given manner in view of the specific circumstances of the case.[563] This kind of extrinsic evidence is admitted for the purpose of enabling the Court to determine the intention of the testator, but not for the purpose of altering the expressed written will of the testator.[564]

*446.* In the case of *Antoniades* the testator had expressed his intention to dispose to his wife all movable and immovable property that the law enabled him to dispose by will; the testator had died leaving a wife and a sister. The first instance Court held that the testator's reference to all property that 'the law enables me to dispose by will' referred to the disposable portion of the estate and could not extend to the whole of the estate; consequently, it held that the spouse would succeed to half of the estate, while the remaining half of the estate would be succeeded by the sister on the basis of the provisions of Cap. 195. However, the Supreme Court reversed the first instance judgment and held that the expressed intention of the testator was to dispose all his property to his wife, if he so could and thus, his wife ought to succeed to the whole of his estate.[565]

*447.* In *Petoufa* the Appellant claimed that the monetary amount found in the safe of the deceased did not fall within the meaning of the term 'moveable property' because it was found in the residence of the deceased; it was argued that since the deceased had disposed to the Appellant his immovable property and anything found therein, the monetary amount found in the safe had also been disposed to him. The Supreme Court, after analysing the intention of the testator and the relationship of the testator and other legatees, rejected the claim and held that the monetary amount was excluded from the legacy that the Appellant had been given and should be given to the remaining legatees.[566] Also in *Pierides* the Court held that a term in the will expressing the intention that all duties, tax, real expenses, legal and executor fees should be paid prior to distribution implied that such fees should be paid pro rata by the legatees and not by the legatee who was given the highest legacy.[567]

## II. Alteration of a Will

*448.* Section 28 of Cap. 195 provides that no obliteration, interlineations, or other alteration made in any will after the execution thereof shall be valid or have any effect.[568] In the absence of a relevant attestation, it shall be presumed that any alterations were made after the execution of the will;[569] where, however, a will has

563. *Charter v. Charter* (1874) LR 7 364.
564. *Grant v. Grant* (1870) LR 5 CP 385. *See*, however, *Re Cohn (deceased) National Westminster Bank Ltd. v. Cohn* [1974] 3 All ER 928.
565. *Antoniades v. Solomonidou* [1980] 1 CLR 441. *See also Ioannou v. Marcou* [1981] 1 CLR 349.
566. *Terzis v. Petoufa* [2011] 1 CLR 336 (in Greek).
567. *Pierides*, App. 284/2009, Judgment of 9 Aug. 2012 (District Court, in Greek).
568. *See* further Regulations 17 and 18 of the Administration of Estates Regulations of 1955.
569. *Cooper v. Bockett* (1844) 4 Moo PC 419, *Greville v. Tylee* (1851) 7 Moo PC 320.

been drawn with blanks left (e.g., for the names of legatees, the amount of legacies) which are afterwards filled up, there is a presumption that the blanks were filled before execution.[570] Evidence may be presented in order to rebut the presumption, including testimony by the witnesses, or a graphologist; the nature of the alterations, the ink used, and the totality of the evidence should be evaluated by the Court in order to conclude whether the alterations were made before or after the execution of the will.

*449.* Alterations to a will shall be valid, even if effected after the execution of the will, whenever they have also been executed in accordance with the requirements set out in section 23 of Cap. 195, or if the signature of the testator and the subscription of the witnesses are made in the margin or some other part of the will opposite or near to such alteration or at the foot or end of or opposite to a memorandum referring to such alteration and written at the end or some other part of the will. Thus, the initialling of a corrigendum by the testator and the witnesses shall be deemed to be as sufficient.[571] Alterations to a will shall further be valid, even if effected after the execution of the will, insofar as the words or effect of the will before such alteration shall not be apparent. It has not been settled whether words should be considered as not being 'apparent', even if their meaning can be found by using recent scientific methods; it is suggested that if the true intentions of the testator may be found by using recent scientific methods, then this should be considered as sufficient.[572]

570. *Christopoulou v. Christopoulou* [1971] 1 CLR 437, District Court.
571. *Koumi* [1975] 1 CLR 239.
572. A different conclusion is supported by *Re Itter* [1950] 130, *Re Ibbertson* (1839) 2 Curt 337, *Re Horsford* (1874) LR 3 P & D 211.

## Chapter 3. Acts *Inter Vivos* related to the Estate

### §1. Estate Planning

*450.* Estate duty was levied in Cyprus in accordance with the Estate Duty Law 67/1962 (and previously the Estate Duty Law, Cap. 319); however, Law 67/62 and the imposition of Estate duty were abolished with the enactment of the Estate of Deceased Persons (Tax Provisions) Law 78(I)/2000. Consequently, the estate of any person who died before 1 January 2000 is subject to estate duty, while the estate of any person who died after 1 January 2000 is not subject to estate duty. In any event, the executor of the will, or the administrator of the Estate of a deceased person who died after 1 January 2000, still has to settle all tax obligations that the estate had at the time of death, arising, *inter alia*, out of the Income Tax Law 118(I)/2002, the Immovable Property Law 24/1980, the Capital Gains Tax Law 52/1980, the Assessment and Collection of Taxes Law 4/1978, and the Special Defence Contribution Law 117(I)/2002.

*451.* In view of the fact that the estate duty tax has been abolished, there are no longer any substantial tax benefits for someone to donate his/her property during his/her lifetime, or proceed in acts *inter vivos* related to the estate. However, a person might wish to set up a trust in order to avoid the application of the provisions of Cap. 195 referring to statutory portion or disposable portion, since trusts are excluded from the estate of the deceased. Similarly, a person might wish to set up a joint account which is also excluded from the estate of the deceased in order to achieve the same results. *Donatio mortis causa* is not often used in practice, since its effect is similar to the effect of legacies.

### §2. Donations

*452.* Donations made during the lifetime of the deceased are not related to the Estate. However, *donatio mortis causa* is directly related to succession law. Section 40 of Cap. 195 provides that any person who is of sound mind and has completed the age of 18 years may dispose of any movable property by a gift made in contemplation of death, if made in the presence of at least two witnesses who have completed the age of 18 and are of sound mind. A gift shall be deemed to be made in contemplation of death where a person who is ill and expects to die soon because of such illness delivers to another person the possession of any of his/her movable property to keep as a gift in case the donor actually dies of that illness. It is noted that *donatio mortis causa* refers only to movable property; the possession of immovable property may not be transferred in this way. Any gift made in contemplation of death shall be treated upon the administration of the estate exactly in the same way as if it were a specific legacy, in accordance with section 40 section 3 of Cap. 195.

*453.* The criterion for the contemplation of death is both objective and subjective; objective in the sense that there has to be a serious illness and subjective in the sense that the donor actually believes that he/she is to die soon because of such illness.[573] A *donatio mortis causa* shall not be invalidated, however, merely because the donor died because of another cause; if for instance the donor donated in contemplation of death specific property because of imminent death by cancer, the donation shall still be valid even if the donor is shot to death before he/she dies from cancer.[574] While section 40 refers only to cases of illness, it is difficult to understand why other cases where there is contemplation of death, such as captivity or imminent death from natural disaster, should not be treated in the same way.

*454.* A gift made in contemplation of death may be resumed at any time by the donor and shall not take effect if the donor recovers from the illness during which it was made, or the donor survives the person to whom it was made. This is due to the fact that *donatio mortis causa* only becomes effective upon the death of the donor.[575] For the donation to be concluded, the donor has to transfer both possession and ownership of the specific movable property to the recipient of the gift[576] or to a third person on the recipient's behalf.[577] Transferring possession without ownership, or ownership without possession, is not sufficient.[578] The transfer of possession may occur either with the delivery of the property to the recipient by hand, as in the case of jewellery, or by delivering the means by which the recipient may enjoy possession of the gift.[579]

*455.* In the case of *Stivadorou* the Supreme Court analysed the consequences of a donation to the executor of the will of the deceased – albeit which occurred during the lifetime of the deceased – of a number of shares owned by the deceased. The deceased had signed the relevant form for the transfer of shares; however, these had never been actually transferred to the recipient, nor had they been registered in the recipient's name. The Supreme Court held that the donation was invalid and noted that:

> *in the case of movables, the delivery of the property from the donor to the recipient seals the donation. The donor does everything he had to do in order for the property to be transferred to the recipient. In the case of shares, their transfer is subject to an act by a third person. The object of the donation are the shares. Their delivery to the recipient is the main demonstration of the intention of the donor to donate them. The signature of the transfer form is the second. So long as these two elements coexisted, the Law would not take into account of the non registration of the shares, because the donor had done everything in order to donate the property; the donor in this case had not done*

573. *Re Craven's Estate* [1937] Ch 423, *Duffield v. Elwes* (1827) 1 Bligh 497.
574. *Wilkes v. Allington* [1931] 2 Ch 104, *Mills v. Shields* [1948] IR 367.
575. *Irons v. Smallpiece* (1819) 2 B & Ald 551, *Agnew v. Belfast Banking Co* [1896] 2 Ir R 204.
576. *Re Cole* [1964] Ch 175.
577. *Re Korvine* [1921] 1 Ch 343.
578. *Hawkins v. Blewitt* [1798] 2 Esp NPC 663.
579. *Mustapha v. Wedlake* (1891) 8 TLR 160.

*this. We conclude that by not delivering the title of the shares to the recipient, the donor left the donation incomplete and consequently, the shares remain owned by the deceased.*[580]

## §3. Trusts

*456.* Trusts are essential for estate planning, since an individual may, through the use of a Trust, bypass the provisions regarding statutory or disposable portion, or may enable persons who have not yet been born, or constituted, to inherit bypassing the relevant provisions of section 31 of Cap. 195. Trusts are not considered as part of the Estate of the deceased. The term trust denotes the legal relationship created *inter vivos* or on death of a person (the settlor), when assets have been placed under the control of a trustee for the benefit of a beneficiary or for a specific purpose. The trust property constitutes an independent fund which is available only for the beneficiaries or for charitable or other permitted purposes. The trustee–beneficiary relationship is the foundation of the trust, and the trustee has the power and the duty to manage, employ, or dispose of the assets in accordance with the terms of the trust. The Trustee Law, Cap. 193 and the International Trusts Law 69(I)/1992 are the main legal instruments with respect to the setting up of trusts.[581] In *Eliades* the deceased had established a trust for the benefit of himself, his spouse, and his grandchildren. The District Court considered that by virtue of section 650 of the Immovable Prop erty (Tenure, Registration, and Valuation) Law, Cap. 224, trusts referring to immovable property are valid only if they are registered in the Land Registry. Since the trust in question had not been registered in the Land Registry, its property had never been validly included in the trust. Accordingly, the immovable property was part of the estate of the deceased.[582]

## §4. Insurance Contracts

*457.* Life insurance is a contract between the policyholder and the insurer, where the insurer promises to pay a designated beneficiary a sum of money upon the death of the insured person. While case law on life insurance policies is not conclusive, it would seem that the insurance contract becomes part of the Estate, if there is no named beneficiary.[583] If there is a named beneficiary, however, the insurance contract should be treated as a beneficiary trust and should not become part of the Estate. In *Karpasitis* the District Court confirmed that if a person has intentionally

580. *Stivadorou v. Hatzikosta* [2002] 1 CLR 497 (in Greek). *See also* I. Nicolaou, 'Donation. A Comparative Overview' *Cyprus and European Law Review* [2013]: 112ff (in Greek).

581. For an introduction to the Cypriot trust *see* A. Neocleous, 'Cyprus: An Ideal Jurisdiction for Trusts', *Cyprus Law Review* 20 (1987): 3125–3146, E. Neocleous & P. Aristotelous, 'Trusts', in *Introduction to Cyprus Law*, ed. Andreas Neocleous & Co LLC, 3rd edn (Limassol, 2010,): 963–989.

582. *Eliades*, App. 277/2011, Judgment of 25 Apr. 2012 (District Court, in Greek).

583. *Terzian v. Terzian* [2003] 1 CLR 1252 (in Greek).

concluded an insurance contract for the benefit of a named third person, then the compensation owed by virtue of the insurance contract is not part of the estate of the deceased.[584]

§5. JOINT ACCOUNT

*458.* The Supreme Court has held that if the deceased had opened a joint account, in the sense that each of the spouses had the right to withdraw from the account, then the surviving spouse is automatically entitled to the remaining balance of the account; thus, the joint account is not part of the Estate of the deceased.[585] It was further held that the fact that the deceased retained control over the joint account during his/her lifetime could not change the fact that a donation had occurred during the lifetime of the deceased; since the donation occurred during the lifetime of the deceased there was no obligation to conform to the provisions of Cap. 195.[586] Thus, in the absence of proof that there was contrary intention of the deceased,[587] a joint account should be excluded from the estate and should directly become the property of the surviving account holder.

584. *Karpasitis*, App. 62/2008, Judgment of 23 Nov. 2009 (District Court, in Greek).
585. *Iacovides v. Schiza* [1967] 1 CLR 323.
586. *Young v. Sealey* [1949] 1 All ER 92.
587. As in *Marshal v. Crutwell* [1875] LR 20 Eq 328, in which the joint account had been opened merely to enable the administration of the family affairs while the husband was ill.

# Chapter 4. Acquisition and Administration of the Estate

## §1. The System of Acquisition

### I. Introduction

*459.* The rights and liabilities attaching to the estate of the deceased, including the statutory portion and the undisposed portion, shall be deemed to have been vested in the personal representative of the deceased from the date on which the deceased died, in accordance with section 25 of the Administration of Estates Law, Cap. 189. Thus, the estate of the deceased is not directly acquired by the heirs or the legatees; such heirs or legatees shall only acquire their share when the deceased's property has been distributed by the administrator or executor in accordance with the provisions of Cap. 189. The personal representatives shall represent the estate of the deceased for the purposes of legal proceedings,[588] either as Plaintiffs or as defendants; neither the heirs of the deceased[589] nor the deceased's creditors[590] may file an action or represent the estate in any legal proceedings.[591] Any legal proceedings against the estate of the deceased should be against the administrator or the executor, as the case may be, of the estate of the deceased and not against the heirs, or legatees of the deceased.[592]

*460.* When a person dies intestate the District Court shall authorize one or more persons to administer his/her estate by providing them with 'letters of administration', namely a written authority to administer the estate of the deceased. If the deceased had made a will, such shall have effect, in accordance with section 14 of Cap. 189, only after it has been proved.[593] Where the testator has appointed in his/her will another person to act as executor of his/her will, the Court may grant administration of the estate of the deceased to such person by granting a 'probate'. Where the testator has not appointed an executor or where the appointed executor has renounced probate or has become incapable, the Court may grant to an administrator the right of 'administration with will annexed'. Applications for grants of probate or letters of administration are made, in accordance with Regulation 9 of the 1955 Regulations, before the Registry of the District Court in the jurisdiction of which the deceased permanently or habitually resided at the time of death, and if no such place of residence may be established or if the deceased has no such place of residence in Cyprus, the Registry of the District Court of Nicosia.

*461.* An application by the executor or the administrator has to be made as soon as possible after the death of the deceased, either personally or through a lawyer in accordance with Form 1 of Annex A of the 1955 Regulations. The application

588. *Panayi v. Mandrioti* [1963] 2 CLR 167.
589. *Demetriades* [2011] 1 CLR 2148 (in Greek).
590. *Emin v. Turkish Bank of Nicosia Ltd* (1963) 2 CLR 74.
591. *Philippou v. Stylianou* [1992] 1 CLR 448 (in Greek), *Christodoulou v. Loizou* [2005] 1 CLR 887 (in Greek).
592. *Polykarpou v. Polykarpou* [1982] 1 CLR 182.
593. *Cacoyiannis v. The Republic* [1988] 3 CLR 1860.

should contain details about the estimated value of the movable and immovable properties of the deceased, and the personal details of the persons who are entitled to such property. An application for administration, if the deceased died intestate, has to be accompanied by an affidavit in accordance with Form 6 of Annex A of the 1955 Regulations, while an application for grant of probate or administration with will annexed has to be accompanied by an affidavit (with the will attached) in accordance with Form 2 or 3 of Annex A of the 1955 Regulations, depending on the case.[594]

## II. Applications for Grant

*462.* Section 4 of Cap. 189 provides that a Probate Registrar shall send to the principal probate registry, that is, the Supreme Court Registry, a notice of every application made in the registry for a grant as soon after such application has been made; no grant shall be made by the Probate Registrar until he/she has received a certificate from the principal probate registry stating that no other applications appear to have been made in respect of the estate of the testator or intestate. The Chief Registrar, that is, the Registrar of the Supreme Court should examine all notices of applications for grants received from the several other probate registries for the purpose of ascertaining whether an application for a grant in respect of the estate of the same deceased person has been made in more than one registry. As provided in Regulation 25 of the 1955 Regulations no subsequent application for a grant may be examined before deciding whether a previous application ought to be accepted.[595]

*463.* Upon receiving an application for a grant of probate or letters of administration with will annexed, the Probate Registrar should inspect the will, in accordance with Regulation 12 of the 1955 Regulations, and be satisfied that the formal requirements for making a valid will have been complied with. If a will has not been executed in accordance with the provisions of Cap. 195, then the Probate Registrar should refuse probate (Regulation 14 of the 1955 Regulations). A Probate Registrar has the discretion to request any necessary information from the applicant, in order to avoid any errors or fraud; in practice the Probate Registrar usually requires for a certificate of death and heirs signed by the President of the Community Council of the community where the deceased resided. If the President of the Community Council does not personally know the deceased or his/her heirs, then he/she should mention his/her sources of information in the certificate. In addition, in cases that the deceased has died intestate or had not appointed an executor of his/her will, the Probate Registrar should require the written consent of heirs of the deceased who are not authorized as administrators that they consent to the authorization of the

594. *Syggelou v. Loizou and another*, Civil App. 254/2015, Judgment of 18 Dec. 2017 (in Greek).

595. *Ioakeim*, App. 61/2015, Judgment of 13 May 2015 (in Greek), *Danou v. Michael* [2012] 1 CLR 118 (in Greek).

administrators. The Probate Registrar may further request, in accordance with Regulation 32 of the 1955 Regulations, that a notice of the application is published in newspapers, or sent to the heirs by registered mail.

*464.* If the grant for probate or administration is not contentious, or in case that the contention has been disposed of, the Probate Registrar may make a grant in common form in the name and subject to the directions of the Court and under the seal of the registry in accordance with section 13 of Cap. 189; the grant shall have an effect over the estate of the deceased in all parts of Cyprus. Grants for probate may be made only after seven days from the submission of the application, while grants for administration may be made only after fourteen days from the submission of the application, unless the Court directs otherwise. The executor or administrator should provide sufficient guarantee to the Probate Registrar, with two or more guarantors, which should amount to twice the value of the property of the deceased, as such is estimated in the affidavit. However, the Probate Registrar may, at his/her discretion and in accordance with Regulation 22 of the 1955 Regulations, restrict the amount of the guarantee, or restrict the number of guarantors, or even request for additional guarantors so that the individual responsibility of each guarantor is restricted. The prior submission of a certificate issued by the Director of the Inland Revenue Department stating that he/she does not object to the grant is also required.

*465.* If there is a contention whether a grant of probate or administration should be made, or if the Probate Registrar appears doubtful whether an application for grant should be accepted, or where any question arises in relation to a grant, the Probate Registrar should refer the matter for the directions of the District Court; in such a case the Court may, by virtue of section 13 of Cap. 189, either direct the Probate Registrar to proceed with the matter in accordance with such instructions as the Court may deem necessary, or may forbid any further proceedings by the Probate Registrar leaving the party applying for the grant to apply to the Court. Section 24 of Cap. 189 further stipulates that where an application for a grant has been refused by the Probate Registrar, despite the fact that there was no opposition, the applicant may apply by motion to the Court for a review of the decision of the Probate Registrar. Upon the hearing of such motion the Court may summon the persons who made the affidavit in connection with the will or in connection with the application for letters of administration, or take any further evidence that may be considered as necessary, either of its own motion or on the application of any person.

*466.* In the case of *Papachrysostomou* the Appellant applied for a grant for letters of administration of the estate of the deceased, as a representative of the deceased's wife.[596] However, the Probate Registrar refused the application by noting that the deceased had divorced his wife by the Islamic mechanism of divorce known as Talaq. The Appellant applied by motion to the District Court for review, arguing that the divorce was invalid and that therefore the marriage had never been dissolved. The motion for review was also dismissed. On appeal, however, the Supreme Court held that the Probate Registrar had no jurisdiction to decide whether

596. *Papachrysostomou v. Mathieson* [1998] 1 CLR 760 (in Greek).

the declaration for divorce was valid or not, since such jurisdiction may only be exercised by a competent court. Furthermore, it was held that the motion for review provided under section 24 of Cap. 189 is not the proper procedure to decide questions governing the substance of succession to the estate of a deceased, such as designating the heirs; such questions should be considered at the adjudication of an action between the parties.

## III. Priority to a Grant

*467.* Priority to a grant for probate is governed by Regulation 30 of the 1955 Regulations which provides that the persons appointed as executors by a will have priority. Where a person appointed executor by a will: (i) survives the testator but dies without having taken out probate of the will, or (ii) is called to take out probate and does not appear, or (iii) renounces probate of the will, his/her rights shall wholly cease in accordance with section 16 of Cap. 189, and the administrator of the deceased's estate shall take place as if the deceased had never appointed such person as an executor. The Court may of its own motion or on the application of any person claiming an interest under a will, by virtue of section 15 of Cap. 189, give notice to the executors to come in and prove the will or to renounce probate and they, or some, or one of them should come and prove or renounce accordingly within fourteen days after notice.

*468.* Section 18 of Cap. 189 further provides for the cases where the Court may grant administration with will annexed; these are the following: (i) where no executor has been appointed, (ii) where the executor appointed in the will has died in the lifetime of the testator or after his/her death without proving, (iii) where the executor has renounced or been called by the usual process of the Court and did not appear, (iv) where the appointment of an executor is void for uncertainty, (v) where the executor is incompetent by reason of minority, lunacy, or other disability or is resident out of jurisdiction, or (vi) where the Court exercises the discretion given to it by section 17 of Cap. 189 to grant administration with will annexed to a legatee; in the latter case the Court should have regard to the rights of all persons interested in the estate of the deceased and may limit such administration in any way.[597]

*469.* If there are no executors, the statutory heirs of the deceased or the heirs to the portion of the estate which is not disposable have priority to a grant; if the Court considers that such persons should, for any grounds, not obtain a grant, the legatees and then the creditors of the deceased have priority; in the unlikely event that there are no legatees or creditors or if the Court considers that such persons should, for any grounds, not obtain a grant, the Republic should obtain a grant for administration with will annexed. If the only executor of the will is a minor, administration with will annexed shall be granted to the person having the care of the minor or to such other person as the Court thinks fit, in accordance with section 22 of Cap. 189,

597. *See also Hjisavva v. Hjisavva* [1965] 1 CLR 151.

until the minor attains the age of 18 years. In any event a grant of probate or administration shall not be granted to more than four persons in respect of the same property by virtue of section 23 of Cap. 189. Section 23 further provides that if the heirs or legatees are minors or if a life interest arises under the will or intestacy, probate or administration shall be granted either to a public officer with or without another person or to not less than two persons. If there is only one personal representative, not being a public officer, then the Court may appoint additional personal representatives for as long as the beneficiaries are minors, or the life interest subsists and until the estate is fully administered.

*470.* If the deceased died intestate, priority to a grant is as follows in accordance with Regulation 31 of the 1955 Regulations: (a) spouse, (b) children or descendants per stirpes, (c) parents, (d) full blood siblings or descendants per stirpes, (e) half-blood siblings or descendants per stirpes, (f) grandparents, (g) full-blood uncles and aunts and descendants per stirpes, (h) half-blood uncles and aunts and descendants per stirpes, (i) the Republic, (j) creditors. However, the Court may always exercise its discretion by virtue of section 17 of Cap. 189 which provides that where the deceased died wholly intestate, administration shall be granted to one or more persons interested in the residuary estate of the deceased, if they so apply; it is further provided that if by reason of insolvency of the estate of the deceased or of any other special circumstances, it appears to the Court to be necessary or expedient to appoint as administrator some person other than the person who would have been entitled by law to the grant of administration, the Court may, in its discretion, appoint as administrator such person as it thinks expedient and by limiting such administration as it thinks fit. Section 17 thus empowers the Court in a proper case to bypass the priority stipulated by Regulation 31.

## IV. Caveat and Probate Actions

*471.* An interested person may object to the grant by filing a caveat to the Probate Registrar; the caveat is essentially a written notice to the Court that it should not allow any further proceedings regarding the estate of the deceased, without first notifying the person who files the caveat. The Probate Registrar should not make a grant to the applicant, unless the caveator withdraws the caveat, or fails to bring a probate action within a period of three months, or unless a competent Court so orders. The caveat is valid for a period of three months within which the caveator may file a probate action; the commencement of an action, though not extending the duration of a caveat, shall prevent the sealing of any grant until a decision of the Court is issued. It has been held that the caveator may not file an action for administration if the three-month period has lapsed.[598] The person applying for a grant may also institute proceedings for a grant or probate by the way of action or of counterclaim; other persons having an interest in the inheritance, such as creditors, legatees, or next of kin or persons claiming through such creditors or beneficiaries

598. *Triantafyllides v. Karaoglanian* [2010] 1 CLR 2014 (in Greek). *See*, however, *Parisinou v. Charalambides* [1998] 1 CLR 781 (in Greek).

by assignment or otherwise, may also bring an action claiming that the estate be administered in Court in accordance with section 54 of Cap. 189.

*472.* Probate actions, namely actions for the grant of probate or letters of administration of the estate of a deceased, or for the revocation of such grant or for a decree pronouncing for or against the validity of a purported will,[599] are governed by special procedural rules. Rule 13 of Order 2 of the Civil Procedure Rules provides that the sealing of a writ of summons in probate actions shall be preceded by the filing of an affidavit by the plaintiff or one of the plaintiffs,[600] in verification of the endorsement of the writ; Rule 13 of Order 2 is of a mandatory nature.[601] Rule 5 of Order 2 further provides that in probate actions the endorsement should show whether the plaintiff claims as creditor, executor, administrator, legatee, heir, or in any other and what other character. Any person not named in the writ may intervene and appear in the action if it affects his/her interests, by virtue of Rule 8 of Order 16, by filing an affidavit showing how he/she is interested in the estate of the deceased. Where the plaintiff disputes the interest of the defendant, this should be alleged in the Statement of Claim in accordance with Rule 5 of Order 20. Rule 24 of Order 19 further provides that every Defence should plead the substance of the case on which the defendant intends to rely and if it is pleaded that the testator was not of sound mind, particulars of any specific instances of delusion should be delivered before the case is set down for trial.

*473.* Regulations 42 and 43 of the 1955 Regulations are relevant: Regulation 42 provides that the persons who object to a grant of probate may only raise the following grounds: (i) the purported will had not been executed in accordance with the provisions of Cap. 195, (ii) the deceased was not of a sound mind at the time the will was made, (iii) the will was made because of fraud or undue influence, or (iv) the deceased was unaware or had not approved of the content of the purported will. Additional grounds may be put forward only by approval of the Court. In any matter of practice or procedure not covered by Cap. 189, the 1955 Regulations or the Civil Procedure Regulations, the practice, and procedure of the Probate Division of the High Court of Justice in England for the time being shall apply in accordance with section 58 of Cap. 189.[602]

## V. Originating Summons

*474.* Section 53 of Cap. 189 provides for the right of personal representatives or any of them, creditors, legatees, next of kin, or persons claiming through such creditors or beneficiaries by assignment or otherwise, to apply to the Court by originating summons for the determination of any of the following questions or matters: (i)

599. An action for non-contentious grants, or an action by the creditors of the estate for debts, or by persons who had contractual relations with the deceased or other similar actions, is not considered as probate action.

600. *Re Luke* (1909) 25 LTR 825.

601. *Demetriou v. Prodromou* [1983] 1 CLR 301.

602. *Theodossiades* [1970] 1 CLR 207, *Terzian v. Terzian* [2003] 1 CLR 1252 (in Greek).

any question affecting the rights or interests of the person claiming to be creditor, legatee, next of kin, or heir, (ii) the ascertainment of any class of creditors, legatees, next of kin or others, (iii) the furnishing of any particular accounts by the personal representatives and the vouching of such accounts, (iv) the payment into Court of any money in the hands of the personal representatives, (v) directing the personal representatives to do or abstain from doing any particular act in their character as personal representatives, (vi) the approval of any sale, purchase, compromise, or other transaction, (vii) the determination of any question arising in the determination of the estate.[603] An application for originating summons may be made at any time.

*475.* It has been held that an application for originating summons is not the proper forum for deciding on issues falling under the definition of a 'probate action'.[604] Furthermore, the Court has discretion, in accordance with Rule 4 of Order 55 of the Civil Procedure Rules, not to determine any issues raised by the originating summons, if it considers that they ought to not properly be determined by originating summons. In *Georghiou* the District Court held that the request to correct the register of members of a company should not be considered by originating summons, in view of the fact that the ownership of the shares in question and the facts of the case were highly controversial; this approach was affirmed by the Supreme Court.[605] An application for originating summons should be supported by an affidavit and any required evidence in accordance with Order 55 of the Civil Procedure Rules. The Court may direct that the summons should be served to the interested parties. Applications for originating summons (but not probate actions) may be heard and determined in Chambers by virtue of section 53 section 3 of Cap. 189.[606]

## VI. Limited Grants

*476.* Grants may be limited in duration, in respect of property or for a special purpose by virtue of section 19 of Cap. 189. In accordance with Regulation 28 of the 1955 Regulations the Registrar should always refer an application for limited grant for the directions of the Court. The general principle is that a person who could apply for an unlimited grant may not properly apply for a limited grant. In *Michael* the defendant who was appointed as the executor by will had been granted a probate by the Probate Registrar; the will provided that a rather small part of the immovable property of the deceased would be left to a person who was not a relative. The heirs of the deceased filed an action against the executor of the estate of the deceased challenging the validity of the will. Subsequently, and while the action was pending, one of the heirs applied for a grant for administration of the estate of

603. *Wortham v. Tsimon* [2001] 1 CLR 1442 (in Greek).
604. *Efstratiou* [1997] 1 CLR 751 (in Greek).
605. *Georghiou v. Frederick School Ltd* [2004] 1 CLR 866 (in Greek). *See also Clerides v. Crentou* [1996] 1 CLR 432 (in Greek).
606. *Hjisavva v. Hjisavva* [1965] 1 CLR 151.

the deceased for the part of the estate that had not been disposed by will. The District Court held that it was not possible to grant both probate and letters of administration for the same estate. The Supreme Court, however, reversed the judgment of the District Court; it was held that since the will referred to a small part of the estate for which the executor had been appointed (and thus the grant was limited), there was no reason why letters of administration could not be granted regarding the part of the estate for which there was no contention. Subsequently, however, a different section of the Supreme Court held that such findings of their colleagues in the Supreme Court should be considered as having been expressed *obiter* or *per incuriam*, since in accordance with Regulation 25 of the Administration of Estates Regulations it is not possible to grant letters of administration for the same estate for which probate had already been granted.[607]

*477.* Limited grant may also be granted if the personal representative is abroad. Section 21 of Cap. 189 provides that if at the expiration of twelve months from the death of the deceased, any personal representative to whom a grant has been made is residing out of the jurisdiction of the Court, the Court may, on the application of any creditor or person having an interest in the estate, grant to him/her special administration of the estate. If the personal representative returns to and resides within the jurisdiction of the Court while any legal proceedings to which a special administrator is a party are pending, the personal representative shall be made a party to such legal proceedings. An advocate may also lawfully represent both executors and administrators of the estate by a limited grant, while they reside out of Cyprus, or even if they reside in Cyprus,[608] so long as the heirs consent and the Court has approved such representation.

*478.* Section 20 of Cap. 189 provides that where any legal proceedings, regarding the validity of a will, or for obtaining or revoking any grant are pending, the Court may grant administration of the estate of the deceased to an administrator who shall have all the rights and powers of a general administrator, other than the right of distributing the residue of the estate; such administrator, called administrator *pendente lite,* shall be subject to the immediate control of the Court and act under its direction. The power to grant administration *pendente lite* refers only to cases of pending probate actions (therefore, excluding not contentious claims) and their aim is to safeguard that the estate of the deceased shall be properly administrated as, and if, needed, despite the fact the probate action is pending;[609] an administrator *pendente lite* should ideally be a neutral person.

*479.* In *Terzian* the Appellants, heirs of the deceased, had applied for a grant of administration *pendente lite*, so as to collect sums from insurance companies for the payment of debts of the estate and for recovering possession of an apartment which

607. *Kyriacos Danos v. Frixou Michael* [2012] 1 CLR 118 (in Greek).
608. *Papachrysostomou v. Mathieson* [1998] 1 CLR 760 (in Greek).
609. *Smith v. Smith* [1867] 31 JP 248.

was part of the estate. The Supreme Court held that a grant of administration *pendente lite* was justified.[610] There are further cases where no person has been interested to administer the property of the deceased and as a result it is not possible for third parties to file or continue an action against the estate of the deceased. Such persons may apply before the Court in order for an administrator to be appointed *ad litem*, namely only for the purposes of representing the estate in the specific action.[611] A person may be appointed as administrator *ad litem* only so long as he/she consents.[612] An appointment of an administrator without his consent is contrary to fundamental principles of justice.[613]

## VII. Renunciation

*480.* Where an estate vests in and devolves upon an heir, such heir may unconditionally renounce the estate at any time, in accordance with section 51 of Cap. 189, within three months from the time when he/she first became aware of the death of the deceased and of the fact that he/she is an heir to such deceased. If an heir has renounced the estate after the lapse of the three-month period, such renunciation is invalid.[614] Renunciation may be effected by filing with the Registry of the Court a declaration. An heir who has renounced the estate shall incur no liability in respect of the debts of the deceased and shall receive no benefit from the estate of such deceased. Section 51 section 3 of Cap. 189 further provides that any renunciation which is made by an heir with the object of defeating the rights of any of his/her creditors may be set aside by the Court on the application of any creditor and upon proof of such object; the above provision refers to the creditors of the heir and not to the creditors of the estate, since the heirs are not personally liable for any of the debts of the estate.

## VIII. Heirs under Disability

*481.* Whenever any person habitually resident in Cyprus dies, either in Cyprus or abroad, the President of the Community Council of the community where the deceased had his/her habitual residence should, in accordance with section 48 section of Cap. 189, make all reasonable inquiries to ascertain who the heirs of the deceased are. If any of the heirs of a deceased person are under disability, the President of the Community Council should forward to the Probate Registrar of the district within which the deceased resided, a report containing an announcement of the death of the deceased, the date of death, the names of the heirs specifying which of them are under disability or absent from Cyprus, the names of some of the nearest relatives of the deceased, and a list of the property left by the deceased, stating

610. *Terzian v. Terzian* [2003] 1 CLR 1252.
611. *Re Ganning* [1936] 40.
612. *Pratt v. London Transport Board* [1937] WN 43, *Lean v. Alston* (1947) KB 467.
613. *Aresti v. Marfin Popular Bank Co Ltd*, Civil App. 178/2011, Judgment of 25 Oct. 2016 (in Greek).
614. *Stavrinides v. The Republic* [1987] 3 CLR 1228.

approximately the value of such property; the list of the property should, where possible, also include money owed to the deceased. Where the President of the Community Council finds amongst the property of the deceased, any money, securities, or jewellery which together with the value of the other property of the deceased shall exceed the sum of EUR 170,94 (CYP100), he/she should take possession of the same giving a receipt thereof to the heirs and bring such property to the Probate Registrar.

*482.* Where the value of the property of the deceased leaving heirs under disability does not exceed EUR 17093.88, the Court may order that the estate be administered summarily in accordance with section 49 of Cap. 189. The Probate Registrar or such other public officer as the Court may appoint shall have the powers and duties of an administrator. Upon the death of any intestate person leaving heirs under disability and property exceeding EUR 10256.33 (CYP 6,000), such property shall, until administration is granted, vest in the President of the District Court of the district where the deceased originally resided and, if he/she was resident abroad, then in the President of the District Court of Nicosia. Section 46 of Cap. 189 further provides that if the deceased died wholly intestate and leaving heirs under disability, the purpose of the above provisions is to safeguard the interests of the disabled person; however, the extent to which such provisions might still prove useful is doubtful, since they are rather outdated.

## IX. The Special Procedure of section 27 of Cap. 189

*483.* Section 27 of Cap. 189 lays down a special procedure; where no letters of administration have been granted in respect of an estate and the person died intestate, leaving no heirs under disability, or, if there are such heirs, property not exceeding EUR 10256.33 (CYP 6,000) in value and so long as an order has not been made for summary administration under section 49 of Cap. 189. It would seem that the special procedure laid down in section 27 of Cap. 189 may in principle be followed only in small estates, although its use in larger estates might potentially be adopted for a transitional period. Such procedure is generally the following: the estate of the deceased shall stand charged with his/her debts and liabilities and shall subject to such charge vest in and devolve on the heirs. The heirs shall be liable to pay the debts and liabilities of the deceased up to the value of the property of the deceased they received or up to the value of the proceeds from the sale of such property. The Court may call upon the heirs to take out letters of administration or to account for the distribution of the estate.

*484.* For a period of eighteen months after the death of the deceased, no property of the deceased shall be sold or transferred by the way of execution for debt or otherwise to any person other than an heir of the deceased; there is an exception for perishable commodities, property sold, or transferred in payment of the debts and liabilities of the deceased, or immovable property exchanged or transferred by the Director of Lands and Surveys in exercise of his/her powers in accordance with sections 28 to 33 of the Immovable Property (Tenure, Registration, and Valuation) Law,

Cap. 224. Where letters of administration are granted in respect of an estate, the property of the deceased shall no longer vest in the heirs, but the administrator, with the exception of property appropriated to an heir, or property sold or transferred in accordance with section 27.

## §2. The Administration of the Estate

### I. Powers and Obligations of the Personal Representatives

*485.* The executor or the administrator of the Estate shall, by virtue of section 31 of Cap. 189, be considered as the personal representatives of the deceased and as trustee of the movable and immovable property of the estate.[615] Personal representatives have the power to sell, mortgage, or charge any part of the immovable property of the deceased, as may be necessary for paying the funeral and testamentary expenses and all just debts of the deceased, by virtue of section 32 of Cap. 189; such powers may be exercised without leave of the Court, so long as they are exercised within the limits of the law.[616] The personal representatives should, in accordance with section 41 of Law 189, administer the property of the deceased by: (i) collecting and gathering the estate with all reasonable speed, (ii) paying the funeral and testamentary expenses if any and all the just debts of the deceased in order of priority, (iii) having the residue of the estate carefully valued and carrying out the provisions of the will, (iv) filing the accounts of the estate to the Court, and (v) distributing the statutory portion and the undisposed portion according to the law.[617] Such powers shall be analysed further in the subsequent paragraphs.

*486.* The personal representative has to collect and gather the estate with all reasonable speed. In order to achieve this, the personal representative may commence judicial proceedings against any debtors of the estate. In accordance with section 43 of Cap. 189 the personal representative shall open an account with a bank for the estate administered by him/her; all money received by the personal representative shall be paid into such account, and no payments shall be made by him/her except by cheque; funeral and testamentary expenses, as well as debts of the estate, should be paid by cheque. The President of the District Court may exempt the personal representative from compliance with the provisions of section 43, whenever compliance would cause special hardship to the personal representative because of the circumstances of the case. With respect to the payment of the debts of the estate, the order of priority in accordance with section 42 of Cap. 189 is the following: (i) payment of funeral expenses and expenses incidental to the acceptance, discharge, and remuneration of the capacity of a personal representative, (ii) expenses of the medical treatment of the deceased during his/her last illness and wages due to the domestic servants of the deceased, not exceeding six months wages, (iii) secured debts according to the order of their priority, and (iv) any other debt. It should be

615. *Cacoyiannis v. The Republic* [1988] 3 CLR 1860, *Ward v. Roubina* [1970] 1 CLR 88.

616. *Loannou v. Demetriou* [1983] 1 CLR 892.

617. F. Michaelides, 'Powers of Personal Representatives', *Cyprus Law Tribune* 3 (1969): 30–33.

noted that in Cyprus heirs have no personal liability for the debts of the estate; such debts are paid only to the extent that there are sufficient assets in the estate. If there are not sufficient assets, the heirs do not have personal liability for the debts of the deceased.

*487.* A personal representative should file an inventory of the estate, in accordance with section 40 of Cap. 189, within such period as the Court might direct; the inventory should be accompanied by an affidavit in accordance with Form 17 of the 1955 Regulations. If there is a valid will, the personal representative should carry out its provisions, reducing the legacies proportionately if it appears that the testator has disposed by will of more than the disposable portion. By virtue of section 44 §1 of Cap. 189 specific legacies shall take rank and be liquidated after the payment of the just debts, but before the general legacies, unless the will shows a contrary intention; a legacy is considered to be specific if it refers to a specific part of the estate which might be separated from the remaining estate. There is a presumption that a legacy is general, unless such is particularly specialized by the testator, so as to be separated from the remaining estate.[618]

*488.* Thus, jewellery or monetary accounts shall be considered as general legacies, unless the testator refers specifically to jewellery or jewels which have specific and identifiable characteristics, or to money being deposited in a specific account, so as to be identified and separated from the remaining estate.[619] Specific immovable property would also be considered as specific legacy. The beneficiary of specific legacy would also be entitled to any increase in the legacy, such as interest or rents, from the date of death of the deceased.[620] If it appears that the value of the specific legacies exceeds that of the disposable portion, the reduction and abatement of such legacies shall be effected in the following manner: the objects of the specific legacies shall be sold and from the proceeds of sale, the monetary sum equivalent in value to that of the disposable portion shall be set apart and distributed among the specific legatees in proportion to the value of their respective legacies.

*489.* The personal representative should further file the final accounts of the estate, including vouchers and an affidavit in verification, to the Court in accordance with section 45 of Cap. 189 within two years from the date that the grant of probate or administration was made; if the administration of the estate has not yet been completed within the two-year period, the personal representative should file a statement to the Court explaining the grounds for non-completion and should further file such additional statement and accounts every six months until completion. Accounts filed in the court should be scrutinized by the Probate Registrar and, if it appears that there are improper, unvouched, or unjustifiable entries or otherwise such account is not a full and proper account, then the Probate Registrar should give

618. *Kirby v. Potter* (1799) 4 Ves 748.

619. *Richards v. Richards* (1821) 9 Price 219, *Fontaine v. Tyler* (1821) 9 Price 98, *Georghiou v. Malapani* [2004] 9 JSC 427 (in Greek), District Court.

620. *Re Compton* [1914] 2 Ch 119.

notice to the personal representative to remedy such defects; if the personal representative fails to remedy such defects to the satisfaction of the Registrar, he/she shall be deemed to have failed to file an account. The Court may, further, of its own motion appoint a competent person to examine any accounts which are complicated. Accounts should be available, free of charge, to the inspection of all persons interested in the administration of the estate.

*490.* Finally, the personal representatives should distribute the estate to the heirs in accordance with the provisions of Cap. 195. The personal representatives may, by virtue of section 47 of Cap. 189, give notice, by advertisement in the Official Gazette or any newspapers as the Probate Registrar may order, of the intention to make any transfer or distribution of the estate; the notice may require that any interested persons should send to the personal representative within a period of no less than two months, particulars of their claim in respect of the property in question. At the expiration of the time fixed by the notice, the personal representatives may transfer or distribute the property or any part thereof to which the notice relates to the persons entitled thereto and shall not be liable to any person of whose claim they had not had notice at the time of transfer or distribution. For the purposes of facilitating the distribution of the estate among the beneficiaries, the Court has discretion, following an application by the personal representative, order, in respect of any part of the estate, the sale, lease, mortgage, surrender or release, division, or other disposition thereof, as it might be expedient.[621]

*491.* Personal representatives should always exercise their duties honourably and fairly; if they waste or convert to their own use any part of property of the deceased, they shall be personally liable.[622] Furthermore, their own personal representatives shall, in case they die, be liable and chargeable in respect of such wastage or conversion in accordance with section 35 of Cap. 189. However, personal representatives who made payments and dispositions in good faith shall be indemnified and protected in so doing, in accordance with section 36 of Cap. 189, notwithstanding any defect or circumstance affecting the validity of the representation; furthermore, the personal representative who acted under the revoked representation may retain and reimburse himself/herself in respect of any payments or dispositions made by him/her, which the person to whom representation is subsequently granted might have properly made.

*492.* Where a representation is revoked, all payments and dispositions made in good faith to a personal representative before the revocation shall be a valid discharge to the person making the same; on the contrary, if any person to the defrauding of creditors or without full consideration obtains, receives, or holds any property of a deceased or effects the release of any debt or liability due to the estate of the deceased, he/she shall be liable to the full extent, in accordance with section 30 of Cap. 189, after deducting: (i) any debt due to him/her from the deceased, at the time

621. *Hjipetri v. Aletraris* [1973] 1 CLR 166.
622. *See also Vasiliou v. Vronti and others*, Civil App. 12/2011, Judgment of 20 Nov. 2015 (in Greek).

of death, without fraud and for valuable consideration and (ii) any payment made by him/her which might properly be made by a personal representative.

## II. Removal and Substitution of Personal Representatives

*493.* The powers of the personal representatives normally cease once the administration of the estate has been completed, namely once the estate has been distributed and the final accounts of the administration have been filed and approved by the Court.[623] The personal representative may, however, be removed by the Court for wilful neglect or misconduct in the administration of the estate, either of the Court's own motion or on the application of any person interested in the estate by virtue of section 52 of Cap. 189. The Court may grant letters of administration to a person for the purposes of carrying out the due administration of the estate in the place of any personal representative who has been removed, or has died, or has become incapable to act. Where the administrators of the estate were more than one and the other has died, or been removed, or become incapable to act, the remaining administrator might apply before the Court for an order enabling him/her to act as a sole administrator of the estate.

*494.* In *Paraskevaides* the Supreme Court reiterated that the wilful negligence of the administrator of the estate should amount to deliberately and purposely doing something which he knows is a breach of trust, consisting in a failure to perform his duty as a trustee. The court should not revoke a grant of administration unless it is satisfied that the administrator has acted improperly. While, however, on the facts of the case it could not be determined that there was deliberate action on behalf of the administrator of the estate which would amount to a breach of trust, the relationship between the administrator and some of the heirs had become hostile so as to endanger the proper carrying out of the administration and the safeguard of the interests of the estate and of the heirs. It was held that where the relationship between administrator and heirs has collapsed, such hostility might become a determining factor. The Court held that it had inherent jurisdiction to terminate the administrator in such a case.[624]

*495.* Where more than one executor had been appointed and one of them has died, or been removed or become incapable to act, the remaining executors shall automatically carry on the administration of the estate as if they had been the only executor appointed by virtue of section 37 of Cap. 189. Section 38 further provides that an executor of a sole or last surviving executor shall also act as the executor of such testator; however, this provision shall not apply if such sole executor had not proven the will of his/her testator, or if another executor who had not before proven the will of the testator subsequently proves it. An executor of a sole or last surviving executor shall also act as the executor of every preceding testator so long as the

623. *See also Pierides v. Keshishian* [1996] 1 CLR 224 (in Greek).
624. *Michaelides and others v. Paraskevaides and another*, Civil App. E34/2016, Judgment of 7 Jul. 2017 (in Greek).

chain of such representation remains unbroken; the chain is broken by: (i) an intestacy, (ii) the failure of a testator to appoint an executor, or (iii) the failure to obtain probate of a will, but is not broken by a temporary grant of administration if probate is subsequently granted. Every person in the chain of representation to a testator has the same rights and obligations in respect of the estate of that testator as the original executor would have had.

# Selected Bibliography


**Books**

**In Greek**

Emilianides, A. *The Cypriot Law of Marriage and Divorce.* Athens-Thessaloniki: Sakkoulas, 2006.

Emilianides, A. Katsaros C. (eds), *The New Charter of the Church of Cyprus*. Nicosia: Hippasus, 2013.

Emilianides, A. *Cypriot Succession Law.* 3rd end, Nicosia: Hippasus, 2015.

Karatsis, S. *The Claim for Contribution to Matrimonial Property.* Limassol: Limassol Bar Association, 2007.

Konnari, E. *Family Law: A Concise Approach.* Limassol: Stalkon Publishers Ltd, 2002.

Liasides, S. *Family Law*, *v.* I, Nicosia, 2005, IIa, Nicosia, 2006, IIb, Nicosia, 2011, IIIa, Nicosia, 2007, IV, Nicosia, 2008.

Liasides, S. *Recognition, Registration and Execution of Foreign Judgments in Family Law Cases and other Civil Cases.* Nicosia, 2009.

Liasides, S. *A Family Law Textbook.* Nicosia, 2010.

Liasides, S., *Family Law Issues*. Nicosia, 2013.

Liasides, S. *Civil Union (Law 184(I)/2015). Legal Aspects*. Nicosia, 2016.

Liasides, S. *Studies in Family Law*. Nicosia, 2017.

Patera-Dimosthenous, E. *The Right of Communication in Modern Family Law. An Interdisciplinary Approach.* Athens: Nomiki Vivliothiki, 2017.

Serghides, G. *Grounds for Divorce. v.* I-II Nicosia, 2007.

Society of Lawyers of Northern Greece. *The Grounds for Divorce in accordance with Greek and Cypriot Law.* Thessaloniki: Sakkoulas, 1993.

Serghides, G. *Matrimonial Property Relations of Spouses and Various Legal Issues.* Nicosia, 2010.

Tornaritis, C. *The Marriage Law in General and Especially the Law of Mixed Marriages in Cyprus.* Nicosia, 1986.

Trokanas, T. *The Cypriot Law of Medically Assisted Reproduction.* Athens: Nomiki Vivliothiki, 2016.

**Other than Greek**

Emilianides, A. *Law and Religion in Cyprus*. 2nd edn, The Hague: Kluwer, 2014.

## Selected Bibliography

Emilianides, A. *Annotated Legal Documents on Islam in Cyprus*. Leiden: Brill, 2014.

Serghides, G. *Internal and External Conflict of Laws in Regard to Family Relations in Cyprus*. Nicosia, 1988.

### Articles

### In Greek

Chrysostomides, K. 'The Validity of the Marriage and the New Legislation'. *Cyprus Law Review* 25 (1989): 3893–3905.

Emilianides, A. 'The Evolution of the Law of Mixed Marriages in Cyprus since Frankish Rule'. *Cyprus Studies* 2 (1938): 197–236.

Emilianides, A. 'Which is the Current Legal Status with Respect to the Adjudication of Cases on Nullity of Marriage?' *Cyprus and European Law Review* 1 (2006): 113–127.

Emilianides, A. 'Jurisdiction for the Adjudication of Matrimonial Property Disputes of Members of a Religious Group'. *Cyprus and European Law Review* 4 (2007): 153–170.

Emilianides, A. 'Problems Arising from the Application of the Residence Criterion for the Local Jurisdiction of the Family Courts'. *Cyprus and European Law Review* 5 (2007): 412–420.

Emilianides, A. 'The Family Law Provisions of the Charter of the Church of Cyprus'. *Family Law Review* 2 (2011): 21–30.

Emilianides, A. 'The Dispute between Church and State for the Revision of the Family Institutions'. In *History of the Republic of Cyprus*. ed. Papapolyviou v. III, 1980–1989, Nicosia: Phileleftheros, 2011, 110–115.

Emilianides, A. 'Homosexuality and Human Rights in the Cypriot Legal Order' in *Sexualities: Views, Studies and Experiences in the Cypriot and Greek Space*. eds C. Phellas et al, Athens: Polyxromos Planitis, 2014: 130-151.

Emilianides, C. 'Succession in Cyprus'. *Corpus* de Jure *Cyprii* 2 (1988): 445–469.

Gavrielides, R. 'Historical Evolution of the Development of Grounds of Divorce in accordance with Cypriot Law'. *Cyprus Law Review* 41 (1993): 6127–6132.

Liasides, S. 'Observations and Comments on the New Charter of the Church of Cyprus'. *Family Law Review* 1 (2011): 23–34.

Loucaides, L. 'Grounds for Divorce'. *Cyprus Law Review* 4, no. 4 (1983): 681–696.

Nicolaou, E. 'The Family Law Evolution: Custody, Maintenance of Minor Child and of Spouse'. *Cyprus Law Tribune* 1 (1992): 51–65.

Nicolaou, E. 'The Cypriot Law of Marriage and Divorce'. *Family Law Review* 2 (2010): 5–17.

Serghides, G. 'Mediation in Family Law Disputes: Is there a Necessity of Applying it in Cyprus'. *Cyprus Law Tribune* 1 (2001): 40–59.

Serghides, G. 'Observations on the Cypriot Marriage Law of 2003'. *Cyprus Law Tribune* 1 (2004): 48–75.

Serghides, G. 'Mixed Marriages in Cyprus'. *Cyprus Law Tribune* 2 (2005): 103–122.

## Other than Greek

Anderson, J.N.D. 'The Family Law of Turkish Cypriots'. *Die Weit des Islams* 5 (1958): 161–187.

Demetriou, A. & Hadjiyiorki, C. 'Family Law'. In *Introduction to Cyprus Law*, ed. Andreas Neocleous & Co LLC, 3rd edn (Limassol, 2010), 841–877.

Emilianides, A. 'Interracial and Interreligious Laws in Cyprus'. *Revue Hellénique de Droit International* 11 (1958): 286–306.

Emilianides, A. 'The Case for Amending the Current Legal Framework'. *Cyprus and European Law Review* 11 (2010): 135–145.

Nicolaou, E. 'Recent Developments in Family Law in Cyprus'. In *The International Survey of Family Law*, ed. Bainham, A. The Hague: Kluwer, 1998, 121–134.

Savvides, L. 'Sex Discrimination in Family Law in Cyprus'. *Cyprus Law Review* 4 (1983): 708–714.

Serghides, G. 'Grounds for Divorce under the Law of Cyprus: The Road to Europe'. *Paneuropean Law Review* 1 (1997): 31–43.

Serghides, G. 'Reflections on Some Aspects of the Family Law of the Turkish Community in Cyprus'. *Cyprus and European Law Review* 11 (2010): 156–163.

Serghides, G. 'Cyprus Family Jurisdiction Ratione Personae and Ratione Materiae'. *Family Law Review* 2 (2011): 4–17.

Tornaritis, C. 'On the Applicable Law in Case of Mixed Marriages'. *Revue Hellénique de Droit International* 19 (1966): 289–293.

Tornaritis, C. 'The Right to Marry and Found a Family, especially under the Law of Cyprus'. In *Mélanges Offerts à Polys Modinos* (Paris, 1968), 320–330.

Tryfonidou, A. 'The Legal Position of LGBT Persons and Same-Sex Couples in Cyprus' *The Cyprus Review* 29 (2017): 183-213.

Tsikkinis, L. 'Succession'. In *Introduction to Cyprus Law*, ed. Andreas Neocleous & Co LLC, 3rd edn Limassol, 2010, 923–962.

Tsikkinis, L. & Neocleous, M. 'Cyprus'. In *International Succession*, ed. Garb, L. & Wood, J., 3rd edn. Oxford: Oxford University Press, 2010, 199–216.

Xenofontos, X. 'Human Rights Aspects of the Law of Marriage and Adoption in relation to Turkish Cypriots'. *Cyprus and European Law Review* 11 (2010): 146–155.

## Selected Bibliography

# Index

*The numbers here refer to paragraph numbers.*

**Index**

Made in the USA
Monee, IL
25 June 2026

55761007R00129